Irrationality in Health Care

Irrationality in Health Care

What Behavioral Economics Reveals
About What We Do and Why

Douglas E. Hough

STANFORD ECONOMICS AND FINANCE
An Imprint of Stanford University Press
Stanford, California

Stanford University Press
Stanford, California

Song lyrics at the beginning of Chapter 8:
  The Song That Goes Like
  From MONTY PYTHON'S SPAMALOT
  Lyrics by Eric Idle
  Music by John Du Prez and Eric Idle
  Copyright © 2005 Rutsongs Music and Ocean Music
  All Rights Reserved Used by Permission
  Reprinted by Permission of Hal Leonard Corporation

Special discounts for bulk quantities of Stanford Economics and Finance are
available to corporations, professional associations, and other organizations.
For details and discount information, contact the special sales department of
Stanford University Press. Tel: (650) 736-1782, Fax: (650) 736-1784

Printed in the United States of America on acid-free, archival-quality paper

Library of Congress Cataloging-in-Publication Data
Hough, Douglas E., author.
    Irrationality in health care : what behavioral economics reveals about what we
do and why / Douglas E. Hough.
        pages cm
    Includes bibliographical references and index.
    ISBN 978-0-8047-7797-1 (cloth : alk. paper)
    ISBN 978-0-8047-9340-7 (pbk. : alk. paper)
      1. Medical economics—United States.   2. Medical care—United States.
    3. Health behavior—United States.   4. Economics—Psychological aspects.
    I. Title.
      RA410.53.H669   2013
      338.4'73621—dc23
                                                                    2012039953

Typeset by Thompson Type in 10/15 Sabon

DEDICATION

To Katerina and Kai,
who I hope will have a better health system when they need it

CONTENTS

ANOMALIES

PREFACE AND ACKNOWLEDGMENTS

The epiphany came slowly. I know that is an oxymoron, but there is no better way to describe it. I was trained as a mainstream, neoclassical economist, transfixed by the discipline's combination of mathematics and real-world applications. To me, economics provided a superb set of tools for analyzing and understanding the world—thinking on the margin, opportunity costs, the fundamental theorem of welfare economics. And in the 1970s, when I was in graduate school, economics was so successful that it was extending its intellectual reach beyond the analysis of markets to the whole range of human behavior—the family, education, urban problems (such as crime and urban renewal).

It seemed obvious then that mainstream economics offered the best way to analyze the myriad of problems that were plaguing the U.S. health care sector. My colleagues and I at the Center for Health Policy Research at the American Medical Association devised all sorts of economic theories of physician and hospital behavior—even though none of us had ever actually seen the management or operations of a physician practice or a hospital. Other health economists, some with more practical experience than us, were also using neoclassical economics to explain what was going on in health care. We were following the path blazed by the giants in the field: Kenneth Arrow (Arrow 1963), Victor Fuchs (Fuchs 1975), Mark Pauly (Pauly 1968), and Uwe Reinhardt (Reinhardt 1972).

When I moved into the consulting world, I continued to use these concepts. They certainly seemed more useful than the other strategy tools that we had. But I began to get the gnawing suspicion that the assumptions and models of mainstream economics were not all that appropriate for analyzing the financing and delivery of health care in the United States. Patients certainly did not have the usual characteristics of a consumer: They were not knowledgeable about the characteristics and benefits of the services that they were buying; they seemed disconnected from the purchase decision because their health insurance was paying for most of their care; and there was not a lot of evidence that the health care services that they received delivered sufficient value for the rapidly growing expenditure. Likewise, physicians were not acting like the profit-maximizing businesspeople that we all were hypothesizing: They were motivated by a much more complex set of goals, and many resisted viewing themselves as suppliers in a market. Finally, hospitals (at least the ones I consulted with) certainly did not fit the theory of the firm that we were taught in school.

But, as Nobel laureate Milton Friedman has argued, scientific theories do not have to be perfect; they just have to be better than the alternatives. And, in the 1970s and 1980s, there were no viable alternatives to neoclassical economics for analyzing health care. Then in 1986 I stumbled across a curious article in the premier journal in economics, *The American Economic Review*, "Fairness as a Constraint on Profit Seeking: Entitlements in the Market," by Daniel Kahneman, Jack Knetsch, and Richard Thaler (Kahneman, Knetsch, and Thaler 1986). Fairness had never been an area that had drawn much attention in mainstream economics, but the results of the authors' experiments resonated with the kinds of behavior I was seeing in health care.

As a consultant, my job was not to read and think deep thoughts about the issues of the day but to help clients solve problems. So I started to read the nascent literature in behavioral economics only casually. Then, I moved to Johns Hopkins University, to run the Business of Medicine program and teach the medical economics courses. At first, I taught the standard material, assigning the usual microeconomics textbooks and journal articles in health economics. The students—all in health care, many of them faculty in the medical school—dutifully completed their assignments but increasingly disagreed with the assumptions and models of neoclassical health economics. As a result, I started to introduce some of the research on behavioral economics—even though none of it dealt with health care. The students responded immediately. So, I added more and more, until I had to offload most of it into a new course on behavioral economics and health care.

My new course has been a real eye-opener for me. The students, who have extensive clinical or administrative experience in health care, have been enthusiastic in applying behavioral economics to health care. Through assignments I gave them, discussions in class, and my own thinking, I began to assemble a series of what I called "anomalies" in health care—behavior that neoclassical economics could not explain or could not explain very well. (I used the term *anomalies*, in part, as a tribute to Richard Thaler, who pioneered a section with that title in *The Journal of Economic Perspectives*.) I began to realize that behavioral economics was much more useful in explaining these anomalies.

In addition, I scoured the health economics literature to see the extent to which the field had begun to apply the tenets of behavioral economics. I found only a few examples in the past decade, such as Richard Frank (Frank 2007), George Loewenstein (Loewenstein 2005), and Kevin Volpp (Volpp et al. 2008; 2011). Their excellent work has begun to encourage other health economists to explore the value of this new discipline.

I wrote this book for four purposes. First, I wanted my colleagues in health economics to appreciate the power of behavioral economics and to use it to advance the field. Second, I wanted physicians and leaders of health care institutions to recognize how their decisions are often affected by a set of biases that can derail their efforts on behalf of patients. Third, I wanted health policy makers to see how they can apply the tools of behavioral economics to improve the delivery and financing of health care. Finally, I wanted to introduce lay readers to the concepts of behavioral economics and to help them see how these concepts applied to the challenges we face in the U.S. health care system.

It would be overconfidence bias on my part to expect that I can accomplish all four goals. In the end I will be satisfied if this book helps to start a different conversation on how to improve the state of the U.S. health care system. I welcome your thoughts.

ACKNOWLEDGMENTS

Every book results from the work of many people, even if only one name is on the title page. This book is no exception. It is usually good politics for an author to thank his editor in the acknowledgments. In this case, my thanks are heartfelt, as well. Margo Beth Fleming was supportive of this project from the beginning and used an extraordinary combination of support and cajoling to get a deadline-challenged author to say what he wanted to say in a way that would appeal to actual readers. I also want to thank my two peer reviewers, Richard Scheffler and an anonymous referee, who also were both supportive and appropriately critical of earlier drafts. Ryan Fongemie did an excellent job of designing the figures from my sometimes sketchy ideas.

I need to thank Dr. Ned Calonge, Dr. Peter Pronovost, and Professor George Loewenstein for their time and valuable insights that illuminated the ways in which behavioral economics can explain what is going on in health care and health care reform. I also want thank to four faculty colleagues at Johns Hopkins University: Steve Sisson, for being an articulate and reflective diagnostician; Ed Bessman, for his insightful and iconoclastic views on medicine and economics; Harold Lehman, for his expertise in medical decision making; and Todd Dorman, for his unvarnished comments on my chapters on physician decision making.

I could not have written Chapter 2 had it not been for two people (in addition to Dr. Calonge): Dean Lucy Marion, PhD, RN, FAAN, for her insights on the workings of the U.S. Preventive Services Task Force and the controversy surrounding the 2009 mammography guidelines; and Dean Janet Allen, PhD, RN, FAAN, for making the introductions to the USPSTF that I never would have gotten in any other way.

Finally, I want to salute each of the students in my behavioral economics course in the fall of 2011: Anna Diller, Vinnie Gopaul, Kristi Guenther, Jin Won Noh, Olumayowa Osibodu, Kaustubh Radkar, Abhishek Raut, Matt Scally, Sumeet Srivastava, Carrie Stein, Femi Taiwo, Tiffany Wandy, and Kim Weatherspoon. Their intelligence, intellectual curiosity, and enthusiasm made me realize that my initial ideas on behavioral economics and health care actually made some sense.

Irrationality in Health Care

1 WHAT IS BEHAVIORAL ECONOMICS — AND WHY SHOULD WE CARE?

It is time, therefore, for a fundamental change in our approach.
It is time to take account—and not merely as a residual category—
of the empirical limits of human rationality, of its finiteness in
comparison with the complexities of the world with which it must cope.
—Herbert Simon (1957)

The health care industry in the United States is peculiar. We spend close to 18 percent of our gross domestic product on health care, yet other countries seem to get better results—and we really don't know why. Most health care products and services are produced by private organizations, yet federal and state governments pay for about half of these services. More starkly, those who consume health care do not pay for it, and those who do pay for that care do not consume it. That is, patients pay less than 15 percent of their care at the point of purchase, the rest being picked up by their employers, private insurance companies, Medicare, or Medicaid (which have no need for physician visits, medications, or surgeries themselves). Health care is also peculiar on the supply side. Unlike in every other industry, the people who fundamentally determine how resources are allocated—that is, the physicians—rarely have any financial stake (as owners or employees) in the resources that they control in hospitals, nursing homes, or other facilities.

It is no wonder, then, that economists like myself are fascinated by this industry and are turning our theoretical and empirical tools to all aspects of demand and supply. Although we have made some headway in understanding the health care industry, the standard tools do not seem to be helping us to understand much about the behavior of patients, physicians, and even society as a whole. In this book I will offer a new economic lens that I hope will provide more clarity in diagnosing the problems facing the business side of health care. This lens—behavioral economics—is helpful in understanding the "micro" decisions that we make as patients and that physicians make as they care for us. In addition, it yields insights into the "macro" decisions we make as a nation regarding how we organize and pay for health care. I will introduce the concepts of behavioral economics by discussing a series of what I call "anomalies," that is, behavior—both individual and societal—that just does not seem to be rational. For example, we will consider:

- Why would requiring everyone to buy health insurance make everyone—including those who don't want to buy health insurance—better off?
- Why do patients insist on getting a prescription, shot, test . . . when they go to a physician with an ailment—yet many patients do not adhere to their diagnostic and treatment regimens?
- Why do tens of thousands of patients die each year in the United States from central line–associated bloodstream infections—even though a simple five-step checklist used by physicians and nurses could reduce that number by two-thirds?

My point is not that these anomalies occur because people are stupid or naïve or easily manipulated. Rather, it is that we—as consumers, providers, and society—need to recognize the power of arational behavior if we are to improve the performance of the health care system and get what we pay for.

MAINSTREAM ECONOMICS AND ITS ASSUMPTIONS
Most economists practicing today learned their trade in what is known as the neoclassical tradition. We were trained in a school of economic thought

that traces its heritage back to Adam Smith and *The Wealth of Nations*, published in 1776. In this world, markets—properly organized—allocate scarce resources to their highest and best use through the application of Smith's famous "invisible hand." The primary role of the government is to ensure that markets are properly organized and operated and then to get out of the way. Buyers and sellers, in seeking to further their own gains and with little or no conscious intent to improve public welfare, will be led to maximize their "utility" (economists' term for happiness or satisfaction) or profit. In fact, using both graceful exposition and elegant mathematics, neoclassical economists have been able to prove what became known as the "fundamental theorem of welfare economics," that a competitive market will generate a Pareto-optimal allocation of resources. That is, this market-generated allocation will yield the highest collective value of those resources. They proved that any deviation from that allocation would benefit some buyers and sellers only at the expense of others.

As you might imagine, this finding has been used to justify capitalism and the market economy. At the same time, it has been used to explain the evils of monopolies (because monopolies typically raise prices above what would be charged in a truly competitive market) and to defend the intervention of the government to limit pollution (because private markets typically do not factor in the costs of pollution to society).

This theory of economics rests on a number of critical assumptions about the structure of the market and the behavior of buyers and sellers in the market. It is important for the discussion here to describe these assumptions, why they are important, and how the theory can fail if the assumptions are not valid. The first—and most fundamental—assumption is that everyone is rational. That is, standard economics assumes that buyers and sellers, individuals and organizations, always act in their own best interests. If participants in the market are not always rational, then they will not make decisions that promote their well-being (either satisfaction/happiness on the part of consumers or profits on the part of sellers), and mainstream economists will be at a loss as to how to proceed.

Second, mainstream neoclassical economics assumes that all participants in the market know their preferences. Again, it would be difficult for a consumer to maximize his or her preferences without knowing what they were. Third, the theory assumes that all participants in the market have full information—about the products in the market, their features and drawbacks, and the prices being offered by various sellers. Understandably, if consumers are not aware of the alternatives that face them, it will be difficult for them to make the right decisions. Similarly, sellers need to know about the preferences of consumers and the range of products being offered by competitors if they are to offer the right product at the right price and sell their wares.

A somewhat less intuitive assumption of standard economics is that consumer preferences and decisions are path independent. The preferences that consumers have and the decisions that they make should not depend on how they arrive at those preferences or decisions. For example, a consumer's willingness to buy a particular car should not depend on whether he saw a more expensive or less expensive car first or whether he saw a blue car (a color he loves) before or after a green car (a color he despises). If consumer preferences and decisions are based on these external and seemingly irrelevant factors, then one has to question the validity of his choices.

Finally, even mainstream economists admit that consumers and producers sometimes make mistakes. Even so, these economists assume that the mistakes are random and not systematic. So, if people miss the mark in making decisions that improve their situation, sometimes they will be above the mark, and sometimes they will be below—and we have no way to predict what mistakes they will make.

It may be pretty obvious that these assumptions do not accurately describe reality all of the time or, in fact, most of the time. People do not always act rationally; they often do not have full information about the products or services they may want to purchase; and occasionally they may not know exactly what they prefer. Mainstream economists have spent a lot of energy over the past several decades analyzing what happens when these assumptions are violated. Going into this work will take us too far afield. However, we should note a rather profound argument made by two prominent economists—Milton Friedman and Leonard Savage—regarding the importance of assumptions.

In an influential article written over sixty years ago, Friedman and Savage (1948) confronted the contention that bad assumptions lead to bad theory. They argued that economic theory does not assert that people act exactly as the assumptions claim that they do; instead, it is sufficient that people only act *as if* they were obeying the assumptions. Friedman and Savage argue that this "as if" nuance is crucial. They maintain that any theory should be evaluated on the accuracy of its predictions, not on the reality of its assumptions. If the assumptions allow the economist to develop a theory that yields results that outperform other theories, then the assumptions themselves are irrelevant.

Friedman and Savage support their argument by their now-famous analogy of a billiards player. A scientist might want to predict the path of a ball struck by an expert billiards player during a match. Friedman and Savage offer that it might be possible to develop mathematical formulas that predict the optimal force and direction of the cue and all the balls on the table. Such a theory of billiards behavior may require an assumption that the player knows and uses these formulas, more correctly that the player acts *as if* she knows and uses the formulas. As Friedman and Savage argue, "It would in no way disprove or contradict the hypothesis, or weaken our confidence in it, if it should turn out that the billiard player had never studied any branch of mathematics and was utterly incapable to making the necessary calculations" (p. 298), as long as the assumption was necessary for the development of the hypothesis and the theory predicted the results of the billiards shot better than any competing theory. The implication of this line of reasoning for economics is that the realism of the assumptions may not matter if the theory of behavior that uses these assumptions generates the most accurate predictions.

Given this criterion, mainstream neoclassical economics has held up very well over the past several decades compared to other competing economic theories. It has dispatched radical political economics (aka Marxism) following the fall of the Soviet Union and the Berlin Wall. It has proved to be more discriminating than institutional economics, which has failed to generate much interest since John Kenneth Galbraith retired. Evolutionary economics, despite the best efforts of renowned economists such as Sidney Winter and Richard Nelson, has not yet generated testable hypotheses that rival neoclassical economics.

THE CHALLENGE OF BEHAVIORAL ECONOMICS

Then came behavioral economics. This field was formed largely through the work of Daniel Kahneman and Amos Tversky in the 1970s. Ironically, Kahneman and Tversky (who died in 1996) are behavioral psychologists, not economists. Kahneman and Tversky first became known to most economists through a 1979 article, "Prospect Theory: An Analysis of Decision Under Risk," in the highly respected and mathematically rigorous journal, *Econometrica* (Kahneman and Tversky 1979). In that article, they presented the first explication of the tenets of behavioral economics. Despite its scarcity of mathematics, the article is the most frequently cited article ever published in *Econometrica* and the second most frequently cited article in the economics literature in the past forty years (Kim, Morse, and Zingales 2006).

What Kahneman and Tversky termed *prospect theory* has since evolved into what is generally referred to as behavioral economics. It has offered an interesting, and often compelling, alternative to mainstream neoclassical economics. First, it makes assumptions about human behavior that have greater face validity to both economists and laypeople. For example, it acknowledges that not everyone is rational, at least not all the time. Rather, buyers and sellers, individuals and organizations, do not always act in their own best interests. In addition, behavioral economics assumes that people do not have what neoclassical economists call a *utility function*, which maps all of the available goods and services and other contributions to happiness into a permanent set of preferences for each individual. Instead, behavioral economics assumes that people learn their preferences through experience, via trial and error. In addition, they make their decisions based on their current situation (which acts like a reference point), not from some overarching utility function.

A further assumption is that incomplete information abounds. Neither buyers nor sellers have all the information that they would like. Sometimes, the buyers do not have enough information, such as when they are buying a used car from the original owner. Sometimes it is the sellers that lack information, such as an insurance company writing a life insurance policy for an individual; the buyer knows his behavior, health history, and other risk factors, but the insurer does not.

Behavioral economists have found that preferences are, indeed, path dependent. Economic decisions are often influenced by factors independent of the individual: Buyers buy differently if they are shown a more expensive house before a less expensive house, a fully equipped car before a stripped-down model, a fifty-two-inch LCD television before a more modest set.

Not only does behavioral economics assume that buyers and sellers are not always rational; the theory also has a fundamental tenet that deviations from rational choice are systematic and can be predicted. This aspect of behavioral economics ultimately sets it apart conceptually from mainstream neoclassical economics and provides the focal point for testing the relative effectiveness of the two approaches for viewing human behavior.

I should note one final difference between mainstream neoclassical economics and behavioral economics. Neoclassical economics has largely been a self-contained discipline, developed by economists, for economists. If neoclassical economists have borrowed concepts from another field, it's been mathematics. On the other hand, behavioral economics owes a very large intellectual debt to the discipline of psychology, especially behavioral psychology. By the nature of its assumptions, behavioral economics depends fundamentally on the perspective, hypotheses, and empirical studies of behavioral psychologists. In fact, there will be times in this book in which it is not clear whether we are looking at behavioral economics or behavioral psychology phenomena—and that is by design.

THE CONTRIBUTIONS—SO FAR—
OF BEHAVIORAL ECONOMICS

In the next chapters we will be exploring the full range of explanations and predictions that behavioral economics can offer. However, I want to illustrate the relative power of behavioral economics here by examining three areas in which this theory provides explanations that are superior to mainstream neoclassical economics: decision biases, the power of the default, and the special value of zero.

First, let's take a look at decision bias. Everyone makes mistakes, even neoclassical economists. What behavioral psychologists have demonstrated—and behavioral economists have used—is that people tend to make bad decisions in a particular way. (Note that I used the word *tend*; what behavioral psychologists have found are tendencies, not immutable laws of behavior. People cannot be as predictable as atoms, so psychology and economics cannot be as definitive as physics.) For example, a host of psychology studies have found that most people are overconfident about their abilities. In a famous study, university students in Oregon and Stockholm were asked to rate their driving compared to other students (Svenson 1981). About 80 percent of the American students thought that they were safer than the median student driver, and about 75 percent thought they were more skilled than the median student driver. Only 12.5 percent thought that they were less safe than the average, and only 7.2 percent thought that they were less skilled than the average. (The Swedish students were somewhat less confident than their American counterparts.) Perhaps the researcher just stumbled on a group of NASCAR protégés, but more likely this finding is an example of a "Lake Wobegon" effect, where all the children are thought to be above average.

We could write these results off as the wishful thinking of inexperienced, callow youth. But a recent study of attorneys shows that overconfidence bias may be endemic. Jane Goodman-Delahunty and her colleagues (Goodman-Delahunty et al. 2010) surveyed 481 litigation attorneys in the United States. They were asked two questions about a current case: "What would be a win situation in terms of your minimum goal for the outcome of this case?" and "From 0 to 100%, what is the probability that you will achieve this outcome or something better?" Sixty-four percent of the attorneys gave confidence estimates that exceeded 50 percent, which—as Goodman-Delahunty and her colleagues note—may not be surprising given that attorneys are trained to be zealous advocates for their clients and thus are likely to be optimistic about the case's outcomes.

The attorneys were then recontacted when their cases were resolved. Fifty-six percent of the time, the outcomes of the cases met or exceeded the attorney's minimum goals. However, in 44 percent of the cases the actual outcomes were less satisfactory than the minimum goals that the attorneys had set earlier. (By the way, there were some attorneys who were underconfident, but they were far outnumbered by the correctly confident and overconfident ones.) Ironically, only 18 percent of the attorneys said that they were very disappointed or somewhat disappointed in the outcome of the case. Now, that's confidence.

In breaking down the results, Goodman-Delahunty and her colleagues found the greatest gap between the prior estimate and the subsequent outcome was for those attorneys who expressed the highest confidence that their goal would be achieved. That is, those who were the most confident before the case was decided were the most likely to be wrong.

Finally, one would hope that attorneys would learn from their mistakes—but they did not, according to this study. More senior, experienced attorneys were as overconfident as their junior colleagues. In an attempt to assist the respondents in calibrating their confidence estimates, the researchers asked 212 of the 481 attorneys in the initial survey to provide reasons why their litigation goals might not be achieved. Those who gave reasons were just as likely to be overconfident as those who did not.

If rampant overconfidence were not enough, Justin Kruger and David Dunning conducted a variety of experiments that supported Charles Darwin's statement in his *The Descent of Man*, "Ignorance more frequently begets confidence than does knowledge" (Kruger and Dunning 1999). Groups of undergraduate volunteers from Cornell University were given various tests of logical reasoning and grammar. At the end of the test, the participants were asked to estimate how their score would compare with that of their classmates. As with the studies already described, participants overestimated their ability and performance, placing themselves on average between the sixty-fifth and seventieth percentile. The unique contribution of Kruger and Dunning is that they disaggregated the respondents by performance quartile and analyzed those responses. Those in the highest two quartiles of performance accurately predicted their ability and performance. However, those in the bottom half dramatically overestimated their results. For example, in the grammar test, those in the bottom quartile scored at the tenth percentile but estimated their ability in grammar in the sixty-seventh percentile and their performance in the test itself in the sixty-first percentile. Kruger and Dunning concluded that "this overestimation occurs, in part, because people who are unskilled in these domains suffer a dual burden. Not only do these people reach erroneous conclusions and make unfortunate choices, but their incompetence robs them of the metacognitive ability to realize it" (p. 1121).

You may be thinking at this point, "This is all very interesting—and perhaps disturbing for our nation—but what does it have to do with economics?" Remember the assumptions of neoclassical economics: Decision makers are rational and have sufficient information to make decisions, and if they do make mistakes, they are random ones. What the decision bias research seems to indicate, though, is that even if people have enough information about a situation (such as their ability to perform) they are apt to overestimate the likelihood of a favorable outcome. As a result, they may make economic decisions—when to get into the stock market, what career to pursue, when to cancel a project that is not meeting expectations—that do not turn out as well as expected. They get into the stock market too late, after the most significant gains have occurred, because they think that they have a knack for picking stocks. They enroll in graduate programs in the humanities and believe that they will be one of the lucky few who get that tenure-track position at a prestigious university. They keep pushing on a risky design project, despite the cost overruns, missed deadlines, and product test failures, because they are so convinced in their own ability to pull off a miracle.

And if, like the surveyed attorneys, they do not learn from their mistakes, then we have a real problem. This tendency to avoid learning is compounded by another finding of behavioral psychology: hindsight bias. Commonly known as "I knew it would happen," hindsight bias manifests itself in two ways: Once an event occurs, its occurrence appears obvious to everyone; and, second, after the event people believe that their earlier prediction of the likelihood of the event was much more accurate than it actually was. Baruch Fischhoff (1975) identified this phenomenon with a series of experiments in the 1970s. In one, he asked college students in Israel to predict the impact of President Nixon's historic visits to China and the Soviet Union, by giving probabilities that certain events would occur (for example, "President Nixon will meet Mao at least once," or "The USA and the USSR will agree to a joint space program"). After the visits, he resurveyed the students, asking them to recall their prior predictions, as if they did not know the outcome. Not surprisingly, the students increased their probabilities that the events that occurred would occur and lowered their probabilities that the events that did not occur would occur.

Other researchers have confirmed the presence of hindsight bias in both laboratory and naturally occurring studies, using historical events (both contemporary and long-past), sporting events, scientific studies, life events (such as buying a house), elections, medical cases, and legal cases. That is, hindsight bias occurs with both well-known and obscure events, events for which the respondents have a stake and those for which they were completely disinterested, and events for which the respondents were complete novices or recognized experts. As an example of the latter, Philip Tetlock (2005) investigated the accuracy of political pundits. In a meticulous study, he examined 82,361 forecasts of 27,451 events made by 284 experts regarding U.S. and international politics, economics, and national security issues. He found that the experts performed not much better than a coin toss, a random prediction. As interesting as that result is, the importance of his study here is the reaction of the experts after their predictions were confirmed or mistaken. They misremembered their original predictions, weighting them more heavily in favor of the event that actually occurred. This tendency was most prevalent among those experts who made the most aggressive, "big" predictions. (By contrast, the experts underestimated the correctness of their rivals' predictions.) Tetlock reported that one expert explained the phenomenon as, "We all once believed in Santa Claus. You don't think I keep track of every screwy belief I once held" (p. 183).

In a more economic context, Gavin Cassar and Justin Craig (2009) investigated how entrepreneurs suffer from hindsight bias. It is common knowledge that most start-up businesses fail, for a variety of reasons— bad ideas, bad market, bad luck. Neoclassical economists predict that every entrepreneur makes calculations along the way to determine whether to remain in business; in particular, she is always calculating whether the marginal benefits of staying in business (such as the future probability and rewards for success) exceed the marginal costs (including out-of-pocket costs and the foregone opportunity to direct her energies elsewhere). Once the marginal costs exceed the marginal benefits, the rational entrepreneur closes the business and uses the lessons from the failure to decide whether to start a new venture. Cassar and Craig found, however, that failed entrepreneurs do not follow the standard economic path. They interviewed 198 entrepreneurs whose start-ups failed. Before their start-ups failed, the entrepreneurs were asked, "On a scale of zero to one hundred, what is the likelihood that this business will be operating 5 years from now, regardless of who owns and operates the firm?" The mean number was 77.3, which is what you would expect from optimistic, risk-taking entrepreneurs. After the business failed, the entrepreneurs were asked, "When you got involved in this start-up, what was the probability that it would become an operational business?" This time the value was 58.8, well below their original estimate and strong evidence of hindsight bias.

By lowering their remembered probability of the success of their enterprise, the business leaders lost an opportunity to learn that perhaps they were too optimistic in gauging the prospects for their idea. Perhaps more disturbing, Cassar and Craig found that those failed entrepreneurs who had previous start-up experience did no better than first-time entrepreneurs in avoiding hindsight bias. The implications can be profound. As a society, we may want entrepreneurs to take risks and overcome the odds of failure, but we probably do not want them to fail to learn from their mistakes and take too many risks.

So why are so many people susceptible to hindsight bias? Hartmut Blank and his colleagues (2008) propose three related reasons. The first is "the impression of forseeability," that in retrospect everyone knew—before the event—how things would turn out. ("It was obvious that Barack Obama would win the 2008 presidential election.") The second is "an impression of necessity," that it was inevitable that things would turn out the way they did. ("Given the collapsing economy, it was impossible for John McCain—or any Republican—to win in 2008.") The third reason is "memory distortion," that people just forget—but they do so in a particular direction. ("No, you're wrong. I never thought that McCain would win.")

Most observers consider hindsight bias to be a problem for decision making. If people cannot remember their inaccurate predictions, then they cannot revise them and make better decisions in the future. Therefore, we should explore whether hindsight bias can be mitigated. The conclusion, according to a number of studies, is "not really." Hindsight bias has not been diminished even if the participants are explicitly instructed to ignore the actual outcome, or to pay more attention, or to work harder. Warning participants about the existence of hindsight bias does not work, even if done repeatedly. Pohl and Hell (1996), for example, conducted repeated hindsight bias experiments with groups of students, explaining between each experiment the nature of hindsight bias and the student's own bias in previous experiments. Nevertheless, the students exhibited the same amount of hindsight bias. The researchers then conducted the experiments with colleagues at Professor Pohl's cognitive psychology department at his university; even they succumbed to hindsight bias. The only replicable method for reducing hindsight bias has been to have participants give reasons why the opposite outcomes or nonchosen alternatives might occur, that is, for them to argue against the inevitability or obviousness of their selected outcome. And that is a lot of work.

Now that we have considered decision bias, let's turn to another powerful tenet of behavioral economics: the power of the default (Thaler and Sunstein 2008). Many situations have an unavoidable initial position; we have to start somewhere. Cars are driven on the left or on the right side of the road. We use English measurements or the metric system. Features in insurance policies are either standard or options. The candy bars can be placed in the middle of the store or at the checkout. What behavioral economists have demonstrated is that where you start makes a difference: The initial (default) position is extraordinarily powerful.

Two famous studies illustrate this point. The first, "Do Defaults Save Lives?" conducted by Eric Johnson and Daniel Goldstein (2003),

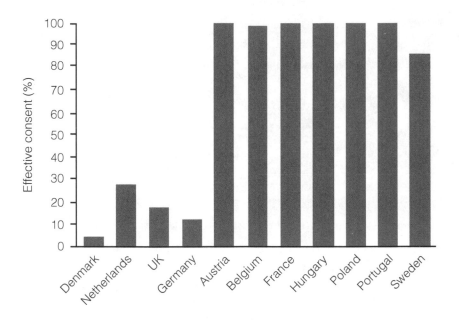

FIGURE I.I
Organ donor rates, by country.

SOURCE: From Johnson, Eric J., and Daniel Goldstein. 2003. Do defaults save lives? *Science* 302: 1338–39, Figure: Effective consent rates, by country. Reprinted with permission from AAAS.

examined the rate at which adults in European countries register to be potential organ donors. Figure 1.1 shows the startling results. In four of the countries—Denmark, the Netherlands, the United Kingdom, and Germany—between 4 and 27 percent of adults are registered organ donors. In the other seven countries, it's between 86 and 99 percent. Although there are some cultural and historical differences among these countries, there seems to be nothing that could explain these extraordinary differences in organ donor consent rates. Johnson and Goldstein's explanation: In the first four countries, adults who want to be organ donors must sign up, whereas adults in the other countries are automatically registered. The first method is called "opt-in" or "explicit consent," whereas the second is called "opt-out" or "presumed consent." Neoclassical economists would argue that such differences would persist only if people were not informed of the initial assignment or told how to change their status or if it were expensive—in time or money—to make a change. For example, perhaps the citizens of Belgium do not know that they have been automatically enrolled as organ donors, or maybe it is difficult to opt out of being a donor (perhaps by making the disaffected donor go to City Hall on a particular day of the month and suffer through waits similar to a Department of Motor Vehicles office in the United States). It turns out that none of these conjectures explains the seemingly anomalous behavior. It is fairly easy to opt out in the opt-out countries.

Before turning to potential reasons for these results, consider another, more economics-related study. Bridget Madrian and Dennis Shea (2001) were interested in the retirement savings behavior of employees. They were fortunate to come across a natural experiment occurring with a large U.S. corporation. The company was changing the structure of the 401(k) retirement program it offered its employees. The original program was set up similar to that in most organizations: Participation in the program was limited to employees who had worked at the company for at least one year; once eligible, employees could contribute up to 15 percent of their pay to the plan, with the first 6 percent receiving a 50 percent match from the employer. That is, for every $2 contributed by the employee, the company would kick in $1, up to 6 percent of the employee's wages or salary. To enroll, the employee would have to complete a form, choose a contribution rate, and then choose how to allocate the contribution among nine investment options.

In 1998 the company made two major changes to its 401(k) program. First, all employees were eligible to participate in the program from their first day of work, but the company's contribution did not start until the employee's one-year anniversary. Second, all newly hired employees were automatically enrolled in the 401(k) program, with 3 percent of their wages or salary contributed to the program and all invested in the program's money market fund. (Existing employees could choose this option, as well.) The automatically enrolled employees could opt out easily or could change the contribution rate or investment selection at any time.

It might be nice to think that the company made this change because of its concern for its employees' long-term welfare. That might be, but the primary reason was that so few nonexecutive employees were signing up for the original 401(k) plan that the plan was failing the nondiscrimination tests required by the IRS so that employee contributions could come from pretax dollars. Regardless of the company's intentions, the change worked. Prior to the new arrangement, 57 percent of employees with one year of tenure would sign up for the 401(k) program; over time, more would sign up, so that by their tenth year, more than 80 percent of employees were in the program. When the new plan became effective, 86 percent of new employees enrolled in the plan. That is, the participation rate of new employees immediately reached the level of long-tenured employees.

There were two other interesting manifestations of the default mechanism in this natural experiment. First, whereas 76 percent of participants in the new program contributed the default rate of 3 percent of their income into the 401(k), only 12 percent of participants in the old program contributed that percentage; in line with the default theme, though, about 37 percent of participants in the old program contributed 6 percent (the limit of the employer match). Second, 80 percent of participants in the new program allocated all of their contributions into the default money market fund, compared to only 5 percent of those in the old program.

So, what explains the persistent difference in behavior related to organ donation and retirement plan participation? Johnson and Goldstein, and Madrian and Shea, argue that the default position has amazing power to guide people's behavior. They argue that part of the default's power is that it can act as an implicit recommendation or endorsement by the government or company. ("The company must think that it is a good thing for me to invest 3 percent of my income in this retirement plan, and to put it all in the money market fund. Who am I to disagree?") Another factor may be just inertia. People in Poland or Portugal might intend to opt out of the organ donation program but never quite get around to doing so. Also, this behavior may be an example of the "endowment effect," which will be discussed in detail in Chapter 2. Briefly, behavioral economists have found that people place a surprisingly high value on whatever they are initially allocated and require a significant premium to change. So, employees in the corporation that changed its 401(k) program had two sets of employees: the old employees, whose "endowment" was nonparticipation in the program; and the new employees, whose endowment was participation in the program with a 3 percent contribution into a money market fund.

Finally, Richard Thaler and Cass Sunstein, in their book *Nudge* (2008), argue that defaults are a way by which the potentially ill-formed preferences of people can be given a push—a "nudge." We will consider their work in more detail later, in Chapter 3, but we should note here that the selection of the default can have profound implications for consumer choice, individual welfare, and societal interests.

The third contribution of behavioral economics that I want to discuss here is the special value of zero. In neoclassical economics, a price of zero has no particular significance. In effect, it is just $1 less than $1, just as $9 is one less than $10. Behavioral economists have found, however, that a price of zero has an extraordinary effect on people's behavior. For example, Kristina Shampanier, Nina Mazar, and Dan Ariely (2007) conducted a series of experiments that explored the impact of varying the relative prices of various products. All of the experiments found the same result, so describing one of these experiments should be sufficient. Participants were offered $10 and $20 gift cards for Amazon .com at various prices. When they were offered a $10 gift card for $5, a $20 gift card for $12, or neither, 29 percent selected the $10 card and 71 percent selected the $20 card. (I performed the same experiment with my students and found basically the same result. Those who picked the $10 card said they did so because it was a 50 percent discount, whereas the $20 card was only a 40 percent discount. Those who choose the $20 card told me that that card saved them $8, whereas the other card saved them only $5.) Shampanier and her colleagues then lowered the price of both gift cards by $4, so that the price of the $10 card was then $1 and the price of the $20 card was $8. This alteration changed the results slightly, with 36 percent selecting the $10 card and 64 percent choosing the $20 card. Then, the researchers lowered the price of the cards by $1 each, so that the price of the $20 Amazon.com gift card was $7 and the price of the $10 gift card was $0—free. The result was astounding: One hundred percent of the participants chose the $10 gift card. Shampanier and her colleagues offered several explanations for the phenomenon. We will consider these alternative explanations in much more detail in Chapter 5.

There exist real-world examples of this magical value of a zero price. Consider the opening of a Chick-fil-A restaurant. This very successful fast-food chain has over 1,500 locations in the United States and distinguishes itself with its emphasis on chicken sandwiches and creative advertising (for example, with billboards showing cows petitioning passersby to "Eat Mor Chikin"). A feature of the opening of a new location is that the first 100 customers receive a prize of one Chick-fil-A Meal (consisting of a Chicken Sandwich, Chick-fil-A Waffle Potato Fries, and a drink) per week for a year. This event has gotten so popular that the company has now had to institute formal rules regarding the giveaway, including:

If more than 100 people are . . . prepared to participate in the Giveaway as of 6 a.m. local Restaurant time on the Wednesday before a Thursday grand opening, the First 100 Participants and Alternates must remain at the Sponsor-designated area at the Restaurant during the entire Giveaway Period to receive a Prize. Exceptions are made for short bathroom breaks and/or to comply with any applicable legal requirement, or otherwise in the sole discretion of Sponsor. Each Participant and Alternate will be given a wristband with his or her Number written on it. The wristband must be worn at all times during the Giveaway Period. During the Giveaway Period, if any Participant is disqualified or leaves the Restaurant for any reason, an Alternate will take the former Participant's place and become a Participant, starting with Alternate Number 1 and continuing as needed to Alternate Number 10. Participants and Alternates may have up to 5 Guests remain at the Restaurant during the Giveaway Period provided that they sign the Release and Waiver, comply with Sponsor's instructions while at the Restaurant and do not create a decorum or safety issue.[1]

So, people are camping out for twenty-four to forty-eight hours for the chance to get free meals that are worth about $6 per week. This phenomenon is certainly an excellent example of the special value of zero. I expect

---

[1] © CFA Properties Inc.

that Chick-fil-A would not be getting this response—or this publicity—if it had distributed 50 percent, 75 percent, or even 90 percent off coupons to every household in its new location's market.

Finally, let's consider another example of the special value of zero, but one that leads to a much different lesson. Uri Gneezy and Aldo Rustichini (2000a) investigated a case in which the price for a service went from zero to a positive amount—and demand went up, against the predictions of neoclassical economics. They examined the behavior of parents at ten day-care centers in the city of Haifa in Israel. The centers were open from 7:30 am to 4:00 pm. If parents were late in picking up their children at the end of the day, teachers had to wait with the children until the parents arrived. As expected, the centers were having a problem with parents being late. With the centers' permission, Gneezy and Rustichini performed a twenty-week experiment. In the first four weeks, they recorded the number of parents arriving late to retrieve their children. In the next twelve weeks, a fine of 10 new Israeli shekels (about US$3) was imposed in six of the ten centers for those parents who were late by at least ten minutes. For the remaining four weeks of the experiment, the fine was removed. The result: almost a doubling of the number of late arrivals! And the number of late arrivals did not drop in the last four weeks of the experiment, when the fine went to zero.

The researchers hypothesized that what was happening was that a social norm had turned into an economic norm. Prior to the imposition of the fine, parents may have viewed their being late as an imposition on the teachers, who were not being paid extra to stay overtime. That is, the parents may have felt that they were violating a social contract with the teachers by being late. When the fine was imposed, the parents may have viewed the fine as nothing more than a price for a transaction. Once the fine became a price, the parents then started to use an economic norm to calculate the value of their time versus the fine. In effect, the parents began to think of the fine as the price for after-hours day care services. The fact that parents' behavior did not return to the prior norm once the fine/price was eliminated suggests that the economic norm became too powerful, or what Gneezy and Rustichini called, "Once a commodity, always a commodity" (p. 14).

IF BEHAVIORAL ECONOMICS IS SO GOOD, WHY HASN'T IT TAKEN OVER?

The three areas we have just discussed—decision biases, the power of the default, and the special value of zero—have demonstrated that behavioral economics can provide insights that mainstream economics either cannot duplicate or it just ignores. If this is the case, then why hasn't behavioral economics usurped the place of neoclassical economics and become "mainstream"? There are a number of very valid reasons. First, despite these and a host of other successes, behavioral economics is still a relatively young branch of the discipline; it's just a little over thirty years since Kahneman and Tversky's path-breaking article in *Econometrica*. As such, behavioral economists and psychologists are still in the process of developing a comprehensive alternative theory of human behavior and decision making. Sometimes, all we have are a conjecture and some interesting results. Sometimes, these conjectures and results overlap and even conflict. The challenging task over the next several decades is to develop a unified theory that provides the foundation for behavioral economics, one that can provide a credible alternative to mainstream, neoclassical economics.

In fact, much of behavioral economics to date focuses on the demand side of behavior, not the supply side. Although this field has yielded some insights into the behavior of producers and sellers, neoclassical economics still better explains the preponderance of supply behavior. As I just noted, there are holes and inconsistencies and errors of interpretation in behavioral economics that need to be addressed. As scientific historian Thomas Kuhn (1965, 1962) pointed out a half century ago, scientists are reluctant to abandon their existing paradigm for another until the existing paradigm fails to predict key questions in the field, whereas the competing paradigm does. We are not quite there yet in economics.

One indicator that behavioral economics has not reached the level of neoclassical economics is that there is not—yet—an introductory economics textbook in wide circulation that uses a behavioral economics framework. And, as Nobel laureate Paul Samuelson has said, "I don't care who writes a nation's laws, or crafts its advanced treatises, if I can write its economics textbooks" (Weinstein 2009).

This is not to say that mainstream economists are ignoring or dismissing the insights of behavioral economists. In fact, over the past decade the research of these economists has been published in the premier journals in the field—*American Economic Review*, *Quarterly Journal of Economics*, and even the *Journal of Political Economy*.

A second reason why behavioral economics has not supplanted neoclassical economics is that a good deal of the empirical studies that have tested the theories of behavioral economists and psychologists have been conducted only on university students. The reason: Much of the work of behavioral psychology and economics has been through experiments, and it is much easier to populate experiments with students who are looking to make a few dollars or to get extra credit in their psychology class than to entice an equal number of adults. To no one's surprise, a number of studies and meta-analyses have shown that college students are not representative of the adult population and that their behavior may be driven by different preferences and constraints than is that of more mature people (Sears 1986; Henrich, Heine, and Norenzayan 2010).

Despite these problems—which I consider to be growing pains rather than fatal flaws—I contend that behavioral economics explains much of human behavior more accurately than does mainstream economics. In particular, I intend to show in this book that this field is particularly rich in expanding our understanding of how individual patients and physicians make medical decisions and how society creates health policy.

BEHAVIORAL ECONOMICS AND HEALTH CARE

The principles of behavioral economics have only begun to be applied to health care. Richard Frank (2007) presented a thoughtful research agenda for the discipline in a chapter written for a volume analyzing the application of behavioral economics in various fields. Peter Orszag (2008) laid out some provocative ideas on health care from a behavioral economics perspective in a speech he gave before becoming the director of the Office of Management and Budget for the Obama administration.

George Loewenstein and his colleagues have been adapting some of their extensive work in behavioral economics to health care, and we will be discussing his work throughout this book (Loewenstein 2005; Loewenstein, Brennan, and Volpp 2007; Volpp et al. 2009a).

Kevin Volpp, a physician and health economist and director of the Center for Health Incentives and Behavioral Economics at the University of Pennsylvania, has been conducting perhaps some of the most extensive experimental work in this new field. Two of his studies are worth describing here, as they indicate how behavioral economics both fits within the tradition of economics (by recognizing the power of prices to affect human behavior) and breaks out of that mold (by demonstrating how traditional approaches in economics fail to account for the complexity of decision making). The first study examined the impact of financial incentives on smoking cessation (Volpp et al. 2009b). Volpp and his team recruited 878 smokers who were employees of a multinational company and who were interested in kicking the habit. Half were randomly assigned to receive only information about community-based smoking-cessation programs, and the other half were given a series of financial incentives ($100 for completing a community-based program, $250 for smoking cessation for six months after the program, and another $400 for an additional six months of smoking cessation). The good news was that the incentivized group had almost three times the quit rate as the control group; the bad news that the quit rate was still rather small: 14.7 percent versus 5.0 percent for the first round of cessation and 9.4 percent versus 3.6 percent for the second round. In a sense, this experiment was very much within the realm of neoclassical economics, with participants expected to make decisions based on marginal benefits and marginal costs. However, as we shall see in Chapter 4, human decision making is much more complex than anticipated in standard economic models; as Kevin Volpp and his team noted in this study, interventions more sophisticated than price need to be applied.

Professor Volpp, along with another team that included George Loewenstein, pursued such an approach in a study involving weight loss (Volpp et al. 2008). They randomly assigned fifty-seven healthy individuals with a body mass index between thirty and forty into three groups, each with a goal to lose sixteen pounds in sixteen weeks. The first was the typical control group, with the participants enrolled in a weight-monitoring program with monthly weigh-ins. Those in the second group were enrolled in the same weight-loss program but with a daily lottery if the participant met his or her weight loss goal. (This incentive tests the participants' sense of loss aversion, a key concept in behavioral economics that we will discuss in the next chapter.) The third group was given a "deposit contract," in which the participants had to contribute some of their own money (between $0.01 and $3.00 per day), which was matched by the program but was at risk if a participant failed to meet the stated weight-loss goal. (As we shall see in Chapters 3 and 4, these so-called commitment devices, based on the tenets of behavioral economics, can be effective tools in influencing decision making.) The study found that those in the incentive groups lost more weight after sixteen weeks than did those in the control group (14.0 pounds for the deposit contract group and 13.1 pounds for the lottery group, versus 3.9 pounds for the control group). Unfortunately, three months after the end of the program, participants in the incentive groups gained back some of their weight, although the mean total loss was still greater than in the control group. (These results foreshadow a discussion we will have in Chapter 5 about intrinsic and extrinsic motivation and the crowding out effect.)

These two studies by Kevin Volpp and his colleagues illustrate both the promise and the limitations of behavioral economics. As I hope this book will demonstrate, the principles and tools of behavioral economics can explain—much better than mainstream, neoclassical economics— the decisions and actions of people when health care is involved. At the same time, it is a young and imperfect science. As a result, some of its hypotheses will be found wanting, and some of its empirical studies will be contradicted. Nevertheless, I believe the field will yield important insights that will help improve health care in the United States.

CONCLUSION

In this book, we will be considering how three different areas of health care behavior can be explained by behavioral economics: public policy, patient behavior, and physician behavior. In some cases there are actual studies that have been undertaken that demonstrate this impact. In others, the behavior can be explained by the general findings of behavioral economics, but there are not yet formal studies in health care to confirm our conclusions. (In that sense, one secondary purpose of this book is to establish a research agenda of interesting questions in health care that behavioral economics can answer, either through laboratory or natural experiments.) I should temper your expectations a bit, though. Unlike some recent books, I will not be contending that the tenets of behavioral economics are a revelation and represent a singular perspective that is vastly superior to any other explanations of behavior in health care. Instead, I have a more modest goal, to establish that the application of behavioral economics will expand our understanding of why the U.S. health care system operates as it does. Perhaps we can then use the principles of this field to improve the behavior of patients and physicians and to improve our collective decisions about allocating scarce resources in this area. I should warn you, though, that many of the findings of behavioral economics research suggest that the sometimes nonrational behavior that we see is so ingrained that it will be difficult to change. Even so, I promise you that it will be worth the effort to see what this new field can do.

2 KEEPING WHAT WE HAVE, EVEN IF WE DON'T LIKE IT

The summer of 2009 was unusually hot—in terms of politics. In the first six months of the Obama administration, Congress had passed a $787 billion economic stimulus plan, the Lilly Ledbetter Fair Pay Act (to facilitate pay discrimination lawsuits), the Helping Families Save Their Homes Act (to assist homeowners facing foreclosure), the Credit CARD Act (to reform practices of credit card companies), and the Supplemental Appropriations Act (which included the "Cash for Clunkers" program). In addition, the House of Representatives and the Senate were vigorously debating a massive overhaul of the U.S. health care system.

It was in this atmosphere that the Congress adjourned for its summer recess. Representatives returned to their districts, and many held "town hall" sessions with their constituents, as they had for years. This year was different, though. Those attending the sessions were in no mood for the calm back-and-forth of prior years. They were mad, and they wanted their representatives to know it. In late July 2009, Bob Inglis, then congressman for the Fourth Congressional District in South Carolina, held a town hall meeting in Simpsonville, a suburb of Greenville. Inglis was a conservative Republican and an opponent of the sweeping health care legislation working its way through Congress. That made no difference to these constituents. At that moment, he represented Washington and all that was wrong with the system. (In fact, in 2010 he lost the primary election for his seat to a "Tea Party" candidate.) At one point during the town hall meeting, an elderly man stood up and told Representative Inglis, "Keep your government hands off my Medicare." Inglis later told *The Washington Post*, "I had to politely explain that, 'Actually, sir, your health care is being provided by the government.' But he wasn't having any of it" (Rucker 2009).

Liberal pundits and late-night comedians made fun of this constituent. What kind of idiot doesn't know that Medicare is a federal program? Does he not see the direct benefits that he is getting from the government that he rails against—Social Security, defense and security, the interstate highway system—not to mention the various tax breaks (such as deducting mortgage interest) that he takes advantage of? Although ignorance could be the explanation, I will argue that something more subtle and potentially more important may be going on here. This gentleman may have been demonstrating one of the major principles of behavioral economics.

In this chapter we will examine two sets of fundamental principles of behavioral economics: the endowment effect/loss aversion (the tendency of people to hold dear what they have, even if they would not choose it now) and anchoring/framing (the sensitivity of people's decisions to how issues are framed and where their reference point is). We will use these concepts to explain three diverse anomalies in health care that all lead back to the same root behavior: (1) Why does the public support many specific aspects of health care reform but not the law that was enacted in 2010? (2) Why did that man in South Carolina object to the federal government getting involved in his Medicare services? And (3) Why was there such an uproar in November 2009 when the U.S. Preventive Services Task Force released its recommendations regarding screening mammography?

LOSS AVERSION AND THE ENDOWMENT EFFECT: WHY PEOPLE HOLD ON TO WHAT THEY HAVE, EVEN IF THEY REALLY WOULD LIKE SOMETHING ELSE

In their groundbreaking article in 1979, Daniel Kahneman and Amos Tversky laid out the basic tenets of behavioral economics (Kahneman and Tversky 1979). To personalize the significance of their work, let's begin by considering the case of Benjamin, a character we will be encountering throughout this book. Benjamin is twenty-seven years old, a recent graduate of the University of Illinois; he works as a database analyst at a trade association in downtown Chicago. He lives in a two-bedroom apartment on the north side of the city with his girlfriend, Elaine. Benjamin is a big sports fan—Bears, Bulls, and especially the Cubs. He also indulges in a little gambling from time to time. He is considering making a $1,000 wager on outcome of the Super Bowl, with a 50 percent chance of winning; if he wins, he gets $1,000 (as well as his $1,000 back); if he loses, he loses his $1,000. Of course, if he does not make the bet, he still has the $1,000. Suppose that Benjamin is considering a more risky bet (perhaps predicting the number of first downs made in each quarter). In this case, suppose that his probability of winning is only 10 percent, but he could receive $10,000 if he bet $1,000. In the terms of mainstream neoclassical economics, Benjamin is defined as being "risk seeking" if he makes either bet and "risk averse" if he does not.

As the mainstream theory says, Benjamin will compare the satisfaction (or "utility") of keeping the $1,000 with the "expected utility" of the bet, where the expected utility is the utility of winning times the probability of winning plus the utility of losing times the probability of losing. As we discussed in Chapter 1, neoclassical economics assumes that Benjamin knows the probabilities, as well as his utility function (that is, how much he likes $10,000 [if he wins the first downs bet], $1,000 [if he wins the game outcome bet], $0 [if he loses either bet], and $1,000 [if he does not bet at all]).

Now, here's the twist that Kahneman and Tversky would introduce to analyze Benjamin's decision making. They would assume that Benjamin really does not know his preferences for every possible situation, only how any change compares to the status quo. In addition, they would argue that Benjamin dislikes losses more than he likes monetarily equivalent gains. In their words, Benjamin is *loss averse*. Finally, although Benjamin may be aware of the objective probability that any event would occur, Kahneman and Tversky posit that he makes his own interpretation of their meaning; in particular, he treats small probabilities as if they are greater than they are, and he weights large probabilities less than the actual probabilities. So, according to Kahneman and Tversky, Benjamin does not maximize expected utility; instead, he maximizes the "prospect" of winning or losing the bets, relative to the status quo.

At first glance, this does not look like a significant difference. In fact, it changes everything. By replacing a "utility function" with a "prospect function," Kahneman and Tversky argue that Benjamin (and other people) do a lot less work in making decisions than neoclassical economists assume. Before acting, all Benjamin has to know is how much he likes the status quo and how he would feel if his circumstances got better or worse.

Prospect theory can be illustrated in the two diagrams shown in Figure 2.1. The diagram on the left shows a hypothetical value function. Note that it starts at zero—the reference point—so Benjamin is considering losses or gains from the status quo. If he experiences gains, those gains generate positive value to him; likewise, losses generate negative value. This may be obvious, but what is not so plain is that as Benjamin experiences higher and higher gains, the additional value he gains is less and less. The same thing happens with losses. As noteworthy, *gains* of a certain amount (say, x, in the figure) generate less value than do *losses* of that same amount; that is, losses count more for Benjamin than do gains. The diagram on the right illustrates how Benjamin translates objective probabilities into subjective ones. The diagram shows that Benjamin puts greater weight on low probabilities and lesser weight on high probabilities.

The notion that Benjamin—as well as others—transforms objective probabilities in a predictable direction derives not from theory but from observation. Most of the evidence comes from gambling, which provide natural and unobtrusive experiments for researchers. Over sixty years ago, R. M. Griffith (1949) investigated the behavior of bettors in 1,386 thoroughbred horse races at Churchill Downs, Belmont, and Hialeah racetracks during the 1947 season. He found that the initial odds placed on the horses were an accurate reflection of their chances of winning the race. However, the betting was not: More money was bet on the long shots—and less on the favorites—than would have been predicted by expected utility theory. In effect, bettors acted as predicted in Figure 2.1. By their seemingly irrational behavior, they improved the odds of long shots and decreased the odds of favorites. The tipping point for

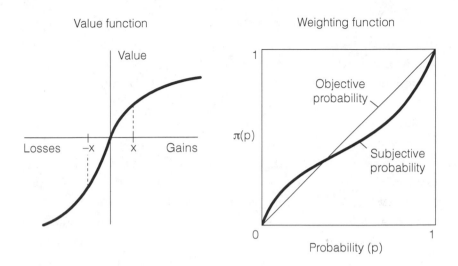

Value function   Weighting function

FIGURE 2.1

The simple analytics of behavioral economics.

SOURCE: Kahneman, Daniel, and Amos Tversky. 1979. Prospect theory: An analysis of decision under risk. *Econometrica* 47 (2) (March): 263–291. Reprinted by permission of The Econometric Society.

overweighting and underweighting the odds occurred when the odds for a particular horse were between 5 to 1 and 6 to 1.

These findings have been confirmed in multiple studies (McGlothlin 1956, Ali 1977). In perhaps the ultimate analysis of this issue, Eric Snowberg and Justin Wolfers (2010) analyzed betting behavior in all 865,934 thoroughbred horse races run in North America from 1992 to 2001, involving 6,403,712 horses. As a baseline, they found that betting randomly would result in a 23 percent loss for the average bettor. A bettor who always wagered on the favorite would lose only 5.5 percent. The average betting losses increased to around 20 percent when the odds were between even and 20 to 1. At longer odds, the losses really piled up, with betting on the real long shots—100 to 1 or worse—yielding a negative 61 percent return. After careful analysis, Snowberg and Wolfers concluded that the behavioral economic theory of subjective probabilities explains bettor behavior more accurately than does the expected utility theory of neoclassical economics.

Observation of actual behavior has also given us the loss aversion hypothesis—that Benjamin hates losses more than he loves gains—comes not from theory but observation. Benjamin is not alone. Tennis great Andre Agassi made the following revelation in his autobiography: "Now that I've won a slam, I know something that very few people are permitted to know. A win doesn't feel as good as a loss feels bad, and the good feeling doesn't last as long as the bad. Not even close" (Agassi 2009: 165).

But loss aversion may not be as secret as Agassi asserts. Even people who love to gamble hate to lose. People exhibit loss aversion regardless of whether they are risk averse or risk seeking. Some of the studies we just discussed provide evidence to this effect. McGlothlin, for example, found that bettor behavior differed by the position of the race in the race card: The later in the day, the higher the tendency to bet on the long shots. In the words of Kahneman and Tversky, "A person who has not made peace with his losses is likely to accept gambles that would be unacceptable to him otherwise" (Kahneman and Tversky 1979: 287).

Of course, not everyone gambles, so the question arises whether loss aversion occurs in other situations. The answer is a definitive "yes." We turn first to investing. Research by Hersh Shefrin and Meir Statman (1985) found that investors tend to sell winning stocks too early and hold on to losing stocks too long. In fact, investors with paper losses are willing to forego the tax advantages of realizing losses to avoid having to accept the loss and move on. In effect, they are hoping that something will happen and their losing stock will become a winner. (A collateral phenomenon that may be in play here is "regret bias," in which investors refrain from selling a stock for fear that its price will increase soon thereafter.)

Joshua Coval and Tyler Shumway (2005) found that even professional traders at the Chicago Board of Trade experience loss aversion. To test for loss aversion, the researchers examined trading behavior at the exchange in the morning and the afternoon. In the morning, roughly two-thirds of the traders made money and one-third lost money. Those who lost money in the morning were 15 percent more likely to take on above-average risk to try to regain their ground. In addition, they were 17 percent more likely to place more trades and 9 percent more likely to make larger trades. Like gamblers on horse races, professional futures traders were hustling to make up their losses because they did not want to end up in the red at the end of the day.

We can find loss aversion outside of gambling and investing. Consider how people respond to changes in price. Neoclassical economists would not foresee any particular reason for consumers to respond differently to increases or decreases in the price of a good. However, if loss aversion holds, consumers should view price increases as a loss and decreases as a gain and—more importantly—respond more to price increases than to price decreases. Several studies have confirmed this effect. For example, Daniel Putler (1992) measured the responsiveness of customers in Southern California to the changing prices of eggs, from July 1981 to July 1983. (Eggs have the advantages of being well known, frequently purchased, readily available, and largely a commodity, so the researcher can concentrate on examining the impact of price on demand.) He found that consumers were much more responsive to price increases than to decreases: A 10 percent increase in price led to a 7.8 percent decrease in demand, whereas a 10 percent decrease in price generated a 3.3 percent increase in demand. So, loss aversion occurs even in the most ordinary products.

One way in which loss aversion manifests itself is in a concept known as the *endowment effect*, that people tend to value something—a thing, a product, an idea—more once they have it than before. Behavioral economists have found the endowment effect in a wide variety of situations. The classic experiment (by Jack Knetsch [1989]) involved coffee mugs and bars of Swiss chocolate. Students from the University of Victoria were divided into three groups. The first group was given a coffee mug (retail price: $4.95) and then asked to complete a short questionnaire. When the students handed in the questionnaire, they were given the option to trade their mug for a 400-gram bar of Swiss chocolate (which sold for around $6 in local stores). The second group was given the bar of Swiss chocolate and then asked to complete the same short questionnaire. When they submitted their questionnaire, they were given the option to trade their chocolate bar for a coffee mug. Finally, students in the third group were given a choice between the mug and the chocolate bar before they completed the questionnaire.

The results of this simple experiment were startling. Of the third group, 56 percent chose the coffee mug, and 44 percent chose the chocolate bar. However, in the first group, 89 percent chose to keep their mug, with only 11 percent willing to trade it for the chocolate bar. And, in the second group, 90 percent chose to keep their chocolate bar and only 10 percent traded the bar for the mug. You would expect the percentages to have been about the same, but the differences were statistically significant and could not be explained by any differences among the students. Knetsch concluded that possession of the mug or chocolate bar—even for the short time involved in completing the questionnaire—somehow changed the perception of the value of the product. In particular, once owned, the mug or candy was truly "owned," such that giving it up represented a loss, a loss that was significantly greater than the expected gain from obtaining the other object. That is, it is loss aversion.

So, you may be asking, after all this, how significant is loss aversion? How much more do people value losses over gains? The answer lies in the simple concepts of *willingness to pay* and *willingness to accept*. Willingness to pay is the maximum price that an individual would be willing to pay for an item. Willingness to accept is the minimum amount that an individual would demand to give up an item. Neoclassical economics assumes that these two values should be close to identical for most goods. The reasoning is as follows. Our friend Benjamin is a big Chicago Cubs fan, and he always sits in Section 314 in the right-field bleachers. We ask him the highest price he would be willing to pay for a ticket in the bleachers; he tells us $45 (his willingness to pay), which we agree to and sell him the ticket. An hour later, we tell him that we want to buy the ticket back and ask him the lowest price he would be willing to accept. Neoclassical economics predicts that the price should be close to $45, give or take transactions costs.

Using the endowment effect, behavioral economics predicts that the two values will be quite different. Willingness to pay represents a measure of the additional satisfaction that the individual expects to receive from acquiring the good, whereas willingness to accept represents the individual's expected loss in satisfaction in parting with it. Economists have been measuring these values for decades, not to prove the tenets of behavioral economics but to get some sense of how people value public goods for which there is no market (such as parks and lakes and hunting grounds). For instance, a 1974 study by Hammack and Brown found that duck hunters were willing to pay an average of $247 to preserve a duck habitat, but they demanded an average of $1,044 to accept the loss of that habitat. A 1986 study by Heberlein and Bishop found that a sample of deer hunters in Wisconsin were willing to pay $25 for a hunting license (which was at the time subject to a lottery because of high demand) but would not sell back their license for less than $172. Subsequent studies, focused on behavioral economics, have confirmed these effects. Daniel Kahneman, Jack Knetsch, and Richard Thaler (1990) found a significant divergence between willingness to pay and willingness to accept with (what else?) undergraduates and coffee mugs. Ziv Carmon and Dan Ariely (2000) really confirmed it with students at Duke University, who were willing to pay $156 on average for tickets to the NCAA Final Four men's basketball tournament (in which the Blue Devils were playing) but demanded a minimum of $2,411 on average to sell those same tickets. To diehard college basketball fans, a fifteenfold difference between willingness-to-pay and willingness-to-accept is obvious, if not to neoclassical economists.

It must be noted that not all researchers have confirmed the endowment effect. John List (2003) conducted a series of studies at sports memorabilia shows in Orlando, Florida, and at the collector pin market at Walt Disney's Epcot Center. He found that inexperienced participants displayed the endowment effect, but most of the experienced dealers and traders did not. This result suggests that people can overcome the endowment effect by gaining experience and expertise.

Finally, one of the ironies of all this evidence about loss aversion and the endowment effect is that people do not seem to believe that it occurs—or that they are susceptible. To this point, Leaf Van Boven, David Dunning, and George Loewenstein (2000) investigated what they called the "egocentric empathy gap," in which people overestimate the similarity of their own valuation of a good with others' valuations. They conducted the now-ubiquitous mug experiment with college students, with half of the experimental group getting a mug and half not. After stating their willingness-to-accept (or pay), participants were asked to estimate the valuation given by those in the other role. Those with a mug said that they would be willing to accept $5.40 to give up their mug, whereas those without a mug said that they would be willing to pay an average of $1.56 for a mug. The mug owners estimated that buyers would pay as much as $2.93, and those without a mug estimated that mug owners would be willing to sell for as low as $4.06. Clearly, both sides were way off.

The researchers then introduced another student as an intermediary—a buyer's agent, who was given $10 and one chance to buy a mug from a single owner, with the agent keeping the difference if a trade were made. Even these highly incentivized agents did not get it right, with only 19 percent of agents' offers being accepted. What is as interesting were the reactions of the owners and agents. Owners were insulted by the low offers of the agents—"How can anyone expect to purchase such a great mug for so little?" Buyers' agents complained about the owners' greed—"How can they possibly think anyone would pay them that much for a mug?" In fact, the researchers reported that one agent "was so upset when she found out that her offer was rejected that she shouted insulting profanities at the mug owners, hollering that she had been cheated out of her money."

In a subsequent study, the researchers asked the owners and agents to rate potential explanations for the behavior of the other party. Both owners and agents—especially those who failed to complete a transaction—attributed the other party's behavior to greed rather than the endowment effect. The researchers concluded that this "egocentric empathy gap" is a robust phenomenon and hypothesized that the gap is resistant to amelioration because people rarely receive "prompt, unambiguous, and accurate" feedback about the subjective nature of valuations of buyers and sellers. Given at best piecemeal feedback, people misinterpret the actions of others. More importantly, they say, the fact that individuals make biased predictions of their own behavior in different roles (an "intrapersonal empathy gap") is likely to exacerbate the "interpersonal empathy gap."

FRAMING AND ANCHORING: WHY PEOPLE OFTEN MAKE DIFFERENT DECISIONS IF THE ISSUES ARE PRESENTED DIFFERENTLY

Given that people view gains and losses differently, it is not surprising that they view alternatives in different ways depending on whether the alternatives are presented as gains or losses. Tverksy and Kahneman (1986) termed this phenomenon *framing*. They argued that "framing is controlled by the manner in which the choice problem is presented as well as by norms, habits, and expectancies of the decision maker" (Tversky and Kahneman 1986: S257). Neoclassical economists would agree about the second part of the statement but not the first. To them, rational decision makers should be able to see through any conceptual smoke screens in the presentation of critical information, whether deliberate or unintentional (absent the proverbial transactions costs).

Unfortunately for the neoclassical economists, framing does seem to make a material difference in how people make decisions. The quintessential example is an experiment that Tverksy and Kahneman (1981) conducted in 1981. They posed the following situation to a group of 307 people:

Imagine that the U.S. is preparing for the outbreak of an unusual Asian disease, which is expected to kill 600 people. Two alternative programs to combat the disease have been proposed. Assume that the exact scientific estimate of the consequences of the programs is as follows:

Half of the group was given alternatives A and B:

If Program A is adopted, 200 people will be saved.

If Program B is adopted, there is 1/3 probability that 600 people will be saved, and 2/3 probability that no people will be saved.

Which of the two programs would you favor?

The other half of the group was given alternatives C and D:

If Program C is adopted, 400 people will die.

If Program D is adopted, there is 1/3 probability that nobody will die, and 2/3 probability that 600 people will die.

Which of the two programs would you favor?

The basic question tests the extent to which the respondents are risk averse or risk seeking; those who choose Program A or C are risk averse, and those who choose Program B or D are risk seeking. The more interesting issue for our purposes is that the two sets of alternatives are identical, except that the first version is presented in a survival frame ("200 people will be saved") whereas the second version is presented in a mortality frame ("400 people will die"). For decision makers who follow neoclassical economic rationality, the presentation should make no difference. For these 307 people, it did. Of the half given the options of Programs A and B, 72 percent chose A; of the half given Programs C and D, only 22 percent chose C. That the data presented to the participants are identical shows how powerful the frame can be in influencing decisions.

Framing can be seen as taking advantage of individuals' sense of loss aversion. For those presented with Programs A and B, Program A looked like a gain (because people were saved), whereas for those given Programs C and D, Program C looked like a loss (because people died). In addition, the study participants were more risk averse when the decision was framed in terms of a gain; they preferred the certainty that 200 lives would be saved (Program A) rather than taking a risk that no one would be saved (in Program B). Conversely, they were more risk seeking when the problem was posed as a loss; the participants were more willing to choose Program D and take the two-thirds chance that all 600 would die for the one-third chance that none would die. In that sense, those in the survey acted like those gamblers at the racetrack who were trying to recover their losses at the end of the day.

The Asian disease paradox has been replicated by others, with similar results. I have asked my MBA-level medical economics students, and even those in public health (who have taken biostatistics and epidemiology courses) succumb to the frame. In a more formal study, political scientists James Druckman and Rose McDermott (2008) ran the experiment with 214 adults and students, in which they also asked demographic questions and self-assessments of the participants' emotional states (including levels of distress, anger, and enthusiasm). The researchers confirmed the Tversky and Kahneman findings. In addition, they found that both anger and enthusiasm lead to more risk-seeking behavior (choosing Program B or D) but that distress leads to more risk-averse behavior (choosing Program A or C). As intriguing, they find that enthusiasm tempers framing, meaning that those who are more enthusiastic tend to be less affected by the frame. On the other hand, increased stress strengthens the framing effect.

In that study, Druckman and McDermott also gave the participants a public finance problem, involving the investment of a government community development grant. In this case, the results were financial gains and losses rather than lives lost and saved. The results confirmed loss aversion and the framing effect. The intriguing finding, though, is that emotions played a much less significant role than in the Asian disease problem. Neither anger nor distress affected decision making; only enthusiasm did, by leading to more risk-seeking behavior (as it did in the previous example). Druckman and McDermott concluded that emotions are important, not just in decision making (which is obvious) but in the decision maker's susceptibility to framing effects. They suggest that emotions may affect life-or-death decisions in much different ways than financial or investment decisions.

The effects of framing are evident in many real-world decisions, both individual and public policy. Eric Johnson and his colleagues (1993) described several insurance-related examples. They noted that consumers tend to dislike deductibles—framing them as losses—certainly compared to rebates—which they frame as gains—even though in the end deductibles may be less costly than rebates. They analyzed a natural experiment—a change in the auto insurance laws in Pennsylvania and New Jersey in the 1990s, to lower insurance premiums in exchange for a reduction in the right to sue. In Pennsylvania, car owners retained full rights to sue but could reduce their premiums by giving up their full rights. In New Jersey, car owners were given lower insurance rates but could buy back the full right to sue through a higher premium. About 75 percent of car owners in Pennsylvania kept their full right to sue, whereas only 20 percent of New Jersey car owners bought back their rights. This natural experiment demonstrates the power of the frame, which itself is a reflection of loss aversion and the endowment effect.

The final concept related to the endowment effect that we need to raise in this chapter is *anchoring*. This concept stems from the observation that an individual's preferences can be rather amorphous initially but become fixed once exposed to a cue, or anchor. This idea—antithetical to the neoclassical assumption of well-established and stable preferences—is what Dan Ariely, George Loewenstein, and Drazen Prelec (2003) term *coherent arbitrariness*. That is, an individual will act as a rational decision maker with "precisely defined and largely invariant" preferences but only after an initial period of malleable and even random behavior. These three behavioral economists conducted a very clever experiment to test for this phenomenon. They showed fifty-five MBA students at the Massachusetts Institute of Technology six products: a cordless trackball, a cordless keyboard, a bottle of average wine, a bottle of rare wine, a book on design, and a box of luxury Belgian chocolates. Each student was then asked whether she would buy each good for a dollar price equal to the last two digits of her Social Security number (a random number, which acted as the anchor). Once the students responded "yes" or "no," they were asked the highest amount they would be willing to pay for each product. According to mainstream economic theory, these amounts should have been totally unrelated to the last two digits of the students' Social Security numbers. Not so. Those students whose two-digit numbers were above the median were willing to pay between 57 and 107 percent more for the products than those whose numbers were below the median. In the most extreme example, those whose last two Social Security digits were in the highest 20 percent were willing to pay a maximum of $55.62 for the cordless keyboard, but those whose last two digits were in the lowest 20 percent were willing to pay only $16.09.

Ariely, Loewenstein, and Prelec argue that anchoring has the following effect on preferences and decisions. If individuals have no precedents or experience in purchasing a particular product or making another kind of decision, their choices will be highly sensitive to anchors—regardless of whether the anchors are relevant to the decision. Once their decision is made, the initial choice will itself act as an anchor over subsequent preferences and choices. These subsequent choices will then follow the patterns of behavior predicted by mainstream neoclassical economic theory.

HEALTH POLICY ANOMALIES

We now have the basic tools from behavioral economics that will enable us to analyze the anomalies that we introduced at the beginning of the chapter. These anomalies could not be explained by mainstream economics, either because the issues are beyond the scope of traditional economic theory or because the standard theory predicts another result. Fortunately, behavioral economics is much more flexible and expansive.

ANOMALY 1: *Why does the public support the specific aspects of health care reform but not the bill that was passed that contained these provisions?*

The Patient Protection and Affordable Care Act (P.L. 111–148) is one of the most controversial pieces of legislation in the history of the United States. Both proponents and opponents saw the health reform law as reshaping the entire health care system in this country, as profoundly as the creation of health insurance or the enactment of Medicare. Supporters perceived an opportunity to provide reliable insurance—and health care—to the estimated 49 million people who were uninsured or underinsured, to minimize disruptions in insurance coverage when people have major life events, and to begin to control the inexorable rise in health care costs. Opponents interpreted the law as unneeded interference into private markets for health care, as well as an unwarranted—and unconstitutional—intrusion of centralized authority in individual decision making.

Nevertheless, the surveys that have been conducted during and after passage of the bill reveal a curious phenomenon: Although there is a sharp divide over the health care reform law, there is significant support for most of the individual provisions. The Kaiser Health Tracking Polls conducted by the Kaiser Family Foundation since enactment of the legislation illustrate this curiosity (2010; 2011; 2012). (Surveys by Gallup and Harris Interactive present similar results.) Every month, the tracking poll asked, "Given what you know about the health care reform law, do you have a generally favorable or generally unfavorable opinion of it?"

TABLE 2.1

Percentage of support for elements of health reform law, March 2012.

Element of law	Very favorable	Somewhat favorable	Somewhat unfavorable	Very unfavorable	Don't know
Provides tax credits to small businesses that offer coverage to their employees	44%	36%	8%	8%	4%
Provides financial help to low- and moderate-income Americans who don't get insurance through their jobs to help them purchase coverage	43	28	10	15	4
Expands the existing Medicaid program to cover low-income, uninsured adults regardless of whether they have children	36	34	12	15	3
Prohibits insurance companies from denying coverage because of a preexisting health problem	45	24	11	17	3
Eliminates out-of-pocket costs for many preventive services, such as blood pressure or cholesterol screenings	42	27	15	13	3
Requires insurance companies that are spending too little money on health care services and too much on administrative costs and profits to give those customers a rebate	32	25	16	19	7
Requires employers with 50 or more employees to pay a fine if they don't offer health insurance to their workers	29	25	15	29	2
Increases the Medicare payroll tax on earnings for upper income Americans	26	27	17	24	6
Requires insurance plans to offer a minimum package of health insurance benefits, to be defined by the government	23	28	15	31	3
Requires nearly all Americans to have health insurance by 2014 or else pay a fine	15	17	12	54	2

SOURCE: "Kaiser Health Tracking Poll—March 2012," (#8285), The Henry J. Kaiser Family Foundation, March 2012. This information was reprinted with permission from the Henry J. Kaiser Family Foundation. The Kaiser Family Foundation, a leader in health policy analysis, health journalism, and communication, is dedicated to filling the need for trusted, independent information on the major health issues facing our nation and its people. The Foundation is a nonprofit private operating foundation, based in Menlo Park, California.

Support and opposition have been closely divided at about 42 or 43 percent on either side, with no discernible trends. Periodically, the Kaiser Family Foundation survey has described to respondents specific elements of the law and asked them whether they feel favorable or unfavorable toward each element. Table 2.1 shows the results from the March 2012 poll, taken around the second anniversary of passage of the law.

In a survey conducted six months after passage of the law (and not repeated), respondents were asked whether particular elements of the law made them feel more or less favorably about the law. These results are shown in Table 2.2.

Neoclassical economics can explain much of this response. When price of a good goes down (especially to zero), quantity demanded goes

TABLE 2.2
Percentage of support for elements of health reform law, August 2010.

Element of law	Percent more favorable	Percent less favorable	Does not make a difference	Don't know
Prohibiting insurance companies from denying coverage to children who have a preexisting health problem	72%	19%	8%	1%
Prohibiting insurers from canceling people's health insurance coverage except in cases where the customer commits fraud	68	15	15	3
Gradually closing the Medicare prescription drug "doughnut hole" or "coverage gap" so seniors will no longer be required to pay the full cost of their medications when they reach the gap	64	14	19	3
Creating an insurance option, or high-risk pool, for those people whose preexisting health conditions currently make it difficult for them to find and buy affordable health insurance	61	20	16	3
Prohibiting insurance companies from setting lifetime limits on the total amount they will spend on a person's health care	56	26	13	4
Allowing children to stay on their parents' insurance plans until age 26	53	26	18	3

SOURCE: "Kaiser Health Tracking Poll—August 2010," (#8093), The Henry J. Kaiser Family Foundation, August 2010. This information was reprinted with permission from the Henry J. Kaiser Family Foundation. The Kaiser Family Foundation, a leader in health policy analysis, health journalism, and communication, is dedicated to filling the need for trusted, independent information on the major health issues facing our nation and its people. The Foundation is a nonprofit private operating foundation, based in Menlo Park, California.

up. So it is not surprising that there is strong support for a provision that "eliminates out-of-pocket costs for many preventive services, such as blood pressure or cholesterol screenings" or for "gradually closing the Medicare prescription drug 'doughnut hole' or 'coverage gap' so seniors will no longer be required to pay the full cost of their medications when they reach the gap." Even in these cases, behavioral economics provides some interesting insights. Thinking back on the discussion of the "special value of zero" in Chapter 1, it is likely that the support stems not just from a reduced price but the "sheer happiness" created by getting something for no out-of-pocket price.

More importantly for this discussion, support for other elements of the law is consistent with the concept of the endowment effect. In fact, some of the strongest support is for those provisions that limit the potential for people to lose their "endowment" of health insurance:

- Prohibiting insurance companies from denying coverage to children who have a preexisting health problem (72 percent said this provision made them more favorable to the law).

- Prohibiting insurers from canceling people's health insurance coverage except in cases where the customer commits fraud (68 percent more favorable).

- Prohibiting insurance companies from setting lifetime limits on the total amount they will spend on a person's health care (56 percent more favorable).

- Allowing children to stay on their parents' insurance plans until age 26 (53 percent more favorable).

With all of this support for individual elements of the health reform bill, then what explains the overall lack of support? Again, behavioral economics provides some insights. First, there is very little support for the linchpin of the bill: the individual mandate. The Kaiser Family Foundation survey in March 2012 found that only 32 percent were very favorable or somewhat favorable of requiring "nearly all Americans to have health insurance by 2014 or else pay a fine." (Previous and subsequent surveys found about the same level of opposition to this provision.) A mandate is perceived as a major loss—of autonomy, independence, the "right to choose"—even if the individual would have bought health insurance on his own accord. As a follow-up question, the Kaiser survey asked those opposed to the individual mandate, "What if you heard that without such a requirement, the cost of health insurance would rise substantially for many people? Would you still have an unfavorable view [of an individual mandate]?" Twenty-two percent of those initially opposed to the mandate (constituting 15 percent of the sample) changed their mind and supported it. However, that still left 50 percent opposed to the mandate. This result demonstrates the power of loss aversion (and echoes Eric Johnson's findings about drivers in Pennsylvania and New Jersey): People adamantly oppose the potential loss of an endowment (the right to make a purchasing decision) even when the consequences are higher prices for health insurance.

Perhaps more fundamentally, behavioral economists would argue that the lukewarm support and strong opposition to the health reform law results not only from support or opposition to specific provisions of the law. Rather, it is a pervasive concern that most people think they will see relatively few tangible gains from the law and may actually face losses. After all, over 80 percent of the respondents to the March 2012 Kaiser Poll already had health insurance. For these individuals, they could see relatively little potential for gain from the reform law (other than the individual provisions already mentioned). This reality is evident from the Kaiser tracking polls. Before passage of the reform bill in March 2010, an average of 38 percent of all respondents thought that the law would make them and their family better off, with an average of 24 percent saying that it would make them worse off and an average of 31 percent responding that it would make no difference to them personally. Since passage, however, the average who stated that the law would make them better off has fallen to 27 percent, compared to 31 percent who thought that it would make them worse off and 36 percent who thought it would make no difference.

If the concept of loss aversion is correct and the measurements of the relative value of losses and gains are accurate, then it is clear that health reform has a difficult road ahead. The 20 percent of the population without health insurance, or with underinsurance, stand to gain from the law. However, the 80 percent with health insurance—who seem to like the coverage that they currently have—see a few gains (for example, protection from exclusions from insurance for preexisting conditions) but fear significant losses (such as Sarah Palin's "Death Panels"). With losses in general valued over gains by a 2-to-1 margin, their perspective on this massive legislation is understandable. Thus, President Obama's repeated declaration that "if you like your health care plan, you can keep your health care plan" is a critical attempt to overcome the endowment effect and tamp down the magnitude of the perceived loss.

ANOMALY 2: *Why did a person in a Congressman's town hall meeting shout, "Keep your government hands off my Medicare!"?*

Now, let's turn back to that gentleman in the South Carolina town hall meeting.

What can behavioral economics tell us about his statement? This is a clear illustration of the endowment effect. Medicare has been such an integral part of the lives of senior citizens in the United States for almost five decades that people forget the controversy involved in its enactment, and—as this gentleman demonstrated—can forget who administers the program. In addition, people have been paying into Medicare through the designated payroll tax, and they are looking forward to "getting back" their premiums. This psychological ownership that people have about Medicare also can explain why poll after poll indicates widespread and fierce opposition to touching this entitlement and why politicians have been reluctant to consider cuts in Medicare to reduce the federal budget deficit.

ANOMALY 3: *Why was there such an uproar in November 2009 when the U.S. Preventive Services Task Force released its recommendations for screening mammography?*

On November 16, 2009, the U.S. Preventive Services Task Force published its revised recommendations regarding screening mammography for breast cancer (U.S. Preventive Services Task Force 2009). The Task Force's previous recommendations had been well received by its target audience—the medical community, especially providers of primary care. This time was different. The American College of Radiology (ACR) immediately denounced the Task Force's report, calling the recommendations "incredibly flawed," "unsupported," "discredited," and "shocking" (American College of Radiology 2009). The chief medical officer of the American Cancer Society declared that the Task Force "took a step backward in the fight against breast cancer" (American Cancer Society 2009). A U.S. Congresswoman railed, "This is how rationing begins. This is the little toe in the edge of the water, and this is when you start getting a bureaucrat between you and your physician. This is what we have warned about" (Lorber 2009). What caused such an outcry?

First, let's look into some background on the Task Force and its processes (U.S. Preventive Services Task Force 2011). It was created in 1984 by the U.S. Public Health Service and codified by Congress in 1998 as an independent government agency within the Department of Health and Human Services. Its mission is "to evaluate the benefits of individual services based on age, gender, and risk factors for disease; make recommendations about which preventive services should be incorporated routinely into primary medical care and for which populations; and identify a research agenda for clinical preventive care." It has issued recommendations in over 100 clinical areas, such as alcohol misuse, depression, hepatitis, and testicular cancer, and it revises each of its recommendations roughly every five years. The Task Force is composed of sixteen members, appointed for a single term of four to six years by the director of the Agency for Healthcare Research and Quality (AHRQ), and includes physicians, nurses, and public health professionals who have expertise in primary care and preventive health.

The Task Force uses an explicit evidence-based methodology, spelled out in a ninety-nine-page procedure manual (U.S. Preventive Services Task Force 2008). Once the Task Force chooses a topic for review, an Evidence-Based Practice Center created by AHRQ develops a systematic evidence report that describes the research and practice literature on the topic. This report is sent to content experts and to federal partner organizations for their review. The report—and outside comments—is presented to the Task Force, which typically votes on draft recommendations at the same meeting. Those draft recommendations are then circulated to federal and primary care partners of the Task Force, as well as to relevant physician specialty societies. Typically, the Task Force adopts final recommendations at its next meeting, and then—rather than simply issuing its recommendations—submits its recommendations and evidence report to a scientific, peer-reviewed journal that applies its usual publication standards to the report.

And so it went for the review of screening mammography for breast cancer. Building on the evidence-based recommendations that it issued in 1989, 1996, and 2002, the Task Force decided in 2007 to conduct its periodic review. It commissioned the Oregon Evidence-based Practice Center (EPC) to prepare the evidence report. In addition to conducting a standard meta-analysis of the research literature, the Center analyzed data from the Breast Cancer Surveillance Consortium (BCSC); the EPC then sent its work to fifteen outside scientists for peer review (Nelson et al. 2009b). After review of the results at its November 2007 meeting, the Task Force asked the six members of the Cancer Intervention and Surveillance Modeling Network (CISNET) to model the impact of different protocols of screening mammography on breast cancer mortality. At its July 2008 meeting, the Task Force approved its recommendations and submitted its report and the EPC and CISNET papers to the *Annals of Internal Medicine* for review and publication. According to the editors of the journal, the report and background papers went through several rounds of revisions over a five-month period, were accepted for publication in September 2009, and were published in the next available print issue on November 17, 2009 (U.S. Preventive Services Task Force 2009; Nelson et al. 2009b; Mandelblatt et al. 2009).

The recommendations represented a significant change from its 2002 guidelines:

- The Task Force recommended against routine screening mammography in women aged forty to forty-nine years. In its previous report, it had included women in their forties in its general recommendation for screening mammograms every one to two years.

- It recommended biennial screening mammography for women between the ages of fifty and seventy-four years, rather than one to two years in the previous report.
- It concluded that evidence about the benefits and harms of screening mammography was insufficient to support any recommendation for women seventy-five years and older, unlike the previous report in which women in this age group were included in the general recommendations.
- It concluded that evidence about benefits and harms of clinical breast examination in addition to screening mammography were insufficient to support any recommendation, as in the previous report.
- It recommended against clinicians teaching women how to perform breast self-examinations, whereas the previous report cited insufficient evidence to support any recommendation.

In developing all of its recommendations, the Task Force tries to balance the medical benefits of screening mammography with the medical harms. As noted in its procedure manual, the Task Force does not consider financial costs. (This distinction will be important later, as we discuss the reaction to the Task Force's recommendations.)

The medical benefits of screening mammography may be obvious—detection of breast cancer at an earlier stage will facilitate treatment that usually requires less extensive procedures, which leads to lower mortality. The medical harms are less apparent. One could be the pain of the mammogram itself; the EPC review identified several studies that showed that many women experienced such pain during mammography, but few surveyed women considered it to be a deterrent to having future screens. Another harm could be radiation exposure over time from multiple mammograms, but the EPC could find little evidence of significant risk. More noteworthy are the anxiety, distress, or other psychological reactions to mammography screening, especially for those women who get false-positive results. The EPC found mixed findings from the fifty-four studies it analyzed, with few showing more than a transient impact.

The fourth potential medical harm from screening mammography is overdiagnosis, which Dr. Gilbert Welch defines as "the detection of abnormalities that will never cause symptoms or death during a patient's lifetime. Overdiagnosis of cancer occurs when the cancer grows so slowly that the patient dies of other causes before it produces symptoms or when the cancer remains dormant (or regresses)" (Welch 2009). As Dr. Welch points out, the challenge of overdiagnosis is that "because doctors don't know which patients are overdiagnosed, we tend to treat them all." Estimates of overdiagnosis of breast cancer range from 10 to 30 percent of those cancers detected.

In its research regarding mammography for women in their forties, the EPC found a 15 percent reduction in breast cancer mortality for those women who had screening mammograms (Nelson et al. 2009). However, they also reported that 1,904 women aged forty to forty-nine would need to be screened to prevent one death from breast cancer, compared to only 1,339 women aged fifty to fifty-nine and 377 women aged sixty to sixty-nine. In addition, they found that 556 women aged forty to forty-nine would need to be screened to diagnose one case of invasive breast cancer, compared to only 294 women aged fifty to fifty-nine and 200 women aged sixty to sixty-nine; likewise, five women aged forty to forty-nine would need to undergo a biopsy to diagnose a single case of invasive breast cancer, compared to three women aged fifty to fifty-nine and two women aged sixty to sixty-nine. In other words, mammography is not as effective for women in their forties as it is for older women.

Guidelines for screening mammograms—who should be screened and how often—have been a point of contention for quite some time. In 1993 the National Cancer Institute (NCI) and the National Institutes of Health (NIH) convened an international workshop to consider guidelines on screening women in their forties. The workshop concluded that there was little evidence in favor of such screening, but this recommendation was overturned by NCI leadership. In 1997, another NIH consensus conference was held, but it was characterized in press reports as a "breast-screening brawl" (Taubes 1997), with one observer noting that the conference was "raucous" and "like no scientific meeting I'd ever seen before." A report in *Science* noted that proponents of screening in their forties included "mainly radiologists, with a few surgeons and a very few epidemiologists," whereas opponents were "mainly epidemiologists and public health physicians." One participant in the conference said that the positions staked out were "almost like a religion for some people." The disagreement has continued, as existing studies have been extended and reanalyzed and new data sources and analytical techniques developed.

Add to this intense scientific dispute the even more intense debate in 2009 about health care reform. On November 7 of that year, the U.S. House of Representatives passed the 1,990-page "Affordable Health Care for America Act," on a vote of 220 to 215. Nine days later, the U.S. Preventive Services Task Force's recommendations were released. The perfect storm was unleashed.

The responses were swift and vehement. On the day that the recommendations were released, the American College of Radiology issued several statements (American College of Radiology 2009). Dr. Carol Lee, chair of the College's Breast Imaging Commission, dismissed the "harms" of mammography (her quotes), stating that the Task Force's conclusions that the harms outweighed the benefits for women forty to forty-nine years of age "is tragically incorrect and will result in many needless deaths." In the same statement, Dr. James Thrall, chair of the College's Board of Chancellors, declared, "I can't help but think that we are moving toward a new health care rationing policy that will turn back the clock on medicine for decades." The American Cancer Society issued a statement that "with its new recommendations, the USPSTF is essentially telling women that mammography at age 40 to 49 saves lives; just not enough of them" (American Cancer Society 2009).

The Task Force was not without its defenders. The National Breast Cancer Coalition issued a statement supporting the recommendations, with its president, Fran Visco, stating that "Women deserve the truth even when it is complicated. They can accept it" (National Breast Cancer Coalition 2009). The American College of Physicians affirmed that the Task Force "is a highly regarded, credible and independent group of experts" and that critics had made "unfair and unsubstantiated attacks" on the Task Force (Stubbs 2009). The media immediately picked up the story. On November 17, Anderson Cooper interviewed Dr. Kimberly Gregory, a member of the Task Force and vice chair of Women's Healthcare Quality and Performance Improvement at Cedars-Sinai Medical

Center and professor of obstetrics and gynecology at UCLA, and Dr. Daniel Kopans, chair of breast imaging at Massachusetts General Hospital, professor of radiology at Harvard Medical School, and vociferous opponent of the Task Force's recommendations (Anderson Cooper 360 Degrees 2009). The interview did not go well for the Task Force. Cooper went after Dr. Gregory, saying that the biggest issue for the Task Force related to routine screenings seemed to be women's anxiety while waiting for the results, "and that seems like kind of minor." In reply, Gregory lapsed into technical jargon, talking about the Task Force's "Grade B" and "Grade C" recommendations. Dr. Kopans jumped in to assert that the Task Force's recommendations "have no basis in science." Later in the interview, Cooper asked Dr. Gregory how there could be a problem with routine screenings even if they identified few cancers. "I mean, if it saves, you know, a handful of women's lives, isn't it still a good thing?" Dr. Gregory pointed out that "a significant number of women" who would be screened would have false positives and have to undergo unnecessary biopsies and additional tests. To which Dr. Kopans countered, "We're not talking about a small benefit here. We're talking about a reduction in deaths of 40 percent."

The Wall Street Journal condemned "a government panel's decision to toss out long-time guidelines for breast cancer screening" (A Breast Cancer Preview 2009). The *Journal* claimed that "the panel—which includes no oncologists and radiologists, who best know the medical literature—did decide to re-analyze the data with health-care *spending* [emphasis in the original] as a core concern." The *Journal* criticized the argument that women in their forties should not be routinely screened because it takes 1,904 screenings on women in this age group to save one life, compared to only 1,339 of those aged fifty to fifty-nine: "To put it another way, 665 additional mammograms are more expensive in the aggregate. But at the individual level they are immeasurably valuable, especially if you happen to be the woman whose life is saved." The *Journal* criticized as "myopic" the recommendation "to cut off all screening in women over 75." "In other words, grandma is probably going to die anyway, so why waste the money to reduce the chances that she dies of a leading cause of death among elderly women?"

As with the Gregory-Kopans set-to, individual medical professionals expressed their opinions with intensity. Marisa Weiss, MD, oncologist in Wynnewood, Pennsylvania, and founder of Breastcancer.org, declared, "I'm riled up; this is a giant step backward and a terrible mistake" (Rabin 2009a). William Rifkin, MD, an internist and editor at Milliman Care Guidelines, opined, "Fears that this report will reduce mammograms assume that mammograms done at a certain age are beneficial. . . . Personal stories or opinions may 'feel right,' but are no substitute for objective research and analysis" (Rifkin 2009). Sheila Rothman, PhD, professor of public health at Columbia University, observed that "People are being asked to think differently about risk. . . . The public state of mind right now is that they're frightened that evidence-based medicine is going to be equated with rationing. They don't see it in a scientific perspective" (Sack 2009). Christine Laine, MD, internist and epidemiologist at Jefferson Medical College and editor of the *Annals of Internal Medicine*, thought that "Americans feel that in health care, more is always better, and more means better outcomes. That's just not true, but it's counterintuitive to a lot of people" (Winslow and Wang 2009).

Politicians seized the opportunity to intervene in the issue. Republicans denounced the Task Force's recommendations: Representative Jean Schmidt (R-OH): "We shouldn't depend on a task force within HHS to tell us what to do" (Lorber 2009); Representative David Camp (R-MI): "This is what happens when bureaucrats make your health care decisions." Some Democrats weighed in; Debbie Wasserman Schultz (D-FL), a breast cancer survivor, said that "We can't allow the insurance industry to continue to drive health-care decisions." The Obama administration quickly distanced itself from the Task Force, with Kathleen Sebelius, secretary of the Department of Health and Human Services, issuing a statement that the Task Force was "an outside independent panel of doctors and scientists who . . . do not set federal policy and . . . don't determine what services are covered by the federal government" (Stein and Eggen 2009, A01). Senator Barbara Mikulski (D-MD) introduced an amendment to the Senate's health reform bill requiring that free annual mammograms and other preventive care for women be included in any health plan, declaring, "We are saying good-bye to an era when simply being a women is treated as a pre-existing condition" (Mikulski December 3, 2009). Senator David Vitter (R-LA) offered an amendment to Mikulski's amendment that directed the government to explicitly ignore the Task Force's recommendations. The amendments were adopted and became part of the final bill that was passed in March 2010.

Dr. Ned Calonge, chair, and Dr. Diana Petitti, vice-chair, of the Task Force were called to testify in front of the Health Subcommittee of the U.S. House Energy and Commerce Committee on December 2, 2009 (Breast Cancer Screening Recommendations 2009). The hearing was an opportunity for both sides of the health reform debate to continue the battle. (In fact, in the four-hour hearing, two hours and forty minutes was taken up by the subcommittee members' opening statements and their own remarks during their allotted question period.) The more notable comments included the following:

Representative John Shimkus (R-IL): This is the canary in the coal mine. This is what we get when we have government intervention starting to dictate health-care policy decisions.

Representative Michael Burgess (R-TX) [and an obstetrician-gynecologist]: The 2,000-page gorilla in the room is this brave new world of health care, which Congress is going to dictate how things are happening. And the recommendations of the United States Preventive Task Force now carry the weight of law, if you will, under the auspices of the secretary of Health and Human Services, or whoever the health-care commissar is, that they designate.

Representative John Shadegg (R-AZ): [Under the just-passed health reform bill], the government would prohibit millions of women from buying coverage for mammograms. The government would forbid private plans from offering mammogram coverage to millions of women.

Representative Tammy Baldwin (D-WI): The task force was doing its job. And as they may admit today, they could have done much more around such a sensitive topic by educating and explaining their recommendations to women across the country. . . . The villain here is the lack of coverage and access to care.

Representative Zachary Space (D-OH): These task force recommendations will not lead to rationing care. . . . I think it's disingenuous to on the one hand defend the status quo, which sees the insurance industry every day making decisions about the lives of their insured based on financial—strictly financial considerations. And then on the other hand, condemn a system because you speculate that these kinds of recommendations will lead to the rationing of care.

Near the end of the hearing, Dr. Petitti confessed, "Quite honestly when I found out that these recommendations were being released the week of the vote that was the big vote [of the House on health reform], I was sort of stunned and then, also terrified. And I think my being terrified was actually exactly the right reaction."

Not surprisingly, the Task Force's recommendations created controversy among American women. Some of the reported comments include the following:

Karen Young-Levi, forty-three: My big fear is that coverage will be diminished and that a very valuable tool to detect something at an early stage could be taken away from me. (Rabin 2009a)

Nancy Moylan, fifty-one: I've been waiting for common sense regarding mammograms for years. . . . It always struck me that most women seemed so relieved to know that they don't have cancer that they never took the next step and said, "Hey, why was I just put through all that anxiety?" (Steinhauer 2009)

Robin Caryn Rabin, *New York Times* columnist: My generation came of age in the late 1970s, in the heyday of the women's health movement, and we were schooled in breast self-exams. . . . We all knew the drill. . . . In a way, doing breast self-exams was more about taking responsibility and ownership of our bodies than anything else. It was a statement about being independent, self-sufficient and self-aware. (Rabin 2009b)

Janine M. Kearns: The recommendations are careless in that they advise that women should not be taught to do breast self-exams. What planet are they on? . . . We need to make these tools more accurate and safe. Whatever it takes. We want to live. (Kearns 2009)

Judy Oppenheimer: After all the good laughs I've had about so-called granny death panels, it came as a shock to find out that the government really does want to kill me. Or, at any rate, doesn't give much of a damn one way or the other. . . . If this recommendation [regarding routine mammograms for those under fifty] had been made 10 years ago, I doubt I'd be around today. 'Your mammogram probably saved your life,' my oncologist said the first time we met. Would it today? (Oppenheimer 2009)

A survey conducted by *USA Today*/Gallup less than a week after the announcement found that 85 percent of interviewed women aged thirty-five to seventy-five years old had heard about the Task Force's recommendations; 47 percent of women aged thirty-five to seventy-five years old strongly disagreed, and 26 percent disagreed with them; and 76 percent thought that the recommendations were "mainly based on the potential for cost savings in the healthcare system."

Behavioral Economics and the Task Force Controversy
This is certainly a fascinating story, but what can behavioral economics inform us about the controversy? The first—and most obvious—behavioral economics concept that can be applied is framing. All of the major parties in this controversy—supporters and opponents of health care reform, advocacy organizations, the medical profession, patients, and even the Preventive Services Task Force itself—applied frames to their perceptions and their arguments. Let's start with the Task Force. To the Task Force, screening mammograms was one of 105 different areas of prevention that it investigates. It uses a strictly scientific perspective to conduct its work and develop its recommendations, from the use of the Evidence-based Practice Centers to conduct the literature reviews and develop the evidence reports to the submission of the final recommendations and background papers to a peer-reviewed medical journal. Dr. Calonge, in response to a question in the congressional hearing (Breast Cancer Screening Recommendations 2009), said, "The

Task Force believes its major charge from Congress, and responsibility to primary care clinicians and patients, is that we set the evidence-based stake in the ground, immune from how much it costs to achieve the benefits associated with a given effective preventive service." Several times during the hearing, Dr. Petitti referred to science: "I'm going to speak to the science," and "the science is . . . ," and "We're scientists." This frame is deeply embedded in the culture of the Task Force and its members. Even when it used the metric of "number needed to screen" to prevent one cancer death, it framed that in a context of clinical, not cost, effectiveness.

The supporters and opponents of health care reform saw the recommendations from a much different frame. The issues raised by the screening mammography guidelines provided a tailor-made opportunity to reopen the ideological battles that had just concluded with the House-passed bill. Opponents framed the Task Force as an integral part of health reform implementation and as a ready-made example of what they saw as the introduction of rationing of health care. They framed the Task Force as the embodiment of the "death panels" that opponents had railed against during the raucous summer. Proponents gamely tried to frame the Task Force's recommendations as an example of the kinds of services that should be available to women but are not because of the lack of universal health insurance. They used it as a barely veiled attack on private insurers that find ways to limit payment for needed services. Clearly, though, the recommendations put health reform proponents on the defensive; hence, Secretary Sebelius's attempt to frame the Task Force as an independent entity with no regulatory powers and Senator Mikulski's amendment to mandate screenings and prohibit the Task Force's recommendations from having any practical effect.

Many advocacy organizations saw the Task Force's recommendations as a threat. They had expended considerable resources trying to imprint their key messages to their target populations: "Mammograms save lives" and "Take the test, not the chance." If you will, they had been trying to "change the frame" so that women would be more inclined to have mammograms. The Preventive Services Task Force was complicating the story, with nuanced messages about "routine" mammograms for some age groups, but not others, and against clinicians "teaching" breast self-exams but not against breast self-awareness. (Recognize, though, that some advocacy organizations, such as the National Breast Cancer Coalition, had been presenting the more complex version of the benefits and harms of mammography.) The recommendations were also coming at a time when research was beginning to raise doubts about the unquestioned value of screening of many diseases (such as the prostate-specific antigen test) (Esserman, Shieh, and Thompson 2009).

The medical profession was in an even more complicated position. Physicians are both scientists and caregivers, and these dual roles are not always compatible. What may be good for an individual patient in terms of resource allocation or risk/reward trade-offs may not be good for the population, and vice versa. So, epidemiologists, who are concerned primarily with populations, are comfortable with framing diagnosis and treatment issues around "the number needed" to diagnose, treat, or save, or to consider risk framed in terms of thousands or millions. On the other hand, clinicians are concerned with individual patients who present with their own idiosyncratic profiles. They need to frame the Task Force's recommendations in the context of these individual patients. Consider the challenge for a primary care physician, who is expected to make a clinical decision and explain the case for and against screening mammograms to an individual patient, when the research findings regarding benefits and harms for certain populations (such as those between forty and forty-nine years old) keep shifting and the organizations these physicians look to for guidance—The American Cancer Society, the American College of Physicians—do not agree.

Finally, patients were applying their own frame to this issue. Not surprisingly, patients are much more similar to primary care physicians than epidemiologists regarding screening mammograms. They rarely will frame issues in terms of population statistics but will focus on individual cases (what Tversky and Kahneman in their very first article [1971] call a "belief in the law of small numbers"). They will more likely frame their opinion as, "I know someone with no family history whose cancer was found from a mammogram when she was thirty-seven," than from statistical considerations. By contrast, because the potential harms from mammograms are more diffused than are benefits, it is unlikely that they will frame the harms as, "I know someone with a family history of cancer who had a false positive and had to have a biopsy, which found nothing." As an example of this kind of framing, Lisa Schwartz and her colleagues (2000) asked 479 adult women about the potential harms of mammography. Ninety-two percent believed that mammography could not harm a woman without breast cancer. Ninety-nine percent believed that false positive results would occur if a sixty-year-old woman had annual mammograms over a ten-year period, but only 38 percent would want information about false positives in making their decision about having a mammogram. Finally, when asked how many false positive results would be acceptable to save a life, 63 percent would tolerate 500 or more false positives and 37 percent would tolerate 10,000 or more. Clearly, the frame for individual women focused on the potential to save a life, not the potential harms of doing so.

Related to framing is the endowment effect, which also can explain much of the behavior surrounding the Task Force's recommendations. In particular, we can see evidence of loss aversion on the part of patients and physicians. For patients, cancer is seen as a catastrophic and irreversible loss, for which aggressive screening and early treatment are imperative. In a separate study, Schwartz and her colleagues (2004) interviewed 500 U.S. adults (360 women and 140 men) regarding their degree of enthusiasm for cancer screening—in general and for specific cancers. Eighty-seven percent agreed that "routine cancer screening tests for healthy persons are almost always a good idea," and 74 percent said that finding cancer early means that treatment saves lives either most or all of the time. Of the surveyed women who had had mammograms, 85 percent reported that they had annual mammograms, 16 percent said they would have them every six months if cost were not a concern, and 79 percent said that there would not be a time when they stop having routine mammograms. Finally, this survey found that 70 percent believed that a fifty-five-year-old woman in average health would be "irresponsible" if she did not have a routine mammogram, and 41 percent said that even an eighty-year-old woman in average health would be irresponsible if she did not have one.

From this perspective, then, the November 2009 recommendations of the U.S. Preventive Services Task Force would be perceived by women as losses, with no apparent gains:

- No routine screening mammograms for women forty to forty-nine years of age.
- No routine screening mammograms for women over seventy-five years of age.
- Screening mammograms only every two years, not every year.
- No teaching of breast self-exam.
- No clinicians conducting clinical breast examinations.

In effect, the Task Force was recommending that most of the things that these women had done—early mammograms, annual mammograms with no age limit, breast self-examinations, periodic examinations by their physicians—were being taken away, with nothing in return. It is no wonder that their reaction against the recommendations was swift and vehement.

Physicians treating adult women would also experience loss aversion from the Task Force's recommendations. As already noted, clinicians focus on the needs of individual patients, not necessarily populations of patients. They want to practice medicine that conforms to the highest professional standards, as reflected in the research literature and practices of others in their medical community. (This is covered more fully in Chapters 6 and 7.) At the same time, they do not want to keep changing their practices every time a new research article is published or a recommendation from a professional organization is issued. Those clinicians most familiar with research understand that studies will occasionally have conflicting results, at least until sufficient data are collected and alternative methodologies reconciled; they will continue current practice until the weight of the evidence is overwhelming. Those clinicians not immersed in the research will likely maintain their practices as well, driven by the endowment effect. After all, if undergraduates will cling to a coffee mug they were given fifteen minutes earlier, a clinician will continue the practice routines that have served her and her patients well.

In addition, medical liability concerns may compel a physician to maintain her practice patterns until the medical community reaches a new consensus.

A final perspective from behavioral economics on the issue of screening mammograms comes from the distinction between willingness-to-pay versus willingness-to-accept. Women in the studies by Schwartz and her colleagues indicated that they were willing to pay something to have greater access to mammograms. However, they were fierce about not forgoing mammograms; they were committed to having annual mammograms, with no age limit. Although the question was not asked regarding mammography, the women in the second study described in the preceding paragraphs were asked what they would do if a physician recommended that they stop having or have less frequent Papanicolaou tests; 59 percent would "try to keep having them," whereas only 41 percent would "agree to have less." That so many would defy the advice of their physician demonstrates the power of the endowment effect.

INTERVIEW WITH NED CALONGE, MD, MPH
Past Chairman, U.S. Preventive Services Task Force
Dr. Ned Calonge was the chairman of the U.S. Preventive Services Task Force when it made its recommendations regarding screening mammograms in 2009. Dr. Calonge was a member of the Task Force from 2003 to 2011 and was chair from 2004 to 2011. He earned his MD from the University of Colorado School of Medicine and his MPH from the University of Washington School of Public and Community Medicine. He was chief, Department of Preventive Medicine, Colorado Permanente Medical Group from 1991 to 2001; chief medical officer, Colorado Department of Public Health and Environment, from 2001 to 2010; and currently is president and CEO of the Colorado Trust.

Did the process for developing the new mammography
recommendations differ from the Task Force's standard process?
The update for mammography went through the usual process, except that it was trying to fill in the evidence gaps from previous reviews. So,

we went out to see if there were any new data. We had it redone by the Oregon EPC. So, that all looks like a normal update process. When we got the evidence report and had the first discussion at a Task Force meeting, we were unable to get the two-thirds vote necessary to accept a recommendation. I think that might be the only time we were unable to get a two-thirds vote, at least during my tenure. So we were kind of stuck. I would like to say that we had a lot of methods for what we were going to do next, but sitting in the chair seat I said, "Well, we're going to have to think about other ways to do this." We threw it back to the evidence group and our staff to say, "Maybe we could use modeling to move this one along." At that point, we reached out to CIS-NET. Since we could not get to a vote, I would say mammography took more than average because we needed additional information in order to make a recommendation.

Why couldn't you get a two-thirds majority?
I think there was real debate, especially for the forty- to fifty-year-old age group. One of the problems we have is there are no absolutes. We had a number-needed-to-screen (NNS) that looked really high, higher than anything else we had ever given an A or B recommendation. So we had these remarkably high NNS, and for some of us that was sufficient to say that this looks like a small net benefit. I think there was a degree of discomfort with doing that, based on the outcome tables that we usually use. Another thing is that if you look at the Nelson paper, the confidence intervals around those NNS were actually pretty large. Each confidence interval included the next group. The uncertainty around the estimates raised uncertainty in the minds of people who were not willing to downgrade to a C [recommendation], and that's what made us unable to vote. So, that's why we said that we needed to do some additional work.

What were the relative contributions of the various harms,
from your perspective as well as the Task Force?
I looked at them as a whole. The false positives are always the Achilles heel of screening tests, but when you're trading off a biopsy versus saving a life or gaining life years, that looks like a reasonable trade-off.

And it could very well look like a reasonable trade-off to most women. We didn't want to make that call for them, and if you just say, all women forty to fifty should get annual mammograms, you're actually making that call for them.

I received a call from a reporter during breast cancer awareness month in November 2010 [a year after the release of the recommendations]. One thing I had found interesting was that the tone had changed in the reporters' questions over the twelve months. The issue about what the Task Force really said and how the evidence came out, I think almost all the reporters I talked to got that. It doesn't necessarily mean that they don't think that women shouldn't have mammograms between forty and fifty, but they certainly understood what we said and what our intent was. But one reporter was a little more confrontational and as we were talking suggested to me that the recommendations were wrong because we were asking women to understand a very complex issue of trading off potential benefits and harm, and she didn't think women could make that distinction. I said that that was one of the most remarkably unempowering things I have ever heard. To suggest that women aren't smart enough to weigh risks and benefits for their own health and make their own health decisions, that's very paternalistic, and quite honestly I can't support that viewpoint. It was interesting because she clearly had never thought about it that way and admitted to me that she was taken aback a little and would have to think about it.

*How did you and the Task Force interpret
the reaction to its recommendations?*
I think the level of what seemed to be a coordinated negative response was not something we had fully anticipated. I think it was pretty clear that the American College of Radiology knew this was coming; we knew the American Cancer Society knew it was coming because we shared it with them; Susan B. Komen for the Cure appeared to know it was coming. There was a little consternation early on that someone had leaked the results. I think it's just an expectation that if you share what you are about to say with this many groups, it may sneak out. It really did seem like there was a well-coordinated reaction, with people

willing to go on TV in all of the major media markets to blast the Task Force.

I would say that we discussed reactions, tried to anticipate them, and were naïve in the degree of reaction that actually came out. There are back-channel discussions that probably will never come to light; but there were lots of rumors among Task Force members that this was a well-funded, well-coordinated misinformation campaign. I can believe that, just to see how well it worked.

I agree that mammography has been oversold. A 15 percent mortality reduction is really poor. If you think about what that number means, if I screen five women who without mammography would die from breast cancer, I save one life, and the other four die in spite of mammography. That's pretty poor performance. And if the radiologists say, "Maybe it's 25 percent," OK, I have three women who are going to die of breast cancer, and one doesn't. The overselling is something I've seen in practice. There are women who would get breast cancer and say, "How could I get breast cancer? I get a mammogram every year." So now we've oversold it to the point where it prevents breast cancer. So, their [American College of Radiology's] reaction was almost predictable.

Do you think the Task Force will go about
its work in a different way in the future?
The new process that we have helps, although it will be interesting to see how well that plays out. The public comment period, where the recommendations statement is not final, I think that's a real important change, and it opens up the system to much more increased transparency. We would have had the "scientific arguments" from the ACR; we could have addressed them in the recommendation statement itself, rather than what we are now doing, which is dueling letters to the editor, which is an inefficient way of addressing issues. And we would have had a pretty good heads-up that we needed to word the recommendations differently in terms of making sure that what we wanted to say was clear to the public. That's an important change.

*To what extent does that make you more vulnerable
to the politicization of the process?*
I think we welcome that. This is science versus advocacy. I think it's
really important to have that dialogue. One of the problems that I'll
admit to as a scientist is that I believe that science and evidence should
sway the day. But the reality is that science and evidence are *part* of the
decision-making process, but they are not the *only* part.

I often think that what would be better for the way we look at preventive services in the [health reform legislation] is to put another process between the Task Force and the coverage decision. Not that they
asked me, but I would not make that direct link. The Task Force would
say what the evidence base is, so that everyone would know what they
are, and there's another group where politics, advocacy, and special interests can have its day, be heard, and influence the coverage decision.
That way you don't perturb the science, and you let these other important factors help sway the coverage decision. You don't push that down
to the scientists, who are trying to make the decision based on the cold,
hard evaluation of the science.

What advice would you give—or have you given—to your successor?
Not all our recommendations garner this level of attention. Go back
to Rep. Waxman's question to me [at the December 2009 Congressional hearing]: How many topics do you have? One hundred and five.
And how many of them have gotten this level of attention? Counting
this one, one.

What we recognize is that any time we say "no," there will be two
categories [of responses]. [Recommendations of] As and Bs are going
to make somebody happy. The Cs, Ds, and Is are going to make other
people unhappy. Anticipating that is really useful. Unhappy usually
translates to goring somebody's ox. We can make sure that we have
at least listened to those constituencies and can acknowledge that and
then say, "But the science doesn't support it." AHRQ has dedicated resources to prepare better messaging around these recommendations.
To their credit, they said "all" recommendations.

But let's be frank, the ones that are really going to get people's attention are things that are not an A or B. My advice is to be real careful around messaging, make sure you listen to the public input, and be prepared for the media issues that are going to come up. I hope that we don't get sandbagged very often.

It would be helpful to have the negative comments beforehand, to create a better message. If you're just going to say "no," or you're just going to do what happened with ACR and this recommendation—an all-out blitz to try to discredit the group and apply political pressure to either eliminate the Task Force or get it to change our recommendations based on their belief—if that's all you want to do, then the public process is not going to work, but at least, we'll be able to say, "We gave these guys a chance, and they said nothing." And I think that's another messaging point.

So my advice was, "Don't sweat the positive ones." When you're going to put something out that says "insufficient," or "small net benefit," or "don't do it," you have to go through the stakeholder process and whether stakeholder groups would be willing to engage in dialogue beforehand. Could we publish joint letters at the same time, so we actually invite the debate and discussion ahead of time, instead of this reactionary all-out war?

We could get rolled on this, but the Task Force will take it in stride. There are a lot of issues about putting people in the room. It could impact the discussion. If it's a high-risk issue—breast screening or childhood screening for inheritable disorders—I think it really impacts discussion in a way that free and open discussion may not occur as easily. The other point is that not everyone can afford to go. You think about who can go to DC and afford to sit there, and it seems like an unfair approach.

SO WHAT? WHAT ARE THE IMPLICATIONS OF BEHAVIORAL ECONOMICS FOR DEBATING AND CREATING HEALTH POLICY?

At this stage of its development, behavioral economics is more highly developed as description than prescription. However, the field does have some insights into how to ameliorate the power of the endowment effect, loss aversion, framing, and anchoring. One nagging concern, though, is whether these human tendencies are learned or innate. Research by Keith Chen and his colleagues demonstrated that capuchin monkeys can experience loss aversion. At the end of the article, the authors speculated,

If these biases are innate, we may be more inclined to believe that they will persist in both common and novel settings, will be stable across time and cultures, and may endure even in the face of large individual costs, ample feedback, or repeated market disciplining. This would greatly constrain both the potential for successful policy intervention and the types of remedies available." (Chen, Lakshminarayanan, and Santos 2006: 535)

If these tendencies in humans are hardwired, then they can be exploited (by those who wish to frame decisions in their favor) but not tempered. On the other hand, if the tendencies are behavioral, then they can be moderated, but they can also be influenced by opportunistic and ideological forces. Unfortunately, the field of neuroscience has made only modest progress in resolving this issue.

The other challenge in offering prescriptions for debates of health policy lies simply in the presentation of information for decision making. As information architect Edward Tufte (2007) has demonstrated throughout his career, there are multiple ways to present information—to clarify or obscure, to make overly simple or overly complex. He has shown that the presence or absence of proper context can significantly skew information. For example, if 1,904 women aged forty to forty-nine need to be screened to save one death from breast cancer, is that a large number or a small number? Likewise, if screening mammograms can reduce mortality of women aged forty to forty-nine years old by 40 percent, is that a large number or a small number given that it means going from 0.04 to 0.025 deaths per 100,000 women? And, as the Asian disease example earlier in this chapter showed, the same data presented—legitimately—in different ways can generate dramatically different responses. Lastly, if the benefits of a health policy such as screening mammograms can be linked to specific individuals ("My sister's life was saved because she had a mammogram when she was forty-three") but the harms (such as overdiagnosis and overtreatment) are diffused across a statistical population, the perceived benefits may overwhelm the harms despite any quantitative calculations. These issues fall well outside the competency of an economist, even a behavioral one.

But we can discuss other implications of the findings of this chapter. First, let's suppose that the tendencies that we discussed are hardwired. In that case, there is significant potential that they can be exploited by those with specific agendas. Of course, in many cases there will be advocates on both sides of an issue. Will these competing frames lead to clarity through competition (as anticipated by mainstream economists, who tout the benefits of competition) or to indecisiveness through confusion (as hypothesized by information theorists)? If the former, the problems of loss aversion and framing resolve themselves without intervention. If the latter, then remedies are called for. Ironically, some of these remedies stem from neoclassical economics.

One remedy could be the use of disinterested, credible, independent agents to assist the public and individuals in making decisions. Agency theory has been a part of mainstream economics for quite some time, to solve what is called the *asymmetric information problem.* Here the issue is not that one side has more information than another but that the information can be framed in ways that can distort effective decision making. An agent with a reputation for honesty and clarity (such as a physician or adviser) can present and interpret information that enables the decision maker to make rational decisions. Ironically, the agents need not be disinterested to be useful in ameliorating the framing phenomenon. James Druckman (2001) demonstrated in a series of variations of the Asian disease experiments that the endorsement of interested entities (like political parties) that represent the viewpoints of the respondents can greatly diminish framing effects. In some sense, it is not that these entities act as true agents, advising the decision makers; rather, they provide signals that can clarify the underlying issues and weaken the power of the frame. One can see how such agents could improve decision making, but what happens in those instances when the credible agents disagree (such as during the screening mammography controversy, when the U.S. Preventive Services Task Force was opposed by the American Cancer Society)? Perhaps then we enter into a second-order agency problem, in which an überagent is needed to provide impartial information about the agents themselves.

Three alternatives to direct agents suggest themselves. The first would be a Wikipedia for framing and anchoring. Issues would be posted (such as the value and harms of medical screenings), and anonymous authors would present and critique alternative frames; as with the original Wikipedia, the process of continuous editing would weed out or expose inappropriate or misleading frames. The second would be a health policy equivalent of Penn & Teller, the iconoclastic magicians who enrage other professional magicians by explaining their tricks. In this case, these entities would present the frames that different sides of a health policy issue are presenting, verify or refute the frames, and perhaps offer alternative frames. People who could play this role include Jon Stewart and Stephen Colbert and their adherents. The third possibility would be a health policy equivalent of Edward Tufte, who has devoted his career to the honest and transparent presentation of information to facilitate decision making. This entity would devise truthful graphics that present data through multiple frames—preferably, simultaneously—so that decision makers would become more aware of the framing and try to discount the behavioral effects discussed in this chapter.

The ideas discussed so far assume that loss aversion, framing, and the like are inherent in human decision making. If, in fact, these behavioral tendencies are learned, remedies would focus on how to moderate their influence on decision making. The first approach would be to increase self-awareness. As various behavioral economics experiments have demonstrated, most individuals are unaware, even oblivious, of the phenomena of the endowment effect, framing, and anchoring. We may perceive biases in other people but not in ourselves. Revealing the nature of framing can provide at least two benefits. One is for everyone to recognize the potential and impact of framing in health policy debates; that is, we should pay attention to "the man behind the curtain." In addition, this effort would remind us to recognize the difficulty of overcoming framing, anchoring, and biases and, before making a decision, to always ask the questions, "What is the frame being presented here?" and "How would the issue look differently if the frame were altered?"

Another possibility would be that independent, socially responsible agencies would present multiple frames of a given issue to decision makers. This agency might be a private organization (like the Cochrane Collaboration, which prepares systematic reviews of medical research) or a federal agency (like the Congressional Budget Office, which provides objective analysis of the fiscal consequences of proposed legislation). For instance, such an agency could implement Dr. Ned Calonge's suggestion that the U.S. Preventive Services Task Force and organizations with opposing points of view issue a joint statement that presents each organization's perspective, conclusions, and recommendations, perhaps with an objective commentary provided by the agency. In addition, the agency could sponsor joint research projects that engage research teams with alternative viewpoints and frames who agree ex ante on the research protocols and criteria for evaluating results. In fact, Daniel Kahneman conducted such an *adversarial collaboration* with another research team who had developed alternative hypotheses related to loss aversion (Bateman et al. 2005).

As may be obvious, these are not "big" ideas for alleviating the effects of the endowment effect, framing, and anchoring. Rather, they are small ideas that involve spreading a culture of awareness about the biasing effects of these principles. It is the pervasiveness of these concepts that can cause decision making to be less than rational, and it will require a pervasiveness of efforts to overcome them.

3 MANAGING EXPECTATIONS AND BEHAVIOR

The United States was built on the promise of individual free will and unlimited opportunity. We Americans treasure abundance, choice, and the pursuit of happiness, and we believe deep in our hearts that access to all three will yield enduring and unalloyed blessings. So we demand more and more choices, whether it's breakfast cereal or houses. If someone forced us to buy a product, we would resist in part because we want to be the one to make the choice. If we were to win the lottery—not the daily one, but the Powerball worth hundreds of millions of dollars—we are convinced that we would be happy for life, whereas, if Congress were to pass a law that we thought was wasteful, unfair, and even unconstitutional, we would think that it heralded the beginning of the end of the republic.

Yet behavioral economics and behavioral psychology have demonstrated that these long-held beliefs may be flat wrong. We oftentimes do better with fewer choices, instead of more. We may actually benefit (at least in the long run) if we are "forced" to buy something that we initially do not want to buy. And our sense of well-being is remarkably stable over time, so that our expectations that major events—both positive and negative—will have a dramatic impact on our lives are considerably moderated by our ability to adapt to changing circumstances. So what we think will give us lasting pleasure may be just a chimera.

In this chapter we will reflect on these issues in the context of health policy and health reform. We will consider three anomalies for which mainstream economics has no real answers but that become understandable from the perspective of behavioral economics. As with Chapter 2, we will begin by introducing some fundamental concepts from behavioral economics and behavioral psychology and then relate them to the health policy anomalies.

PROJECTION BIAS, HYPERBOLIC DISCOUNTING, AND HOT–COLD DECISIONS: REDUCING THE HYPERVENTILATION OVER HEALTH CARE REFORM

As we have noted, mainstream economists assume that people try to make decisions that maximize their welfare. In many cases, that means that people need to have a good idea of what their underlying preferences will be in the future because that's when the results of their economic decisions will play out. In Chapter 2 we demonstrated how our friend Benjamin could be influenced (dare we say it, manipulated) by how issues are framed and anchored at any point in time. Now, we want to see how Benjamin's potentially distorted view of the future—and the past—can influence how he makes decisions.

First, we need to explore briefly the growing science of happiness and well-being. People consistently mispredict what will make them happy or give them a sense of well-being in the future. Over the past thirty years, economists and psychologists have been measuring the extent of this mismatch. In the most celebrated study, Philip Brickman, Dan Coates, and Ronnie Janoff-Bulman (1978) surveyed lottery winners, paraplegic accident victims, and a control group in Illinois in the 1970s. When the participants were asked to rate on a scale of 0 to 5 how happy they were at the time of the survey, the means were 4.0 for the lottery winners, 3.82 for the control group, and 2.96 for the accident victims. Although the order certainly looks right, there was no statistically significant difference in reported happiness between the lottery winners and the controls, and the paraplegics' rating was above the midpoint of the scale. The study participants were also asked to rate how happy they expected to be "in a couple of years," using the same 0 to 5 scale. The surprising result was that there was no statistically significant difference among the three groups (4.20 for the lottery winners, 4.14 for the control group, and 4.32 for the accident victims), despite their outwardly different prospects.

Perhaps we should not put too much emphasis on this landmark study because of its small sample (seventy-three participants in total). Nevertheless, its unexpected results spurred other researchers to examine how people rate their happiness and well-being. In general, these studies have found that people overestimate the impact of major life events—both good and bad—on themselves or on others. For example, Jason Riis and his coauthors (2005) investigated patients with kidney disease who had to have hemodialysis three times a week. They used a very clever methodology devised by Daniel Kahneman, in which forty-nine patients and forty-nine matched healthy adults carried personal digital assistants; at random times they were prompted to rate their mood at the time, from –2 (very unpleasant) to +2 (very pleasant). After a week of promptings, the average mood response was +0.70 by patients and +0.83 by the healthy controls, a statistically insignificant result. Study participants were also asked four positive emotion and five negative emotion questions; again, no statistically significant differences between the two groups. Now comes the really interesting part: At the exit interview, those in the healthy group were asked to imagine that they had been a patient on hemodialysis for at least one year and to estimate what their average mood would be; their average was –0.38, well below the +0.70 that the patients themselves had rated their mood. In their exit interviews, the patients were asked to imagine that they had never had kidney disease or needed hemodialysis and to estimate what their average mood would be; their average was +1.16, well above their own mood (+0.70) and that of the healthy group (+0.83). The authors reached two conclusions: Those with chronic kidney disease who have to suffer through permanent hemodialysis have been largely able to adapt to their condition, and neither they nor healthy people anticipate this adaptation.

As with much of behavioral economics and behavioral psychology, the data on well-being and adaptation do not always speak with the same clarity. One carefully designed and executed study (Oswald and Powdthavee 2008) used a longitudinal data set (the British Household Panel Survey) to measure life satisfaction levels over time for adults who were fully abled, moderately disabled (defined as "disabled but able to do day-to-day activities"), and severely disabled (defined as "disabled and unable to do at least one of the [specified] day-to-day activities"). The researchers discovered that the moderately disabled reported immediately after the disability a life satisfaction score 0.4 points lower (on a 1 to 7 scale) than the fully abled; over time, however, the life satisfaction of the moderately disabled increased 0.2 points (meaning that they recovered about 50 percent of their reduced sense of well-being). The severely disabled reported a 0.6 point drop in life satisfaction immediately after their disability but recovered only 0.2 points (or 30 percent adaptation) over time. Overall, this study found that well-being does adapt—but only partially—to adverse life events.

Despite studies like this, which found only modest adaptation, more studies have confirmed the effect. It became clear that what was needed was not more studies but a framework for understanding them. George Loewenstein, Ted O'Donoghue, and Matthew Rabin (2003) developed the concept of *projection bias* to provide this structure. They noted that Adam Smith in his *Theory of Moral Sentiments* (Smith 1790/2009: 172) alluded to this concept over two centuries ago:

The great source of both the misery and disorders of human life, seems to arise from over-rating the difference between one permanent situation and another. Avarice over-rates the difference between poverty and riches: ambition, that between a private and a public station; vain-glory, that between obscurity and extensive reputation. The person under the influence of any of those extravagant passions, is not only miserable in his actual situation, but is often disposed to disturb the peace of society, in order to arrive at that which he so foolishly admires.

They start with a standard neoclassical economic model of individual behavior, but allow for an individual (say, our friend Benjamin) to fail to recognize how his preferences or needs will change over time. Their model then demonstrates that Benjamin's failure to recognize his projection bias leads to two distortions. First, Benjamin will underappreciate what George Loewenstein has termed a negative *internality*—that if he consumes more Godiva chocolates today, Benjamin will get less pleasure from consuming these treats in the future. Second, Benjamin will underappreciate the role of habit formation in his decision making. Loewenstein and his colleagues show that these two distortions will lead Benjamin to consume too much earlier in his life and too little later in his life, compared to what a rational individual would choose. In addition, they show that projection bias will lead Benjamin to underappreciate day-to-day fluctuations in how he values different goods, which will lead to underbuying or overbuying relative to a rational individual. In particular, Benjamin will be more likely to buy a durable good than will a rational person. Their intuitive argument goes as follows: Suppose Benjamin has been eyeing a Porsche Cayman S (which he cannot afford on his $50,000 salary as a database analyst); his valuation of this car can vary every day, but let's suppose that on average the valuation is not high enough for him to buy the car. If Benjamin were rational, he would never buy the car; however, if he has projection bias, he will buy the car on the one day where his valuation (driven perhaps by advertising or his fantasizing about the thrills he could have with the car on the track) exceeds the purchase price: hence the economics of the midlife crisis (which, in Benjamin's case, comes twenty years early).

For our purposes, projection bias helps to explain the phenomena that we have been considering. Thus, those who have never won the lottery project that their well-being would necessarily be dramatically improved if they were to win the lottery. And healthy people project that life must be unbearable for a patient with kidney disease who has to undergo hemodialysis three times a week. David Schkade and Daniel Kahneman (1998: 340) observe that "if people judge what it is like to *be* a paraplegic by imagining what it is like to *become* a paraplegic, they will exaggerate the long-term impact of this tragic event on life satisfaction." Loewenstein, O'Donoghue, and Rabin are arguing that that is exactly what people with projection bias are doing.

It may be obvious, but a major aspect of projection bias and the absence or presence of adaptation is how people view the future. Neoclassical economists have assumed that people make decisions about the future as if they have what is called an *exponential discount function*. Exponential discounting has two convenient properties: The discount rate is constant over time, and value declines proportionally over time. The implication of these properties is that if our friend Benjamin preferred $100 today to $200 two years from now, he would also prefer $100 six years from now to $200 eight years from now. Unfortunately, this usually does not happen, and, as has been demonstrated (Ainslie and Haslam 1992), Benjamin is more likely to prefer the $200 eight years from now to the $100 in six years. Benjamin's time preferences are what is termed "time inconsistent" and follow what economists call a *hyperbolic discount function*.

Figure 3.1 shows the dramatic difference between these two discount functions. The exponential function decreases gradually over time, whereas the hyperbolic function declines much more rapidly at first, then tapers off. People who exhibit hyperbolic discounting have a higher discount rate and prefer the present much more than the short-term future but have a lower discount rate and are relatively indifferent between years in the long-term future (say, 2027 and 2029). The time inconsistency arises when that long-term future becomes the present, and people really care about whether something happens in 2027 or 2029. To those living in the world envisioned by neoclassical economics, this distinction is irrelevant.

One final point should be made about hyperbolic discounting: It may appear that hyperbolic discounting and projection bias represent the same phenomenon. In some sense this may be true. However, the distinction—and it is a significant one—is that people are generally unaware that they exhibit projection bias, but they may be fully aware that they use (at least implicitly) hyperbolic discounting. That is, people with projection bias are probably making suboptimal decisions, whereas those with hyperbolic discount functions may be making the right decisions—at least for them. This distinction will become significant when we consider the

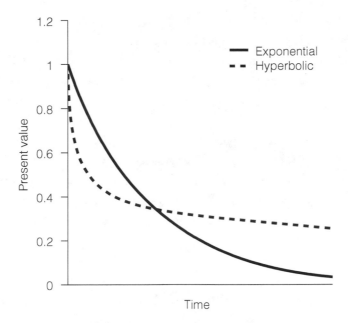

FIGURE 3.1
Discount functions.

implications of these phenomena for health care and health reform later in this chapter.

There are a few more constructs from behavioral economics that we need before we proceed to a discussion of health reform and health care behavior. Stefano DellaVigna and Ulrike Malmendier (2004) developed an elegant model that describes the behavior of consumers and firms when the consumers have time-inconsistent preferences. They divide consumers into two types: "sophisticated," who know that they have time-inconsistent preferences; and "naïve," who do not. The researchers examine two markets in which there is a time mismatch between costs and benefits. The first is the market for what they call "investment goods," which they define as goods for which the consumer pays most of the costs upfront and receives most of the benefits in the future, such as health club memberships and vacation time-sharing. The second is the market for what they call (somewhat erroneously) "leisure goods," for which the consumer receives the benefits up front and pays the costs later. For example, airlines in the early days of credit cards would advertise "Fly now, pay later." DellaVigna and Malmendier cite hotels in Las Vegas, which charge low prices for their rooms and buffet meals (many times "comping" their best customers) to encourage visitors to stay and gamble.

Their model yields some intriguing results. In a market for investment goods, firms will charge a per-usage price that is lower than its actual cost of delivering the service (maybe even making it free) and charge a higher flat fee to recoup their costs. Naïve consumers will be attracted to the idea of low costs and high benefits in the future and will overestimate how often they will use the good. Sophisticated consumers, though, will require something (called a "commitment device," which we will discuss in the next chapter) to make sure that they overcome their hyperbolic discounting and actually use the good as often as they should; hence the relatively high monthly membership fees and low (if not, zero) per-visit prices for most health clubs.

DellaVigna and Malmendier prove that the opposite results hold for a market for leisure goods. Firms will charge low prices at the beginning (for example, "teaser" rates for credit cards or cheap Las Vegas hotel rooms and meals) and much higher prices in the future. Naïve consumers will underestimate their future usage (when the credit card interest rates are higher and the house gets its substantial take at the gaming tables). Sophisticated consumers will demand some kind of commitment device to dampen their usage (such as a modest credit limit).

Not only do people evaluate events differently if they are in the past or the future, but they also rate events differently if the events are in what George Loewenstein (2005) calls a "cold" state or a "hot" state. In cold states, people are more analytical, more reasoned, more rational. In hot states, they are driven more by emotions, feelings, and sensations. What will be of most interest to us here is Loewenstein's notion of a *hot–cold empathy gap*. Those who are in a hot state tend to be unaware of the extent to which their decision making and actions are affected by being in this state, and they tend to believe that they are more calculating and rational than, in fact, they are. This unawareness, in turn, leads people in hot states to expect that their preferences will be more stable than they actually will be when they move to a cold state. For their part, those in cold states seem not to understand how their decisions and actions will be different when they are in hot states. That is, they underestimate the power inherent in these states. As a result, they fail to anticipate being in a hot state or to prepare adequately. For instance, suppose our friend Benjamin gets an invitation to his New Trier High School ten-year class reunion to be held in four months; he wants to attend but feels that he needs to lose fifteen pounds to get back to his seventeen-year-old weight. In this cold state, he devises a plan to lose one pound a week until the reunion. Everything goes well until late one night he's hungry and tired and his body craves that XXL-size bag of M&Ms he bought at Sam's Club and hid in the closet where his girlfriend Elaine cannot find them. In his hot state he thinks that one night of gorging on M&Ms won't make a difference and that he will get back on the diet the next morning; his cold state is nowhere to be seen but wakes up in the morning wondering why he feels so full.

Loewenstein and Leaf Van Boven (Van Boven and Loewenstein 2003) confirmed the hot–cold empathy gap with several experiments. Visitors to a gym were asked to read a story about hikers lost in Colorado without enough water or food and were then asked to describe how unpleasant it would have been for the hikers and what the hikers would regret not packing. Those who completed the survey after they exercised (that is, in a hot state) mentioned the unpleasantness of being thirsty and the hikers' regret at not packing water 50 percent more frequently than those who had not yet exercised (and were still in a cold state). The study participants were also asked about their own feelings, if they had been in the hikers' situation. Again, those who had just exercised were much more likely to say that they would have been bothered by thirst and would have regretted not bringing water. The researchers used the statistical technique of structural equation modeling to examine simultaneously the study participants' predictions of their own feelings as well as that of the hikers; through this technique, Van Boven and Loewenstein were able to determine that people predict the behavior of others largely through the projection of their own behavior and their own current hot–cold state. This result led the researchers to conclude that people tend to overestimate the similarity of their situation with others and especially tend to project their current, albeit transient, hot state onto others. In the words of Adam Smith, "We either approve or disapprove of the conduct of another man according as we feel that, when we bring his case home to ourselves, we either can or cannot entirely sympathize with the sentiments and motives which directed it" (Smith 1790/2009: 133).

ANOMALY 4: *Why do opponents—and proponents—of the Patient Protection and Affordable Care Act believe that the law will have a larger impact on the health care sector than it probably will?*

For many policy issues—the invasion of Iraq, abortion, privatization of Social Security—opinions are strong and debate is heated. Usually, once a decision is made, the issue loses its intensity—not because those who lost have been convinced but because the heat of the moment passes, and people move on. That sense of resolution or closure has not yet occurred in the debate over health care reform. Before the health reform law was passed, the rhetoric was passionate and often overwrought. From the opponents:

- Sen. Judd Gregg (R-NH) (Gregg 2009: A7):

  It would take Sherlock Holmes armed with the latest GPS technology and a pack of bloodhounds to find "reform" in the $2.5 trillion version of the health-care bill we are supposed to vote on. . . . this bill is bad for New Hampshire. According to a recently released report, the Reid legislation could increase insurance premiums in New Hampshire by as much as 93 percent for some individuals. For those who purchase their health insurance from a small business, premiums could increase as much as 25 percent.

- Federation for American Immigration Reform (Illegal aliens 2009):

  The House bill does not include a mechanism to prevent illegal aliens from receiving "affordability credits" that would subsidize the purchase of private health insurance. . . . "The loopholes and omissions in the House bill are not there by accident," continued [Dan] Stein [President of FAIR].

"These loopholes were intended to extend benefits to illegal aliens while allowing Members of Congress to deny those facts to the American people."

- Sarah Palin, from her Facebook page (Palin 2009):

    As more Americans delve into the disturbing details of the nationalized health care plan that the current administration is rushing through Congress, our collective jaw is dropping, and we're saying not just no, but hell no! Who will suffer the most when they ration care? The sick, the elderly, and the disabled, of course. The America I know and love is not one in which my parents or my baby with Down Syndrome will have to stand in front of Obama's "death panel" so his bureaucrats can decide, based on a subjective judgment of their "level of productivity in society," whether they are worthy of health care. Such a system is downright evil.

From the proponents:

- Sen. Harry Reid (R-NV) (Murray 2009: A1) :

    Instead of joining us on the right side of history, all Republicans can come up with is this: Slow down, stop everything, let's start over. If you think you've heard these same excuses before, you're right. When this country belatedly recognized the wrongs of slavery, there were those who dug in their heels and said "slow down, it's too early, things aren't bad enough."

- Robert Creamer, political strategist, Nov. 6, 2009 (Creamer 2009):

    Only one small group of Americans would benefit economically from the defeat of the House health insurance reform bill: the private insurance industry. . . . The House stands on the brink of passing historic legislation that creates a public health insurance option that will end the stranglehold of the insurance industry on our health care system. For the first time, the bill will make health insurance available to almost everyone in America—allowing our country to join the ranks of every other developed nation in making health care a right.

- Rep. Alan Grayson (D-FL), Sept. 29, 2009 (Allen 2009):

    The Republican health care plan: don't get sick. . . . The Republicans have a back-up plan in case you do get sick . . . This is what the Republicans want you to do. If you get sick America, the Republican health care plan is this: Die quickly!

Contrary to expectations, the rhetoric had not cooled down much almost one year later, when the Republicans in the U.S. House moved to repeal the Affordable Care Act (ACA), titling their bill, "Repealing the Job Killing Health Care Act Bill." Again, some words from the opponents:

- Rep. Michele Bachmann (R-MN), Jan. 19, 2011 (Montopoli 2011):

  Obamacare as we know is the crown jewel of socialism. . . . We will not stop until we . . . put a president in the position of the White House who will repeal this bill. . . . I've seen everything from 26% increases on health insurance, to 45% increases on health insurance. . . . We will continue this fight until Obamacare is no longer the law of the land, and until we can actually pass reform that will cut the costs of healthcare.

- Rep. Lamar Smith (D-TX), Jan. 19, 2011 (Health care repeal debate 2011):

  I support this legislation that repeals the Democrats' job-stifling, cost-increasing, freedom-limiting health care law. . . . The Democrats' health care law will produce more litigation and more costly health care.

And from the proponents of health care reform, we heard:

- Rep. Anthony Weiner (D-NY), Jan. 19, 2011 (Ryan 2011):

  You know, I want to advise people watching at home who are playing that now popular drinking game "you take a shot whenever the Republicans say something that is not true." Please assign a designated driver. This is going to be a long afternoon.

- Rep. Nancy Pelosi (D-CA), Jan. 5, 2011 (O'Brien 2011):

  This is our first test of how grassroots Democrats will respond to the Republicans' disgraceful attempt to roll back our progress for America's middle class families. We must hold House Republicans' feet to the fire for taking government funded health care for themselves while voting to deny it to American families.

Despite these vociferous and even strident opinions, the findings of behavioral economics and behavioral psychology presented so far in this chapter strongly suggest that Anomaly 4 will prevail and the reality of the health reform law will be dramatically less than what proponents and opponents are expecting. First, we can turn to projection bias. The research has demonstrated that people badly overestimate the impact that future events will have on them. Let's look at how that might play out with health care reform. Opponents of health reform imagine that a wide variety of evils will be visited on them and society—mandated purchases of health insurance, death panels, socialism—essentially the end of life as we know it. Recognizing that some of these fears were just political rhetoric to sway people and the specific provisions of the legislation, others were sincere concerns of opponents of health reform. Nevertheless, it is highly likely that the reality of health reform implementation will be quite different. Socialism is in the eye of the beholder, and the United States has adopted a number of policies—Social Security, unemployment insurance, Medicare—that were touted as socialism when they were introduced but are enormously popular now; few—even conservative Republicans—would now advocate their repeal.

Death panels are a different story. There was little reality in these fears. The elements of the law that had even the loosest connection to death panels were as follows:

- A provision in a draft bill that would reimburse health providers for engaging in end-of-life counseling with patients under Medicare (ironically, reflecting a policy strongly advocated by Republican Sen. Johnny Isakson of Georgia) but excised by Democrats soon after the controversy arose.

- The Independent Payment Advisory Board, which was charged with limiting reimbursement rates (unless overruled by Congress) if per capita spending growth in Medicare were projected to exceed a target rate.

Mandated health insurance may prove less onerous than projected. People may come to accept it, as they do "mandatory" car insurance or mortgage insurance (although opponents will be quick to point out that no one is required to buy a car or a house). In addition, the mandate is a "soft" one, in that it is a mandate "for those individuals who can afford health care insurance," with affordability defined as costing less than 8 percent of monthly income. Those who do not buy insurance will be required by 2016 to pay a fine/tax of $695 or 2.5 percent of income, whichever is higher. It is unclear at this point how vigorous enforcement will be.

Proponents of health reform are probably as myopic in their expectations. They tout major benefits to the law—insurance for 32 million currently uninsured citizens, creation of health exchanges to improve competition and transparency, development by health providers of accountable care organizations. Although these changes will probably have significant impacts, they likely will not be as momentous as expected. Take the uninsured, for example. A variety of well-designed studies have demonstrated that the presence of health insurance increases health care utilization but not as much as expected: between 8 and 40 percent for outpatient physician services and between 0 (yes, zero) and 15 percent for inpatient hospital utilization (Freeman et al. 2008). An early study of the experience in Massachusetts after that state enacted a similar law in 2006 found that hospitalization for some preventable conditions actually decreased (presumably as the uninsured sought care early and avoided hospitalizations) and that hospital costs increased no more than in other states (Kolstad and Kowalski 2010). In sum, these studies found that many of the uninsured had been able to obtain some health care; their utilization—and, one hopes, their health status—will improve, but it will not be starting from zero.

Likewise, insurance exchanges and accountable care organizations (ACOs) sound like good ideas for improving the U.S. health care system. The exchanges could promote competition and improve consumers' ability to compare premiums and coverage. However, the health insurance market is highly oligopolistic in many areas, and there is little in the Affordable Care Act to encourage insurers to enter new markets. The potential for ACOs is promising, as well. If a new health care payment model rewards coordination and a focus on outcomes rather than inputs, then these ACOs will be valuable mechanisms for delivering care. However, it is likely that relatively few health care organizations will be able to meet this challenge, and the bulk of physicians, hospitals, and other delivery settings will probably be doing what they have always been doing. So, these are good ideas, well-intentioned, but not likely to achieve the extravagant claims that reform proponents have been touting.

These realities are well known and well documented. Then why haven't they penetrated the debates over health-care reform? Setting aside the willfully ignorant and blatantly partisan, we can appeal to behavioral economics. Even though a well-informed public may understand the limitations of health care reform, they are subject to the asymmetric valuation of past and future events. The future holds more promise—or danger—than the past and is certainly more malleable:

- If there weren't death panels in the past, there could be in the future.
- Even if the uninsured had access to some health care services in the past, surely they will seek much more care than previous studies had shown—and with much better outcomes, as well.
- Times have changed, and Social Security and Medicare are bed-rocks of our society, but Obamacare is just too much.
- Sure, health insurers have been able to carve up their own protected territory, but these insurance exchanges will be a new day of competition and transparency.

Then, add the hot–cold empathy gap. Even if projection bias and asymmetric valuation did not exist, people make different decisions in a hot or cold state. As Loewenstein and others have demonstrated, the amazing thing is that people tend to discount the impact of being in these states. As a result, they will not (perhaps cannot) anticipate that their decisions will change when they are in a different state. The ongoing health reform debate has created an atmosphere in which hot-state thinking is enabled. Consequently, projection bias on both sides is amplified, and worst-case scenarios abound.

ANOMALY 5: *Why would requiring everyone to buy health insurance make everyone—including those who don't want to buy health insurance—better off?*

Who wouldn't buy health insurance, given the extraordinary costs of diagnosis and treatment? The price of cardiac bypass surgery is over

$100,000, a vaginal delivery without complications can run between $9,000 and $17,000, and even a visit to the emergency department costs over $1,200. According to the Kaiser Family Foundation (Kaiser Commission on Medicaid and the Uninsured 2010), 61 percent of the 50 million nonelderly uninsured work full-time, and 78 percent earn less than $40,000 per year. Health expenses for these people are likely to be a financial catastrophe. If that is the case, why is there so much controversy over the Patient Protection and Affordable Care Act (PPACA) requirement that everyone have health insurance? The answer, in part, lies in the statistics provided by the Kaiser Family Foundation. Almost 10 percent of the uninsured earn more than 400 percent of the federal poverty level (now at $22,000 for a family of four); 8 percent are single adults living alone, and 25 percent are single adults living together; 19 percent are adults aged nineteen to twenty-five years old, and 21 percent are from twenty-six to thirty-four; and almost 60 percent report that their health is excellent or very good.

For these people, behavioral economics would suggest that projection bias and hyperbolic discounting are in full force. Let's suppose that our friend Benjamin has opted out of his employer's comprehensive health insurance plan. Benjamin is relatively young, making $50,000 a year, and is in reasonably good health. As we saw in the Loewenstein-O'Donoghue-Rabin model, Benjamin probably will consume too much in the near term and too little later in life. He will consider how to spend his income, and health insurance (which he will rarely use unless he has a truly catastrophic event) will provide few immediate benefits compared to sports, concerts, new iPad apps, and other accoutrements of young adult life. In addition, it is likely that Benjamin has (or is acting as if he has) a hyperbolic discount function. He places a much higher value on current consumption than future consumption. So, insurance—with its reward for deferred gratification—will not be high in his set of preferences. Finally, Benjamin's decision whether or not to buy health insurance is usually made in a "cold" state, one in which he (and his girlfriend and most of his friends) are healthy and not expecting to use expensive health care services. Given these forces, it is not surprising that Benjamin has not signed up for his employer-offered health insurance. In effect, he is uninsured by choice.

If Benjamin and those like him choose not to buy health insurance, why would requiring them to do so make both them and everyone else better off? The argument why it would make everyone else better off is straightforward and makes no call on behavioral economics. It follows from the simple concept of risk pooling. For insurance to work, it must be purchased by those who will not have a claim during the period as well as those who do; if those without a claim do not buy insurance, the pool will be made up of claimants, and the system will collapse. Because young, healthy individuals are significantly less likely to experience significant health expenses, they might take the risk and not buy health insurance, leaving the demand to those more likely to use it—not a harbinger of a healthy insurance market.

Behavioral economics can provide an explanation of why it will be in Benjamin's interests to be required to buy health insurance. One buys health insurance in a cold state but usually uses health care in a hot state. As the research has shown, those in cold states often do not appreciate how their preferences will change when they are in a hot state. Once they have a significant health problem, it will be too late to buy insurance. Requiring everyone to buy health insurance creates a commitment device that allows people to overcome their hyperbolic discounting. A significant side benefit to society of this requirement is that the body politic does no better than individuals in overcoming the trap of cold and hot states. The government may impose a rule that those who need health care but did not buy health insurance be required to pay a health provider's retail prices or be denied care. That approach may work in the cold state. But when an uninsured person presents in the emergency department with a possible heart attack, it will be next to impossible for the system—the physician, the hospital, society—to turn that person away. (The Emergency Medical Treatment and Active Labor Act [EMTALA], which since 1986 has required hospitals to provide care to anyone needing emergency treatment regardless of ability to pay, illustrates our embracing of the hot state without consideration of the costs on a hospital if the patient cannot pay.) Thus, we have the paradoxical result that the individual mandate to purchase health insurance benefits both society and the reluctant individual.

THE PARADOX OF CHOICE: WHY
CONTEXT MAKES A DIFFERENCE

We all love choice. This country was built on choice, from manifest destiny to Baskin-Robbins's thirty-one flavors—the more the better. Choice is seen as such a universally positive concept that organizations incorporate it as much as possible. (Hence, those in favor of educational vouchers frame their cause as "parental choice," and supporters of abortion rights for women see themselves as "pro-choice.") Mainstream economists view choice as a fundamental tenet. At best, it allows individuals to maximize their utility. At worst, it can do no harm if individuals choose not to choose or choose not to examine all of their options if it costs too much to do so. In the words of Kelvin Lancaster (1990): "The economist's traditional model of consumer choice . . . implies an inherent preference for variety, since it asserts that, for some range of prices, there is a combination of n goods that is preferred to any combination of fewer goods that costs no more" (190).

Psychologists likewise assert that choice enhances an individual's life in multiple ways. Edward Deci and Richard Ryan (1985) argue that choice reinforces intrinsic motivation (which improves commitment to a course of action), and it allows people to be in control (or, at least, to feel in control) of their lives. In effect, choice generates two benefits from an economic and psychological perspective: Choice yields better outcomes, and choice produces a more satisfying process. Thus, a Hobson's choice, even if it results in what the individual would have chosen herself, will not be as satisfying.

These perspectives were well established until a dozen years ago when a young social psychologist from Stanford University and her dissertation advisor turned them upside down. Sheena Iyengar and Mark Lepper (2000) found that fewer choices might just be better than more. On two consecutive Saturdays they set up a booth inside an upscale grocery store in Menlo Park, California, a store known for its very large

selection of products. In their booth, Iyengar and Lepper alternated dis-
playing a selection of either six or twenty-four exotic flavors of high-end
jams. Customers in the store were invited to taste as many jams as they
wished and were given a $1 discount off the purchase of any of the jams
(which were on the regular store shelves). Standard economic and psychology theory would predict that if more flavors of jam were being displayed, more customers would stop at the booth, they would taste more
jams, and they would be more likely to buy a jam. As it turned out, only
one of these predictions panned out: Sixty percent of those passing by
the twenty-four-flavor booth did stop, compared to only 40 percent of
those passing the six-flavor display. Everyone who stopped tried either
one or two flavors. The biggest surprise, however, was the dramatic difference in purchase decisions: Thirty percent of those stopping at the
six-flavor display subsequently bought a jar of the jam, but only 3 percent of those stopping at the twenty-four-flavor display did so. In a separate study involving choices of gourmet chocolate, Iyengar and Lepper
also found that those with limited choices reported being more satisfied
with their choices than were those with more choices.

The researchers attributed this result to what they called "choice
overload." That is, although people might initially like lots of choices,
in the end—when they have to make a decision or take action—lots of
choices will reduce their ability or willingness to do so. Multiple choices
with multiple attributes that need to be compared tax a decision maker's
cognitive abilities. Iyengar and Lepper also suggest that more choices
make individuals feel more responsible for their choices, perhaps trig-
gering a kind of "chooser's remorse" that creates a fear that they will
not make the absolute best choice. All in all, their research strongly suggests that more is, indeed, less.

At about the same time, Barry Schwartz, professor of social theory
and social action at Swarthmore College, was considering similar issues.
In a thought-provoking article and a popular book (Schwartz 2000,
2004), Schwartz confronted what he provocatively calls the "tyranny of
freedom" and the "paradox of choice." He noted that Americans have
unprecedented choices—of goods, careers, life partners, lifestyles—
yet do not seem to be much happier than earlier generations that had

substantially fewer options. He argued that complete freedom can be debilitating and that true self-determination must be constrained by social convention, habit, or legal rules. In addition, he criticized the standard economics construct of individuals as rational choice machines as being "on the one hand too rich, by giving people credit for more calculation and flexibility than they possess, and on the other hand too impoverished, by failing to appreciate a range of influences on decision making that are not themselves amenable to rational calculation" (Schwartz 2000: 83).

The last decade has seen an explosion of research on the issue of choice. A recent article reviewed fifty such studies that conducted sixty-three experiments about choice (Scheibehenne, Greifeneder, and Todd 2010). The reviewers reported that only sixteen experiments confirmed the choice overload effect that Iyengar and Lepper identified, forty found no statistically significant impact of the number of choices offered, and seven found that people did better (in terms of outcomes and satisfaction) when they had more choices.

Rather than refuting the choice overload hypothesis, these findings reflect the more nuanced research results that have accumulated since the original Iyengar and Lepper work. Simona Botti and Sheena Iyengar (2006) identified three distinct psychological mechanisms by which choice can reduce well-being: information overload, preference uncertainty, and negative emotions. We have already discussed information overload. Preference uncertainty stems from the fact that, despite the assumptions of mainstream economics, people do not always have full, well-defined, and stable preferences before they make a decision. Sometimes, there are "really new products" that are not merely extensions of old products. For these, individuals must first identify the attributes of these products and then translate them into something for which they are more familiar. More routinely, people encounter choices that are new to them but not to the market (for example, first-time home buyers) or for which they will make either a singular decision (such as choice of college) or a rare decision (as in choice of cosmetic surgery). In these cases the decision maker has little or no direct experience with the choice, knows some (but not all) of the attributes (both positive and negative) of the choice, and may not have a clear idea of how she would even evaluate or rank the attributes. So, more choices are not beneficial.

Botti and Iyengar's third mechanism—negative emotion—refers to the reality that not all decisions are happy ones—"Do I like the dark chocolate almond Godiva or the white chocolate with coconut?" Suppose the choice was, "Which flavor of yogurt do you want—celery seeds, tarragon, chili powder, or sage?" Botti and Iyengar conducted that very experiment, with one-half of the study seeing those choices and the other half seeing the more traditional (and appetizing) brown sugar, cinnamon, cocoa, and mint. In each group, half were allowed to choose their flavor and half were handed a flavor. Obviously, those who got the better flavors were more satisfied with the outcome. The more interesting result was that those with the better flavors reported more satisfaction with the outcome if they were able to choose the particular flavor (instead of being given a Hobson's choice), but those with the worse flavors were less satisfied if they had been told to choose. The lesson from these findings seemed to be: "Let me choose, as long as the alternatives are relatively attractive. If the choice is to pick the 'least worst,' let someone else do it."

ANOMALY 6: *Why would giving consumers lots of choices in their health plans be a bad idea?*

Given the discussion we just had, the answer to this anomaly should be obvious. Nevertheless, there are some nuances and aspects of the question that should be addressed. Health insurance is an excellent example of a product for which an abundance of choices might be detrimental to decision making. It is high consequence, so the potential for buyer's regret is high. It is a decision that is made only once a year given that employers and most government health plans offer a single open enrollment period each year, which means that individuals probably will not remember much about their decision process in prior years, the most important policy attributes to them, and their preference rankings. It is a complicated product, with variations in coverage, provider panels, deductibles, coinsurance, and lifetime limits, which rarely yield a universally preferred plan. Finally, there are few decision tools to help decision makers—no *Consumer Reports* on health insurance (at least at the market level), no Angie's List to steer one away from bad insurers and toward good insurers—so individuals must rely on their own memory, insurers' marketing materials, and word of mouth. Yet, despite these obstacles to efficient and effective choice, people prefer more choices to fewer. So, how would we justify limiting the number of choices in health plans?

Fortunately, there is a growing body of research demonstrating the problems associated with wide-ranging options in selecting health insurance. In 2006 the Dutch government significantly revamped its health insurance system, whereby a mix of compulsory social insurance and voluntary private health insurance was replaced by a single market-based system. The key to success of the new structure has been a well-developed demand side of the market. With a grant from the Dutch government, two researchers conducted laboratory experiments to simulate the workings of such a market (Schram and Sonnemans 2011). Participants in the experiment were shown either four or ten policies, which varied by coverage of six possible events (ranging from small probability/severe consequences to high probability/mild consequences). Participants were given a hypothetical health profile, which varied over the thirty-five periods covered in the experiment. To encourage diligence, participants were compensated based on their making appropriate selections relative to their health profiles. This laboratory experiment, while artificial, enabled the researchers to control for factors (such as costs of switching plans or changes in health profiles) that they could not have accounted for in a real-world analysis. The experiments revealed that those who saw the ten-policy frame took more time to decide on an insurance policy, reviewed a smaller proportion of the available information about alternative policies, switched policies more often, and—most significantly from a policy perspective—ended up further away from their optimal choices. Contrary to standard economic theory (but consistent with the behavioral economics and psychology research described in this chapter), more choices made the decision harder and the outcome worse.

In the United States, we have had a natural experiment to test the benefits and downsides of choice—the Medicare Part D program enacted in 2003. Unlike Medicare Part A (hospital coverage) and Part B (physician coverage), Medicare Part D was predicated on beneficiaries obtaining their coverage for prescription drugs through privately offered insurance plans. Despite concern that few insurers would offer plans, just the opposite happened—beneficiaries in each state were offered at least forty-five plans. Medicare beneficiaries were highly incentivized to choose a plan, as 75 percent of the premium costs were paid by the federal government. To select their plan, beneficiaries had to go to a designated Medicare website, which listed the plans and their primary characteristics (for example, premium, covered drugs). At the end of the initial enrollment period, over 90 percent of eligible Medicare beneficiaries had signed up for a plan.

Several health services researchers have analyzed the impact of this program, using opinion surveys, laboratory experiments, and analysis of claims data. Most have confirmed the results identified in this chapter—too many choices generate poorer outcomes. For instance, Tom Rice, Janet Cummings, and Yaniv Hanoch (Cummings, Rice, and Hanoch 2009; Rice, Hanoch, and Cummings 2010) analyzed a survey conducted of adults (over sixty-five and under sixty-five) by the Kaiser Family Foundation in November 2006, the year the Part D program went live. The results are shown in Table 3.1. Four out of five respondents (regardless of age) felt that the program was too complicated, and three out of four senior respondents (and 65 percent of respondents eighteen to sixty-four years of age) favored simplifying the program by reducing the number of plans offered. Also interesting is that 77 percent of seniors and 85 percent of those between eighteen and sixty-four years old were in favor of having seniors buy a plan directly from Medicare itself, which would replace choice with a fixed program like Medicare Part A and B. Seniors, in particular, were wary of the choice problem that they faced. Two-thirds preferred that Medicare select a handful of plans, rather than offer dozens of plans, and 45 percent felt that too many plans were being offered. (To show the confusion surrounding the program, 20 percent of those saying there were too many plans offered also preferred being offered dozens of plans [rather than a handful], and 15 percent of those who thought there were too few plans preferred being offered only a handful.)

TABLE 3.1

Percentage of support for different aspects of the Medicare Part D program.

Question	Full sample	Age 18–64	Age 65+
Think Part D is too complicated			
Somewhat agree/Strongly agree	81.3%	81.8%	78.8%
Somewhat disagree/Strongly disagree	18.7	18.2	21.2
Favor simplifying drug benefit by reducing the number of drug benefits available			
Somewhat agree/Strongly agree	66.3	64.6	75.1
Somewhat disagree/Strongly disagree	33.7	35.3	24.9
Think seniors should be able to purchase plan directly from Medicare			
Somewhat agree/Strongly agree	83.6	84.9	77.0
Somewhat disagree/Strongly disagree	16.4	15.1	23.0
Which statement better reflects your opinion:			
Medicare should offer seniors dozens of drug plans so individuals can select their own plan to meet their needs			33.5
Medicare should select a handful of plans that meet certain standards, to make it easier for seniors to pick among plans			66.5
Do you think people on Medicare have:			
Too many			45.1
Too few			17.0
About the right amount			37.9
Of drug plans to choose from?			

SOURCES: Janet R. Cummings, Thomas Rice, and Yaniv Hanoch, "Who thinks that Part D is too complicated? Survey Results on the Medicare Prescription Drug Benefit," *Medical Care Research and Review*, Vol. 66, Issue. 1, p. 19, © 2009. Reprinted by Permission of SAGE Publications; and Thomas Rice, Yaniv Hanoch, and Janet Cummings, "What factors influence seniors' desire for choice among health insurance options? Survey results on the Medicare prescription drug benefit," *Health Economics, Policy and Law*, Volume 5, Issue 04 (October 2010), pp. 437–457, portion of Table 1, p. 445, Weighted analytic sample descriptive statistics. Copyright © 2009 Cambridge University Press. Reprinted with the permission of Cambridge University Press.

Yaniv Hanoch and his colleagues (Hanoch et al. 2011) conducted a clever experiment to understand how people made decisions regarding Medicare Part D plans. They asked 150 adults (half under sixty-five, half over) to help a hypothetical friend decide on a plan. The participants were shown information on a computer screen regarding either three or nine plans (in a layout similar to what Medicare beneficiaries were shown in their real decision making), and the researchers used tracking technology to measure how the participants made their choices. The researchers found that those facing nine choices accessed less of the information that was readily available and made worse choices than those who saw just three plans. In fact, those having more options were only 25 percent as likely as those with fewer options to choose the lowest-cost plan. That these experimental subjects (who included tech-savvy young people as well as the elderly who have to make a real—and consequential—choice of drug plan) had such difficulty with an exercise much simpler (by a factor of five) than that faced by Medicare beneficiaries suggests that giving consumers lots of health plan choices may not be in their best interest.

Our final evidence of the downsides of choice is an extraordinarily careful analysis of Medicare Part D claims data by Jason Abaluck and Jonathan Gruber (2011). They were able to match the claims experience of 477,000 Medicare beneficiaries with the characteristics of the Part D drug plans that the beneficiaries chose (as well as the plans that were available to them that they did not choose). Their findings were both statistically significant and disturbing from a health policy standpoint: (1) Seniors placed much more weight on the plan premiums than on expected out-of-pocket costs; (2) They seemed to value financial characteristics of the plans far beyond the impact of these characteristics on their own expenses or finance risk; and (3) only 12 percent chose the lowest total cost plan in their state. If they had not made these errors, individuals could have saved 31 percent of their total Part D spending. Through a simulation, Abaluck and Gruber estimated that if Medicare beneficiaries had been presented with only the three lowest-cost plans in their state (instead of the fifty or so choices that they were given), they would have experienced a 17 percent average gain in utility; however, the gains would not have been spread evenly, with 50 percent of population seeing a gain, 18 percent seeing no change, and 32 percent seeing a loss compared to what they had chosen.

All together, these studies—from opinion surveys to lab experiments to analyses of actual behavior—affirm that choice in health care decisions is a decidedly mixed blessing. The challenges of understanding and weighing the diverse attributes of health plans, combined with the potentially dire consequences of making a mistake, make choice a difficult undertaking. As hard as it may be for me, a former market-oriented economist, to admit, perhaps the ministrations of mainstream economists and others are off base, and the "essential wisdom of the marketplace, capitalism, and entrepreneurship" is not appropriate for many decisions in health care. Rather, a more structured system, one that recognizes the cognitive burden on decision makers while retaining their freedom to choose as they will, needs to be developed.

SO WHAT? HOW CAN WE USE BEHAVIORAL ECONOMICS TO INFLUENCE BEHAVIOR— IN A BENIGN AND SUPPORTIVE WAY?

In this chapter we have discussed a wide variety of phenomena in behavioral economics and psychology, all related to how expectations often systematically differ from reality. People mistakenly predict how they will feel if bad things, or good things, happen. They overestimate the impact of events on themselves or others. They make decisions in a "cold" state that they regret later when they are in a "hot" state—and vice versa. They assume that others will think and act as they do, even though they "know" that that is not the case. They believe that more choices will make them better off, even when they don't.

We have shown that these phenomena help to explain some overblown predictions in health policy; for example, by opponents that passage of the Patient Protection and Affordable Care Act will lead to rationing and death panels or by proponents that repeal will doom millions of vulnerable Americans to a world without health care. We also used the tenets of behavioral economics and psychology to present some counterintuitive results—that requiring everyone to buy health insurance would make everyone (including those who don't want it) better off and that limiting choices for health care consumers would also make them better off.

Later in this book we will recall the concepts described in this chapter to address other issues in health care decision making. To conclude this chapter, though, we need to consider the "so what?" question. It is one thing to identify and explain a phenomenon; it is another to suggest possible remedies. First, we need to recognize that remedies may be neither available nor necessary. (This may be the health policy analyst's version of the Hippocratic oath: First, do no harm.) It is critical to determine if the personal and policy health care decisions that we have discussed are the result of errors or just different sets of preferences that have different consequences. For example, take the concept of hyperbolic discounting. If an individual truly discounts the future much more severely than economists predict, then he is deliberately placing a higher value on the present and will accept that consumption in the future will be significantly less than it would have been if he had an exponential discount function. Thus, there is no error, and there are no policy implications. (In effect, "It's not a bug. It's a feature.") On the other hand, if when the future arrives the individual expresses profound regret with his earlier decisions—and expects society or the government to intervene—then we have a problem.

One possible way to solve—or even preempt—this problem is to "debias" people, that is, to educate them about the various biases that they and others have and to suggest ways for them to overcome these biases. Unfortunately, there are at least two obstacles to debiasing people. The first is that people may recognize that other people have cognitive biases but not that they themselves do. Research by Emily Pronin at Princeton University (Pronin, Gilovich, and Ross 2004; Pronin 2007) and others confirm, in Pronin's words, "people's tendency to attach greater credence to their own introspections about potential influences on judgment and behavior than they attach to similar introspections by others." Second, and equally discouraging, is the dearth of debiasing techniques that have been demonstrated to work. Scott Lilienfeld and colleagues at Emory University (Lilienfeld, Ammirati, and Landfield 2009) recently concluded that we have neither the tools to debias people nor the evidence that doing so would improve human welfare.

If education will not work, we are left with what some would call manipulation of the choices that people face or, more benignly, what Cass Sunstein and Richard Thaler call *libertarian paternalism* (Sunstein and Thaler 2003; Thaler and Sunstein 2008). What they mean is that policy makers could recognize the decision biases that people have and build in devices to assist them. For instance, insurance companies or nonprofit agencies could model the impact of the lack of health insurance on those most likely not to buy it; this modeling might show that an average twenty-five-year-old male in Omaha, Nebraska, faces a 5 percent chance of incurring a life-threatening injury over the next ten years or that a thirty-year-old female in Austin, Texas, has a 40 percent chance of incurring $100,000 of health care expenses by the time she is forty. Making the consequences of alternative decisions more salient to individuals can guide them to a decision that they would more likely select in retrospect.

Likewise, policy makers should recognize that unlimited choices are not in most people's best interests. Instead of offering fifty choices of Medicare Part D plans in each market, the federal government could offer only ten (with the selection based on transparent criteria). We should recognize that if people distrust the federal government with enough vehemence, they could be suspicious of the government's "rationing" of their choices. An alternative approach would be to offer fifty choices of plans but present only a subset of six to ten choices at any one time, with the ability of a beneficiary to see more choices if she wanted. Or the government could take advantage of the interesting research finding that simply providing categories of choices (even if the categories or their labels provide no substantive information) significantly improves decision satisfaction and outcomes (Mogilner, Rudnick, and Iyengar 2008). So the government could provide the fifty choices of Part D plans but sort them into ten categories with any label ("Category A," "Jefferson," or "Viognier").

Of course, if a policy maker chooses to go this route and offer fewer than the maximum number of choices potentially available, that creates a second-order set of problems. How many is the optimal number of choices? Is it three, as suggested by Abaluck and Gruber? Is nine too many, as Hanoch and his colleagues found? Which plans should be offered—a random selection, those with the highest market share, those with the highest satisfaction, the cheapest (as recommended by Abaluck and Gruber)? Should the plans have attributes that are quite different from each other, or should they be fairly similar? Unfortunately, the state of behavioral economics and psychology does not allow us to answer these questions with any certainty. What is clear, however, is that decision makers need to be presented with a meaningful list of alternatives, to ensure both an appropriate outcome and satisfaction in the decision process.

On the other hand, as a reviewer of this book noted, many people face the opposite choice problem. Many employers offer health insurance benefits to their employees but provide few, if any, choices of plan. It's the Blue Cross/Blue Shield plan, or nothing. Or it's that plan and a very similar plan offered by another commercial insurer. Based on the research discussed in this chapter, it is clear that consumers prefer some choices (even if they end up selecting the choice that the employer would have offered as the single choice). By offering a few more choices, an employer could offset the additional administrative costs with increased satisfaction of its employees (without increasing health coverage).

Another approach to reducing decision bias and choice overload stems from the discussion in Chapter 1 about the power of defaults. Whether it is organ donations or retirement plan enrollment, establishment of an initial position conveys significant power in directing choices. In their book *Nudge*, Thaler and Sunstein (2008) discuss the critical task of designing what they call the "choice architecture" of a decision. They specifically point out the confusing choice architecture built into the Medicare Part D program and decry the problems that this structure caused. (For instance, they note that the federal government randomly assigned six million "dual eligibles" [that is, those eligible for both Medicare and Medicaid] to a Part D program, so these beneficiaries had no choice at all.) Thaler and Sunstein prefer what they call "intelligent assignment," in which those who do not make a choice of plan are placed in a plan that most closely matches their expected drug needs for the coming year. During the following open enrollment period, Medicare beneficiaries would be sent a list of drugs used during that year and their expenses and would have access to the price lists of the relevant plans in their area. Thaler and Sunstein expect that this plan would enhance one of the major tenets of the Part D program—competition among insurers—and improve the decision-making process for Medicare beneficiaries.

As attractive as the Thaler and Sunstein nudges are, a number of objections arise to having a third party—especially the government—intervene in the private decisions of individuals. The first is that a beneficent nudge can turn into a dictatorial shove, if the nudger believes that the nudgee is not sufficiently responsive to the hints (recall the increasingly severe limitations on smokers' ability to smoke in New York City—first restaurants and bars, now public parks). The second regards the strength of the nudge. Thaler and Sunstein require that the nudges be transparent and easy to change, but it can be deceptively easy for defaults to be set without a person's knowledge (have you ever found the "default" setting for your computer's audio player switched to Quick-Time, RealPlayer, or iTunes?), and it can be made deceptively hard to change the settings by manipulating the decision paths. Thaler and Sunstein acknowledge these possibilities but note that decisions have to be made somehow and that each approach has its problems.

So we are left with the unsatisfying situation in which powerful biases can make it harder for individuals to make their own health decisions and for society to create effective health policy than is anticipated by mainstream economics. In addition, there are few proven remedies to counteract these biases. At best, we have some tools—such as limiting choices and setting defaults—that offer hope, but even these are not foolproof. The good thing is that the situation is ripe for creative behavioral economists and psychologists to develop and test interventions that will nudge individuals and institutions back to rationality.

BIASES AND THE PARADOX OF
CHOICE: TRY THIS AT HOME
I discovered once I started reading the behavioral economics and psychology literature that I began to notice examples of this behavior all around me. And that generated ideas for research projects to test the effects in health care. I hope you will find the same effect.

So, try the following:

1. Identify instances in which you see yourself, family, friends, and colleagues exhibiting these behaviors:
   a. Projection bias (for example, estimating when projects will get done, homework completed).
   b. Hyperbolic discounting (for example, young adults not buying health insurance).
   c. Hot–cold decision making (for example, going out drinking the night before a big exam or client presentation).
   d. Choice overload (for example, a family not being able to decide where to go on vacation).

2. Identify instances in which institutions—your employer, the government—are stymied by these behaviors:
   a. Projection bias (for example, adopting a budget that everyone knows will not be balanced).
   b. Hyperbolic discounting (for example, maximizing quarterly results despite negative long-term consequences).
   c. Hot–cold decision making (for example, making campaign promises that cannot be kept).
   d. Choice overload (for example, offering multiple vendors for defined contribution retirement plans, each of which offers multiple products).

3. Conduct your own surveys, to determine the extent to which your friends, family, and colleagues:
   a. Buy products that have an upfront cost but little or no per-use cost, yet they do not use the product (for example, community coupon books, exercise equipment, museum or organization memberships).
   b. Boast about the size of their income tax refunds.
   c. Feel before and after their favorite sports team loses an important game.

4

UNDERSTANDING
THE STUBBORNLY
INCONSISTENT PATIENT

It's summer 2014. The finals of the World Cup. Rio de Janeiro. Brazil versus the United States. It is an unexpectedly tight match, with the United States managing to tie the Brazilians at 1 to 1 in the sixty-fifth minute. But Landon Donovan has just been assessed a foul for tripping a Brazilian player within the box in front of their goal. As a result, Brazil has been awarded a free penalty kick, with Ronaldinho, their best player, lining up to make the shot. Tim Howard, the veteran U.S. goalkeeper, stands ready to defend. Ronaldinho sets up, takes a deep breath, and arches a hard kick to the right side of the goal. Howard does not move; the kick goes into the net. Brazil 2, United States 1. The match ends that way.

What was wrong with Howard? Why didn't he move? He cost us our first World Cup championship. Sure, it takes only a quarter of a second for the ball to go from Ronaldinho's foot to the back of the goal, but saving those kinds of shots is what Howard is expected to do. How could he just stand there in the most important moment of his career?

As it turns out, Howard (or one of his coaches) may have read the article published seven years earlier, in the *Journal of Economic Psychology* (Bar-Eli et al. 2007). The researchers looked at 286 penalty kicks in top league and championship games and found that 80 percent of the penalty kicks resulted in scores. They then analyzed where the kick went relative to the goalkeeper and where the goalkeeper jumped (if he did). They found that the kick went to the goalkeeper's left 32 percent of the time, to his right 39 percent of the time, and in the center 29 percent of the time. The goalkeeper, on the other hand, went to his left 49 percent of the time, to his right 44 percent, and stayed in the center only 6 percent of the time. The researchers determined that the goalkeeper had a 30 percent chance of stopping a penalty kick if both he and the kick went left, a 25 percent chance of success if the kick went right and he went right, but a 60 percent chance if the kick went to the center and he stayed there. (The goalkeeper would have virtually no chance of stopping the kick if he moved in a different direction from the kick.) They concluded, then, that the optimal strategy for a goalkeeper facing a penalty kick is to stay in the center—just as Tim Howard did.

If that is the case, why do these top goalkeepers follow the optimal strategy only 6 percent of the time? The answer could be in what Daniel Kahneman and Dale Miller (1986) called *norm theory*. In norm theory, people see negative outcomes (in this case, a goal against your team when the goalkeeper did not move) as worse when they can imagine that a better outcome (a jump by the goalkeeper that saved a goal) could have occurred. In soccer, the norm is that the goalkeeper takes an action—moves left or right—when a penalty kick is made. To do otherwise is perceived as allowing a goal to be scored, even if the actual probabilities demonstrate otherwise. The penalty kick researchers termed this mode of thinking *action bias*.

In this chapter we will use the concept of action bias, as well as other behavioral economics and psychology concepts, to explain the sometimes baffling and remarkably inconsistent behavior of patients. Again, as in previous chapters, we will not claim that behavioral economics has the magic answer to solve the riddle of patient behavior; instead, we will try to show that this burgeoning field provides a number of unique insights into human behavior that are not available elsewhere. In particular, in Chapter 3 we saw how people can make poor decisions because they fall victim to a variety of cognitive biases or because they are just overwhelmed by too many choices. In this chapter we consider situations in which the problem is not cognition but rather an internal conflict between a person's considered, "rational" thinking process and her instantaneous, intuitive decision-making process. As with the previous chapters (and this entire book) the topics we will be discussing may seem beyond the traditional purview of the discipline of economics; however, as we have argued before, this narrowness of perspective as to what constitutes economics has been part of the reason why mainstream, neoclassical economics has not been able to explain much of what is going on in health care.

SYSTEM 1/SYSTEM 2: WHY PATIENTS MAKE PUZZLING DECISIONS

Let us return to our friend Benjamin. Sometimes, he makes decisions through a deliberate process of careful analysis. In deciding what college to apply to, he compared schools' location, size, course offerings, reputation, social life, and cost. He and his parents spent many evenings discussing which college would be the best for him and what they could afford. For other decisions, Benjamin makes a snap judgment and goes with it—which movie to go to tonight or which beer to order afterwards. For two millennia, philosophers have debated about these two modes of thought—one based on reasoning and the other on something else. The great nineteenth-century philosopher and psychologist, William James, for instance, distinguished between what he called "empirical thinking" and "associative thought."

The growth of behavioral psychology, along with advances in neuroscience, has generated an explosion of interest in what are called "two-system theories" of thought. Table 4.1 shows two such constructs. The first contrasts what the authors call the "experiential" and the "analytic" system of thinking (Slovic et al. 2004). The second proposes a similar framework but uses the deliberately neutral terms of "System 1" and "System 2" (Kahneman and Frederick 2002). These two approaches may appear quite similar—and may seem like common sense—but they are actually the focus of heated debate among psychologists and neurophysiologists (Damasio 1994; Evans 2008; Keren and Schul 2009;

TABLE 4.1
Examples of two-system theories of decision making.

a. Experiential versus analytic

Experiential system	Analytic system
Holistic	Analytic
Affective; pleasure-pain oriented	Logical: reason oriented (what is sensible)
Associationistic connections	Logical connections
Behavior mediated by "vibes" from past experiences	Behavior mediated by conscious appraisal of events
Encodes reality in concrete images, metaphors, narratives	Encodes reality in abstract symbols, words, numbers
More rapid processing: oriented toward immediate action	Slower processing: oriented toward delayed action
Self-evidently valid: "experiencing is believing"	Requires justification via logic and evidence

b. System 1 versus System 2

	System 1 (intuitive)	System 2 (reflective)
	Automatic	Controlled
	Effortless	Effortful
Process characteristics	Associative	Deductive
	Rapid, parallel	Slow, serial
	Process opaque	Self-aware
	Skilled action	Rule application
	Affective	Neutral
Content on which processes act	Causal propensities	Statistics
	Concrete, specific	Abstract
	Prototypes	Sets

SOURCES: a, Slovic, Paul, Melissa L. Finucane, Ellen Peters, and Donald G. MacGregor, 2004. Risk as analysis and risk as feelings: Some thoughts about affect, reason, risk, and rationality. *Risk Analysis: An International Journal* 24 (2) (04): 311–22, Table 1. © 2004. Reprinted by permission of John Wiley & Sons, Inc.; b, Kahneman, D., & Frederick, S., "Representativeness revisited: Attribute substitution in intuitive judgment" in *Heuristics and Biases: The Psychology of Intuitive Judgement*, edited by Thomas Gilovich, Dale Griffin, and Daniel Kahneman, Table 2.1, p. 51, "Two Cognitive Systems." Copyright © 2002 Cambridge University Press. Reprinted with the permission of Cambridge University Press.

Gigerenzer and Gaissmaier 2011). It is well beyond the scope of this book to review this debate. Rather, we will take the general framework of two-system theories of thinking as given.

As represented by the two theories presented in Table 4.1, experiential or System 1 thinking represents what we typically think of as intuitive or snap judgments. In this mode, we make decisions quickly and almost "without thinking." The decisions come to us seemingly without effort, as if we were on automatic pilot. In this mode, we do not focus on a few components of the decision but instead view the issue as a totality. It is almost thrilling to make decisions this way. If asked, we really have a hard time explaining how we made the decision. Often, the best we can do is to reply, "It just seemed right."

Analytic or System 2 thinking is dramatically different. We are deliberate; we take our time, and we make a concerted effort to think through the problem. We think carefully. We are fully aware of the decision-making process, in part because of the high degree of effort involved. We are driven by the logic of the situation. We use facts and data, comparing the benefits and downsides of each alternative. Reason abounds, and we can articulate the motivations for our decision. It feels to us that we are not beholden to emotion or the frisson that making a snap decision can offer.

Some claim that there is a hierarchy in these modes of thinking. They argue that experiential or System 1 thinking is more basic and primitive; it is what we used on the Serengeti Plain tens of thousands of years ago to detect and avoid predators. They contend that analytical/System 2 thinking is more developed and sophisticated, the product of evolutionary forces and the creation of language and education. Others see the two modes of thinking as both necessary and complementary. Sometimes you use one; other times you use another. A baseball pitcher will probably use System 2 when he is deciding whether to throw a fast ball, curve, slider, or changeup and whether to go up and away, or down and in, to the batter. On the other hand, when the pitcher is at bat, he had better use System 1 when a 90-mph fastball is aimed for his head.

In more momentous situations, both systems are likely to be in play. When you fall in love, System 1 is ruling the day. You are experiencing high "affect" (defined somewhat prosaically as "the specific quality of 'goodness' or 'badness' experienced as a feeling state [with or without consciousness] and demarcating a positive or negative quality of a stimulus") (Slovic et al. 2007) and, in Paul Slovic's terms, "Experiencing is believing." For some people, the decision to get married becomes a System 2 process, as the lovers consider the long-term consequences of their decision. For others, System 1 thinking takes over. For some of these, System 1 works out very well—I met my wife of twenty-four years on a cold January 10 in Chicago; we "knew" it was right by Valentine's Day; we were married on July 1. For others, not so much—witness Britney Spears's fifty-five-hour marriage to a childhood friend in 2004 in Las Vegas. (The judge declaring the annulment cited that Spears "lacked understanding of her actions to the extent that she was incapable of agreeing to the marriage") (Britney Spears 2004).

Mainstream economics clearly is predicated on System 2 thinking. The theory presumes that our friend Benjamin knows his preferences—what he wants and when he wants it. He uses logic and reason to calculate—sometimes explicitly but at least implicitly—the course of action that is most beneficial to him. If he makes a mistake, it is a random one that can be corrected. Behavioral economics, on the other hand, explicitly incorporates System 1 thinking into its methodology. George Loewenstein and his colleagues posit that decision making when risk and uncertainty are involved is more than a cognitive activity; it is, in fact, "risk as feelings" (Loewenstein et al. 2001). As Figure 4.1 indicates, their model looks remarkably similar to the two-system theories of thought. Although they do not remark on it, the boxes at the top (in dark gray) are those that drive mainstream economic theory, and those at the bottom (in light gray) are what behavioral economics adds to the economic model.

Loewenstein and his coauthors recognize that "cognitive evaluation" and "feelings" (that is, System 2 and System 1) can work well together in risk-related situations. For instance, cognitive evaluation/System 2 is often helpful in tempering the fear response that many people have to risky situations, and feelings/System 1 can alert a decision maker that what seems on paper like a beneficial opportunity (from a rational dollars-and-cents standpoint) may carry intangible risks that need to be considered. Nevertheless, their primary interest is in those circumstances in which emotions derail optimal decision making in situations involving risk. For instance, they cite research that indicates that

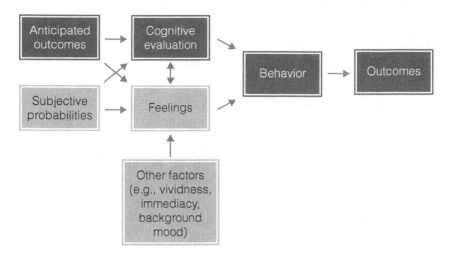

FIGURE 4.1

The Risk-as-feelings model.

SOURCE: Loewenstein, George, Weber, Elke, Hsee, Christopher, and Welch, Ned, 2001, Risk as feelings. *Psychological Bulletin*, 127(2), 267–286.

risky behaviors (such as smoking, drinking, not buying health or life insurance) are only weakly correlated with standard economic measures of risk tolerance (Barsky 1997). That is, a System 2 approach alone does not predict the complete decision-making behavior of individuals.

They cite other research that supports the idea that System 1 thinking will distort decision making. One study demonstrated that the vividness of risky situations will allow these situations to be framed in such a way that consumers can make irrational decisions regarding risk (Johnson et al. 1993). For example, the researchers asked a group of adults (thankfully, not inexperienced undergraduates) about their willingness to buy different kinds of flight insurance. The participants were reminded that terrorism and mechanical failures are sources of danger to travelers (and this was a decade before 9/11). One-third of the group was asked how much they would pay for $100,000 of life insurance in case of their death on an airplane due to "any act of terrorism"; one-third were asked how much they would pay for insurance coverage in case they died on an airplane because of "any non-terrorism related mechanical failure"; and the remaining one-third were asked how much they would pay for flight insurance that paid for "any reason" of their death while on the airplane. Although the last category obviously would include terrorism and mechanical failure, the study subjects did not act as if it were. The mean premiums that the participants said they would pay were $14.12 for terrorism-only insurance, $10.31 for mechanical failure insurance, and $12.03 for any reason insurance. The researchers hypothesized that the vividness of the two specific causes focused the attention of the decision makers much more so than the neutral frame of "any reason." In effect, the emotions embedded in System 1 overrode the analytical calculator of System 2.

Both mainstream and behavioral economics assume that how people perceive risk depends on their experience with risk, that is, whether an adverse event has happened to an acquaintance, a friend or relative, or themselves. With mainstream economics, this experience expresses itself exclusively through modified probabilities (and thus System 2); with behavioral economics, personal experience can affect both System 1 and System 2. Neil Weinstein (1989), in a major review of the research literature on this topic, found an even more complex story. In particular, he determined that people who experience an adverse event generally see such events as happening more frequently and see themselves as future victims. As a result, they express increased interest in prevention. In addition, experiencing an adverse event gets people to think about risk more often and with more attention. However, experience with risk is not correlated with how preventable or serious people think that risks are. Finally, Weinstein found that those experiencing an adverse event have only a short window of time, psychologically, to take actions related to future events and that people are much more inclined to take action if it requires a single act rather than repeated ones. All of these findings speak to System 1 decision making more than that of System 2.

System 2 also seems to fail as a decision mechanism when people are required to evaluate events with low probabilities, which is often the case in risk-related situations. One study conducted five experiments to explore how people judged the safety of a chemical plant (Kunreuther, Novemsky, and Kahneman 2001). These authors found that, even when provided a familiar comparison point (such as the probability of being in an auto accident), participants could not distinguish meaningfully among a one in 100,000 chance, a one in a million chance, and a one in ten million chance (or even among a one in 650, one in 6,300, or one in 68,000 probability event). Only when given a detailed qualitative risk comparison were study subjects able to make accurate assessments.

Another aspect of risk analysis that is relevant here is how individuals perceive benefits vis-à-vis risks. Benefits and risks are different concepts, and you would not necessarily expect them always to be correlated. An idea, event, or technology could have high benefits and low risks (for example, solar power) or low benefits and high risks (for example, handguns), but it also could have both high benefits and high risk (for example, nuclear power), or low benefits and low risks (for example, multivitamins for asymptomatic individuals). Nevertheless, several studies (such as Fischhoff et al. 1978 and Alhakami and Slovic 1994) have found that people perceive a strong inverse relationship between benefit and risk. This relationship is especially powerful when either the perceived risk or benefit is particularly high. These researchers argue that, by creating that connection in their minds, people conflate the two concepts and lose the important distinctions that each brings. In effect, people make their decision making easier by assuming that anything that has high (low) benefits also carries with it low (high) risks.

Let us return for a moment to the concept of affect, which we defined earlier in this chapter. Affect is a powerful driver of decision making, especially in System 1. A fascinating experiment demonstrates the power of affect (Rottenstreich and Hsee 2001). Experimental subjects were told to imagine that they were required to participate in a psychological experiment. Some were told that the experiment involved a chance of a "short, painful, but not dangerous electric shock"; half of these were told there was a 1 percent chance, the other half were told a 99 percent chance. Others were told there was a chance for a $20 cash penalty, again with half told there was a 1 percent chance and half a 99 percent chance. The participants were asked how much they would pay to avoid the adverse event. The results for those facing the affect-poor cash penalty event were straight from mainstream economics (and System 2): Those facing a 1 percent chance of losing $20 were willing to pay an average of $1, whereas those facing a 99 percent chance said $18, both values very close to their arithmetically expected loss. On the other hand, those presented with the affect-rich electric shock event responded much differently—an average of $7 to avoid a 1 percent chance and $10 to avoid a 99 percent chance. That is, the vastly different probabilities of a shock made little difference in how much participants were willing to pay to avoid the shock; the high affect triggered System 1 thinking to emphasize the nature of the adverse event and minimize the relative probabilities.

Ellen Peters (2006) argues that affect performs four key functions in decision making. First, for our friend Benjamin, affect provides information—a different kind of information than what he acquires through System 2. In unfamiliar situations, affect offers cues to Benjamin that provide context; in familiar situations, it reinforces his decision-making process. Second, affect acts as a spotlight, to focus Benjamin on new information, which then allows him to use the information to guide his decision. Third, affect acts as a kind of common currency. Many decisions require complex assessments of trade-offs, and Peters argues that affect helps to translate these difficult choices into simpler evaluations. In effect, it allows Benjamin to really compare apples and oranges. Finally, affect acts as a motivator. Peters cites research that has demonstrated that emotion (which affect is a part of) generates "a readiness to act and the prompting of plans." That is, affect nudges Benjamin to get off the dime and do something.

Before we go on to discuss how System 1/System 2, action bias, affect, and related concepts explain patient behavior, we need to recall a key concept in Chapter 2—framing. Framing is the phenomenon in which the way an issue or problem is presented affects how people make a decision. In the earlier chapter framing was seemingly a quirk that mainstream economics could not explain. Now we have a better understanding of why it occurs. Framing works its magic through the application of affect in System 1 decision making. Remember Tversky and Kahneman's (1981) Asian disease paradox, in which placing the problem in a survival frame elicited much different results than did placing it in a mortality frame. Remember also when James Druckman and Rose

McDermott (2008) replicated the study—and asked questions about the participants' emotional state—they found that both anger and enthusiasm led to more risk-seeking behavior but that distress led to more risk-averse behavior. In addition, they found that enthusiasm moderated framing and that increased stress strengthened the framing effect. As we now have come to realize, all of these factors are being applied through the intuitive, automatic, and opaque decision-making processes of System 1.

ANOMALY 7: *Why do patients insist on getting a prescription, shot, test . . . when they go to a physician with an ailment?*

The short answer is action bias. Patients suffer from action bias in the same way that soccer goalkeepers do. Except for routine, follow-up visits, patients come to the physician when something is wrong. Their normal life has been disrupted by pain, suffering, worry, and anxiety. They come to the physician expecting that something will be done. They expect the physician to make an intervention that will return them to normal life. It may be a prescription, it may be an injection, it may be an order for a laboratory test or imaging study. But it must be something, and it must be definitive.

Of course, action bias is triggered by the operation of System 1. The illness (or suspected illness) is like the electric shock experiment. The malady may be relatively minor and even short lived, but to the patient it can dominate their consciousness. Because, as research has shown, probabilities do not seem to have much impact in a high-affect situation, and people cannot seem to distinguish among low probabilities, reassurance by the physician that there is only a small chance that the problem is serious may not be comforting. The only thing that will reduce the affect is some action, almost any action.

One potential danger to patients of action bias is the apparent inability of people to distinguish materially between benefits and risks. If they assume that diagnostic or treatment modalities that have high benefits also have low risk, they may be demanding health services that carry more risk than they realize. For example, return to the mammography controversy discussed in Chapter 2. The U.S. Preventive Services Task Force withdrew its previous recommendation regarding routine biennial mammograms for women in their forties, which stemmed from a concern that mammograms (which do provide a demonstrable benefit of detecting breast cancer) also carry risks (for example, increased anxiety, follow-up tests and biopsies, unnecessary treatment for false positives) that are not generally recognized by patients. Remember the interview that Anderson Cooper did with Dr. Kimberly Gregory, a member of the Task Force: "But, Dr. Gregory, doesn't it—I mean, if it catches some women who otherwise—who otherwise it wouldn't catch, I mean, isn't it a benefit? I mean, if it saves, you know, a handful of women's lives, isn't it still a good thing?"

A recent study published in *Health Affairs* (Carman et al. 2010) indicates that Anderson Cooper's attitude reflects that of many Americans. The researchers conducted qualitative interviews and focus groups, as well as quantitative surveys, about people's attitudes toward evidence-based health care. All of the methodologies found similar results: Americans believe that all health care meets minimum quality standards (despite an occasional mistake), more care is better care, newer care (that is, newer techniques) is better care, and more costly care is better care. In the words of one interviewee, "I don't see how extra care can be harmful to your health. Care would only benefit you."

As physicians know, many of the maladies they see every day will resolve themselves on their own; in these cases, inaction by the physician—also known as "watchful waiting"—is the most appropriate strategy. Of course, there are instances in which action—sometimes, immediate action—is called for. The physician, through her education and experience, is much more likely than the patient to be able to determine which is which.

Mainstream economics has identified this patient–physician interaction as a "principal–agent relationship." Such relationships arise as a solution to an economic problem known as asymmetric information, in which one side in a transaction (such as a buyer) has substantially less information than the other side (say, the seller) about the characteristics of a good or service. Information asymmetry can derail what otherwise would be a beneficial transaction to both sides because the knowledge-able side will have an incentive to conceal detrimental information and exaggerate positive information; over time, the side with less information may withdraw from the market because it cannot trust the other side. One way to repair this breach is for the party with less information to engage an agent who by interest, training, or expertise has access to the relevant information and can act on the principal's behalf. Clearly, our friend Benjamin relies on his physician to understand his conditions and needs and act in his best interest. Nevertheless, the agency relationship between patient and physician carries its own uncertainties. How does Benjamin know that his physician is fully qualified to act in his interests and is willing and able to do so without conflicts of interest?

Despite the benefits of the principal–agent relationship, the patient will still almost always prefer action to watchful waiting (unless the risks of action are salient and substantial), and the patient will be disappointed if the physician chooses inaction. Then, add to this preference the medical liability environment. Research (DeKay and Asch 1998) has shown that if physicians act rationally (that is, use System 2), they will order more diagnostic tests than necessary to minimize their risk of being sued for malpractice and that the overutilization will actually harm patients. In addition, physicians may be subject to the same biases as patients. Dr. Jerome Kassirer (1989), then editor of the *New England Journal of Medicine*, attributed what he called excessive diagnostic testing to physicians' "stubborn quest for diagnostic certainty," as well as forces imposed on the physician by the U.S. system of health care (such as "pressure from peers and supervisors") and "physicians' personal practices and whims" (including "irrational and ossified habits"). (More on these issues can be found in Chapters 6 and 7.) As a result, physicians will succumb to action bias and join their patients in overutilizing diagnostic tests and therapeutic services. Unfortunately, this mutual reinforcement harms patients in two ways—unnecessary services and a weakening of the agency relationship between patient and physician.

Table 4.2 shows how this bias plays out in reality. In 2008 Americans made 956 million visits to the physician, about 3.2 visits for every

TABLE 4.2

Characteristics of physician office visits in the United States, 2008.

	Number (in thousands)	Percentage
Total	955,969	100.0%
Established patient	841,192	88.0
New patient	114,777	12.0
Reason for visit		
New problem		34.2
Chronic problem		35.9
Pre- or postsurgery		7.2
Preventive care		20.8
Unknown		1.7
Diagnostic or screening service provided/ordered		
One or more	857,030	89.7
Blood tests	468,091	49.0
Other tests (e.g., urinalysis, ECG, biopsy)	406,232	42.5
Imaging	146,453	15.3
Medications provided or prescribed		
0	227,254	23.8
1	216,088	22.6
2	146,290	15.3
3–5	206,754	21.6
6+	142,235	14.9
Unknown	17,346	1.8
Health education services ordered or provided		
None	600,648	62.8
One or more	339,939	35.6
Unknown	15,382	1.6

SOURCE: National Center for Health Statistics, Centers for Disease Control and Prevention 2010.

man, woman, and child in the country. The bulk of these (88 percent) were between a patient and physician who had an established relationship. About one-third were for a chronic problem, one-third were for a new problem, one-fifth were for preventive care, and 7 percent were for a surgical issue. Now, here is the interesting part: In almost nine out of ten cases, the physician ordered or provided one or more diagnostic or screening services. In 49 percent of the visits some kind of blood test was done, such as a "complete blood count" (or CBC), cholesterol, glucose, or prostate-specific antigen (PSA) test. Over 40 percent of the time, the physician ordered another kind of test—urinalysis, electrocardiogram (ECG), Pap smear, biopsy, colonoscopy, test for sexually transmitted disease, or pregnancy test. In 15 percent of the visits an imaging exam was ordered, including 58 million X-rays, 21 million mammograms, 15 million MRIs (magnetic resonance imaging), 15 million CT (computed tomography) scans, and 12 million echocardiograms. Finally, in less than one-quarter of the 956 million visits to the physician were no medications provided or prescribed. That is, 711 million times in 2008 a physician gave the patient, or wrote a prescription for, at least one medication. Patients received one medication 216 million times, two medications 146 million times, between three and five medications 207 million times, and six or more medications 142 million times, for a total of around 2.3 billion prescriptions written from physician office visits in 2008. On the other hand, in only 36 percent of visits were health education services (such as diet, exercise, smoking cessation) provided. (In some sense, the demand for action goes only so far.)

This pattern of tests and medications may be therapeutically appropriate. However, behavioral economics suggests that it is driven as much by the nonmedical psychological needs of the patients (and perhaps the physicians) as it is the exigencies of disease. As a result, the consequence of action bias is higher health care costs—more prescriptions, more lab tests, more imaging, more procedures—with not necessarily better care or outcomes. And here's the depressing thing: If elite professional soccer goalkeepers exhibit action bias when the incentives for success are huge, what are the chances that patient (and physician) behavior will be likely to change?

Of course, mainstream health economists would have a ready-made solution to overutilization of services due to action bias—raise the effective price to patients, through higher deductibles and copayments or more restrictive utilization review (which increases the hassles to patients and their physicians). But behavioral economics—as reflected in the electric shock study—suggests that this policy will not have as much impact as these economists would like to believe.

ANOMALY 8: *Why do many patients not adhere to their diagnostic and treatment regimens?*

If the last anomaly was puzzling, this one is even more peculiar. If patients are eager to receive a prescription or order for a lab test when they come to the physician, then why don't they follow the doctor's orders? There are three ways in which our friend Benjamin can fail to adhere to what his physician has ordered for his care: primary nonadherence (not filling the prescription or not showing up for the lab test), secondary nonadherence (not following the dosage, timing, or instructions of his treatment), and lack of persistence (discontinuing the course of treatment before its specified end). There have been a host of studies of the prevalence of nonadherence, but most have targeted specific patients (for example, the elderly) or conditions (such as HIV), and none is comprehensive or definitive. What the research seems to show is that between 5 and 25 percent of prescriptions are not filled. For example, a recent study tracked 196,000 electronic prescriptions written for 76,000 patients in Massachusetts in 2004 (Fischer et al. 2010). It found that only 77.5 percent of all prescriptions—and 71.7 percent of new prescriptions—were ever filled. The most cited systematic review of research on secondary nonadherence and lack of persistence, published over thirty years ago (Sackett and Snow 1979), found that adherence with short-term therapeutic regimens declines rapidly and that only about half of those on long-term regimens (for example, for chronic conditions) adhere to their therapy. A more recent meta-analysis reviewed 569 studies conducted over a fifty-year period and found that adherence ranged from 4.6 percent to over 100 percent (as some patients took more than the prescribed amount of medication), with a mean adherence rate of 75.2 percent (that is, the mean nonadherence rate was 24.8 percent) (diMatteo 2004). If we apply these findings to the data on physician office visits described earlier, then only 1.8 billion of the 2.3 billion prescriptions written in 2008 were filled, and only 1.3 billion of the prescription instructions were probably adhered to.

Why do so many people not adhere to their medications or ordered tests, especially given their apparent eagerness to have some action taken to alleviate their pain and suffering? A recent study summarized the primary predictors of poor adherence as: presence of psychological problems, presence of cognitive impairment, poor provider–patient relationship, treatment complexity, and monetary costs of the treatment (Osterberg and Blaschke 2005). The authors also cite some other reasons that can be interpreted as manifestations of behavioral economics/psychology. One is "treatment of asymptomatic disease"; that is, those patients who have an illness with no or few manifestations are more likely to not adhere to their treatment. For example, suppose our friend Benjamin had a family history of heart problems, and he himself has elevated cholesterol levels; but he may rarely experience any evidence of his condition (unless, of course, he had a heart attack, which is not likely at his age). As a result, he may not notice any impact of his taking his prescription for Lipitor; likewise, he will probably notice no short-term impact if he fails to take the medication. What Benjamin is experiencing is low affect. Suppose, on the other hand, that Benjamin had back pain, exacerbated by intramural softball in Lincoln Park. Back pain is a high-affect condition, and he definitely will notice when he forgets to take his Flexeril.

A related concept that Osterberg and Blaschke identified is the "patient's lack of insight into the illness." That is, Benjamin might not realize that the symptoms of a chronic disease will wax and wane, but adherence to the treatment regimen is necessary for successful treatment in the long run. For acute and short-term conditions (such as gastroenteritis), he may stop taking his Cipro before the end of treatment if his symptoms improve. Finally, the authors cited the "patient's lack of belief in benefit of treatment" and "side effects of medication." These two predictors of non-adherence correspond to the behavioral economics notion that individuals conflate the concepts of benefits and risks; in this case, patients may decide that medications with significant side effects yield few benefits as well and thus discontinue them without consulting their physicians.

There is significant evidence that supports the behavioral economics hypothesis for nonadherence (and, to be fair, some evidence that is not consistent with this explanation). Several studies note that adherence rates are higher for acute than chronic care, and for short-term than for long-term treatments (Sackett and Snow 1979; Osterberg and Blaschke 2005). Another reports that, in terms of disease conditions, adherence is highest for high-affect diseases such as HIV, arthritis, gastrointestinal disorders, and cancers, and lowest for lower-affect diseases such as diabetes and sleep disorders (diMatteo 2004). The Massachusetts prescription study described in the preceding paragraphs found similar results, with antimicrobials, anti-inflammatories, asthma medications, and antianxiety drugs having the highest levels of adherence for new prescriptions (Fischer et al. 2010). Finally, two studies identify "white-coat adherence," in which patients improve their adherence to medications beginning five days before—and lasting five days after—scheduled appointments with their physician (Osterberg and Blaschke 2005). The affect here is Benjamin's realization that his physician will ask about the medications he is supposed to be taking, and, as many studies have shown, Benjamin is reluctant to disappoint such an authority figure. This affect dissipates, though, after the appointment.

So, what is the impact of nonadherence on the cost and outcomes of health care? In some sense, nonadherence caused by the reduction or elimination of affect of disease may be a good thing, by counteracting the overutilization caused by action bias. At this point, there has been no integrated research on the extent of the offset. However, there have been a number of studies of the singular impact of nonadherence. In a 2003 analysis of the issue, the World Health Organization (Sabate 2003) declared that "increasing the effectiveness of adherence interventions may have a far greater impact on the health of the population than any improvement in specific medical treatments." More specifically, a major review examined sixty-three studies of more than 19,000 patients that measured the impact of patient adherence on the outcome of care (DiMatteo et al. 2002). The authors found that adherence reduced the risk of a poor treatment outcome by 26 percent and that the odds of a good outcome if the patient were adherent were almost three times higher than if the patient were not adherent.

Broad estimates of annual monetary costs for nonadherence among U.S. patients range from $100 billion from hospital admissions due to patients not taking their drugs properly (Osterberg and Blaschke 2005) to $290 billion in avoidable medical spending due to all drug-related problems (including adherence) (New England Healthcare Institute 2009). A recent analysis of a panel of 135,000 individuals with congestive heart failure, hypertension, diabetes, or dyslipidemia over a three-year period found that adherence rates ranged from 34 to 51 percent (Roebuck et al. 2011). The researchers calculated that full adherence would have raised pharmacy spending for these patients, ranging from $429 per person per year for those with hypertension to $1,058 for those with congestive heart failure. However, the nonpharmacy per capita expenditures for these individuals would have decreased dramatically, from a low of $1,860 per year for those with dyslipidemia to $8,881 for those with congestive heart failure. Clearly, nonadherence—for whatever reason—creates significant costs to the system, at least some of which might be alleviated by interventions tied to behavioral economics.

ANOMALY 9: *Why do patients make different treatment choices when benefits and risks are presented in different ways?*

It would appear that patients would be prime candidates to be vulnerable to framing effects. They are in a stressful situation, in which their normal lives have been disrupted by illness; they may be losing control over the course of their lives; and they need to depend on an agent—the physician—and her knowledge of medicine and of the workings of a sometimes dysfunctional health care system. Add to that the action bias and benefit–risk conflation discussed earlier, and we have the ingredients for framing.

Although there have been several studies of framing in health care decisions, there are two that demonstrate most clearly how different presentations yield anomalous results—one three decades ago and the other much more recently. The first, by Barbara McNeil, Stephen Pauker, Harold Sox, and Amos Tversky (1982), investigated the preferences of people for two alternative therapies for lung cancer—radiation and surgery. They recruited three distinct groups of people: 238 men with chronic medical problems (none of whom had lung cancer), 424 radiologists, and 491 MBA students from Stanford Business School. Half of the groups were told the alternative treatments were radiation and surgery, and the other half were told the treatments (labeled "A" and "B" to avoid any connotations tied to radiation or surgery) were medications administered in the hospital and equivalent except for survival rates. Then, half of each group was given the following scenario:

Of 100 people having surgery (or Treatment A) 90 live through the post-operative period, 68 are alive at the end of the 1st year and 34 are alive at the end of 5 years. Of 100 people having radiation therapy (or Treatment B) all live through the therapy period, 77 are alive at the end of the 1st year and 22 are alive at the end of 5 years. Which treatment would you prefer?

The other half of each group was presented with:

Of 100 people having surgery (or Treatment A) 10 die during surgery or the post-operative period, 32 die by the end of the 1st year and 66 die by the end of 5 years. Of 100 people having radiation therapy (or Treatment B) none die during the therapy period, 23 die by the end of the 1st year and 78 die by the end of 5 years. Which treatment would you prefer?

If you look carefully, you will realize that the information in the two presentations is identical; it is just that the first is presented in a survival frame ("90 live . . .") and the second is in a mortality frame ("10 die . . ."). Mainstream economists, with their emphasis on System 2 thinking, would predict that the results should be identical between the two presentations (while allowing that those who had been told the specific treatments might respond differently from those told about Treatments A and B). Behavioral economists know better.

Not surprisingly, the behavioral economists are right. In the survival frame, 82 percent preferred surgery (and 63 percent preferred

Treatment A). In the mortality frame, only 56 preferred surgery (and 39 percent preferred Treatment A). What seemed to be happening was that the prospect of going from ninety living after surgery (or Treatment A) versus 100 living after radiation therapy (or Treatment B) in the survival frame was not as compelling as going from ten dying after surgery (or Treatment A) versus none dying after radiation therapy (or Treatment B) in the mortality frame. In a sense, this is the Asian disease paradox but in a different guise. In addition to confirming the framing effect, this study demonstrates how robust the effect can be. Although the radiologists (not surprisingly) tended to favor radiation therapy over surgery, the framing effect occurred with the same magnitude for all three groups—physicians, patients, and students—despite their significant differences in age, income, education, and experience with illness. This finding suggests that patient preferences for care can be easily influenced by how alternatives are presented. It validates the assumption made by behavioral economics that preferences are formed in the act of deciding and are not immutable as presumed by mainstream economics. More importantly, it illuminates the significant responsibility of health professionals to present diagnostic and treatment alternatives to patients in ways that elicit true preferences rather than responses to framing.

The second study is not as much another study of framing as it is an examination of the power of side effects to modify patient decision making (Amsterlaw et al. 2006). The researchers presented several groups of adults with some variation of the following situation:

Imagine that you were recently diagnosed with colon cancer. Without treatment, people with your type of colon cancer usually die within two years. There are two different surgical procedures that can be performed.

Surgery 1 cures colon cancer without any complications in 80% of patients. It does not cure the cancer in 16% of patients, and the patients die of colon cancer within two years. In addition, 1% of patients are cured of their cancer, but must undergo colostomy; 1% are cured of their cancer but experience chronic diarrhea; 1% are cured of their cancer, but experience intermittent bowel obstruction; and 1% are cured of their cancer, but experience a wound infection that can take up to one year to heal.

Surgery 2 cures cancer without any complications in 80% of patients. It does not cure the cancer in 20% of patients, and the patients die of colon cancer within two years.

Surgery 1 would seem to be superior to Surgery 2 because its cures 4 percent more patients (albeit with complications). Nevertheless, the researchers found that about 50 percent of study subjects preferred Surgery 2, the uncomplicated procedure. The researchers varied the presentation, by combining the complications into a single number, using frequencies instead of percentages, and rewording the question. Nothing materially changed the results. At least 40 percent of respondents preferred the dominated procedure, regardless of the presentation. (The researchers asked the same scenario of a random sample of 119 primary care physicians, and found that almost 40 percent of them chose the uncomplicated, but higher mortality, surgery, suggesting that neither medical training nor practical experience inured physicians from the presentation effect.) In some sense, the results imply framing does not always work because the responses were largely impervious to how the scenario was presented. But for our purposes the key implication is that patients' conflation of benefits and risks (by overweighting the enumerated side effects of surgery) can undermine their rational decision making. The high affect associated with the listing of possible side effects can lead patients to engage System 1 and ignore objective statistics that System 2 thinking would apply.

The results presented in this anomaly, as well as the other anomalies in this chapter, suggest several conclusions. First, patients engage both System 1 and System 2 when they make decisions about their health care. As we have seen, these two systems can be complementary, not competitive, and improve decision making. However, because of the high affect associated with most health care decisions (not always life-and-death but still of sufficient consequence to raise concerns), System 1 appears to engage with more force than System 2. Second, this dominance allows action bias to flourish, which drives the demand for diagnostic and treatment modalities, at least some of which will provide no benefit to the patient and in fact will cause harm. Third, when the affect of illness recedes and System 1 fades into the background, patients may reconsider their treatment decisions and choose to cut back or discontinue their medications or therapy. Although these actions might actually help to counteract the overutilization caused earlier, it is not at all clear that the result will balance in each patient. Finally, it appears that patients are particularly vulnerable to the framing of an illness, its projected course, and treatment options. This vulnerability places a particular burden on health professionals—as the patients' agents—to provide the right amount and mix of information so that patients can make the right decisions in both the short and long terms.

THE EXPERIENTIAL TRIUMPHS OVER THE ANALYTIC: WHY PATIENTS CAN'T DO THE RIGHT THING

The decades of the 1960s and 1970s were the apotheosis of mainstream, neoclassical economics. The discipline had gained a reputation for serious science, given its growing axiomatic and mathematical approaches to individual, market, and societal problems. For many economists, the field had succeeded in modeling and explaining much of human behavior. In fact, economists began invading other social sciences, armed with a toolkit that they thought trumped what other fields could offer. So, we saw new areas of economic study, including the economics of health, education, crime, slavery, and even extramarital affairs, in what became known as "economics imperialism." Economists were at the top of their game.

In 1977 two future Nobel laureates, George Stigler and Gary Becker, wrote an audacious article, "De gustibus non est disputandum" ("There is no arguing about tastes") (Stigler and Becker 1977). In it, they claimed that "no significant behavior has been illuminated by assumptions of differences in tastes" and that by using something called household production functions, "all changes in behavior are explained by changes in prices and incomes, precisely the variables that organize and give power to economic analysis." They concluded with the assertion, "Our hypothesis is trivial, for it merely asserts that we should apply standard economic logic as extensively as possible." In the article, Stigler and Becker outlined rational economic theories of human behavior usually considered outside the discipline's sphere of influence, including habit, fashion, advertising, and addiction.

It is that theory of rational addiction that is of relevance to our discussion here. Stigler and Becker, and later Becker and Kevin Murphy (1988), constructed a model in which individuals rationally choose to become addicted: "We claim that addictions, even strong ones, are usually rational in the sense of involving forward-looking maximization with stable preferences" (p. 675). They allowed that there could be "beneficial" addictions (such as to good music) as well as "harmful" addictions (such as to heroin), but the model worked either way. Becker and Murphy demonstrated that their theory could explain such phenomena as bingeing, the effectiveness of going "cold turkey" to end an addiction, and the role of anxiety and stress in precipitating an addiction. One problem was that their model assumed "time consistency," meaning that individuals' behavior in the future coincides with their current desires regarding this behavior. Two other economists solved this theoretical problem thirteen years later (Gruber and Köszegi 2001), and since then mainstream economists have used these rationality-based theories to explore individual behavior such as obesity, smoking, alcohol consumption, and TV watching.

Not surprisingly, behavioral economists and psychologists have offered alternative explanations for addictive behavior. George Loewenstein was the first modern economist to model explicitly the impact of what he called "visceral factors" on individual decision making (Loewenstein 1996, 2000). He defined visceral factors as "a wide range of negative emotions [e.g., anger, fear], drive states [e.g., hunger, thirst, sexual desire], and feeling states [e.g., pain] that grab people's attention and motivate them to engage in specific behaviors" (Loewenstein 2000: 426). Although Loewenstein did not use this term, these factors work through what we have been calling System 1, or experiential, decision making. He argued that visceral factors have two defining characteristics. First, they often influence people to behave in ways that are not in their overall self-interest. It is not that these factors are always destructive, however. Loewenstein argued that at low levels of intensity, visceral factors improve well-being by leading you to eat when you are hungry or take your hand away from a hot stove. At much higher levels of intensity, though, visceral factors "can be so powerful as to virtually preclude decision making. No one decides to fall asleep at the wheel, but many people do" (Loewenstein 1996: 273). Less dramatically, we are all familiar with the lament, "I knew it was a bad idea to . . . go to that bar last night/eat that extra-large pepperoni pizza/buy those Manolo Blahniks." Although proponents of rational decision making would argue that such behaviors are simply mistakes that can be accounted for in their theory, Loewenstein and others contend that these visceral factors are too fundamental to dismiss as just sources of random error. Rather, they are deep-seated aspects of human behavior and need to be addressed explicitly.

Loewenstein's second defining characteristic of visceral factors is that people tend to underestimate their impact on behavior and decision making. Recall the discussion in Chapter 3 about the hot–cold empathy gap. We discussed a number of studies that demonstrated that those in a "cold" decision state do not accurately predict how they will behave in a future "hot" state. A recent study at the University of Amsterdam looked at the issue from the other end—how well people recall past decision states and the impact of visceral factors on decision making (Nordgren, van der Pligt, and van Harreveld 2006). Study participants performed various memory tasks in stages of fatigue or pain and were asked about their own performance as well as that of others. The researchers found that those still in the most extreme hot state (fatigue or pain) attributed their performance (or that of others) much more to fatigue or pain than did those who performed the task in a more moderate hot state or in the cold state; in addition, those who performed the task in the hot state, but who were asked about their performance when they were in the cold state, responded much closer to those who were always in the cold state. The researchers concluded that the sensory experience of a visceral drive can be intense but dissipates quickly so that it is difficult for a person to recall the extent of the experience.

As a result of the impact of visceral factors, people may not be able to control themselves and will behave in inconsistent and even self-destructive ways. Ted O'Donoghue and Matt Rabin (1999) have added a creative, and important, twist to this familiar story. They developed a model that predicts behavior in situations where people have self-control problems (possibly because of visceral factors); the difference from previous models is that O'Donoghue and Rabin assumed that there are two kinds of people, naïve (who believe that they will behave themselves in the future) and sophisticated (who realize that they will not behave). (You will remember that in Chapter 3 we discussed a similar model by Stefano DellaVigna and Ulrike Malmendier [2004].) The naïves will procrastinate when faced with immediate costs (for example, write that paper, fix the drafty window) and "preproperate" (their neologism for doing something when you should wait) when faced with immediate rewards (for example, go to the movies, play basketball). O'Donoghue and Rabin hypothesize that sophisticates will do both earlier than the naïves. Faced with immediate costs, the sophisticates will realize that delay will be costly and that their behavior will not get any better in the future and will procrastinate less. Faced with immediate rewards, the sophisticates will take advantage of the opportunity and preproperate even sooner than the naïves. When they applied the model to addiction, O'Donoghue and Rabin found some surprising results. The sophisticates will be better able to quit an addiction than the naïves because the naïves will delay quitting in the belief that they will quit tomorrow. On the other hand, sophisticates are more likely to become addicted if they think they will do so at some point ("I know I will eat that bag of M&Ms sometime, so I might as well eat it now").

ANOMALY 10: *Why are bad habits (such as alcoholism, smoking, overeating) easy to form and hard to break, but good habits (such as exercise, eating fresh fruits and vegetables) hard to form and easy to break?*

Take smoking, for example. The rational addiction argument is that our friend Benjamin began smoking as a sophomore at New Trier High School because, given the information he had at the time, he calculated that the lifetime benefits to him of smoking (using the usual time discount factors) exceeded the lifetime costs. If Benjamin's preferences or the costs of smoking go up or the benefits go down, then he will stop smoking. To the objection that an addict like Benjamin wants to stop but can't, Becker and Murphy reply that Benjamin will quit "when he finds a way to raise long-term benefits [of smoking cessation] sufficiently above the short-term costs of adjustment" (p. 693). If Benjamin tries and fails to quit with different treatments (for example, nicotine patches, gum chewing, support groups), they assert that "nothing about rationality rules out such experiments and failures." In addition, they admit (in fact, they argue that their theory demonstrates) that going "cold turkey" may be the only way that Benjamin can kick the habit, but so be it. Their argument is actually more sophisticated than that presented here, but the essence of the argument relies on Benjamin being a rational decision maker who uses System 2 thinking to make optimal decisions.

Paul Slovic and his colleagues (Slovic et al. 2007) dispute "the portrayal of beginning smokers as 'young economists' rationally weighing the risks of smoking against the benefits," and they argue that the experiential system (aka System 1) overwhelms the analytic system (aka System 2) and is driving smokers' decisions. It is George Loewenstein's visceral factors that are the most salient in these decisions. The immediate gratification of the smoke gets Benjamin to ignore the incremental—and long-term—damage that this behavior will do to his health. As evidence that System 1 fails to protect young people from smoking, they cite the surveys that show that 85 percent of adult smokers and 80 percent of young smokers answer "no" when asked, "If you had it to do all over again, would you start smoking?"

On top of System 1 thinking, add projection bias from Chapter 3. The Gallup Organization reports that 75 percent of smokers say they would like to give up smoking. Yet 16 percent say that they have never tried to quit, and 37 percent have tried only one or two times (Jones 2006). Clearly, these smokers fall into the category of expecting to stop soon but having little chance of doing so. Projection bias gives them hope that they will quit sometime, just not now. Fifty-five percent of former smokers reported that they quit in just one or two attempts. So, for the 34 percent of current smokers who have tried to quit three to five times, the 9 percent who have tried to quit between six and ten times, and the 5 percent who say they have tried to quit more than ten times, their optimism is overshadowed by the reality of their consumption and the experience of the majority of former smokers. Their behavior, and lack of success, illustrates the power of the experiential decision-making system.

Also, let's consider hyperbolic discounting from Chapter 3. The Gallup Organization reports that the average smoker started smoking at age eighteen, with only 35 percent reporting that they started when they were older than eighteen (Jones 2007). These findings are not surprising; the inconsistent time preferences of teenagers lead them to heavily discount the long-term risks in favor of more immediate, experiential, System 1 decision making. The application of hyperbolic discounting is also evident in the age profile of current smokers. The percentage of the population who smoke is highest for those in their twenties (at around 28 percent), then drops to around 20 percent for those from thirty to fifty-five and steadily declines to almost zero for those in their eighties (Newport 2010). Of course, one explanation for this pattern is the higher mortality of smokers compared to nonsmokers, so that there are fewer old smokers. But a complementary explanation is that hyperbolic discounting has caught up to older smokers; the health and disability costs that they are facing are much closer in time than when the smokers were teenagers, so more of them are quitting.

Recent research on smoking behavior establishes the salience of this approach in explaining the power of bad habits (Sayette et al. 2008). The researchers recruited about 100 smokers and split them into two groups: the "hot group," who were told to abstain from smoking for twelve hours prior to the first session; and the "cold group," who were allowed to smoke normally. In the first session, those in the hot group were told to pick up the pack of cigarettes they had brought with them, light and hold—but not smoke—a cigarette for thirty seconds and rate their urge to smoke. (Talk about torture!) Those in the cold group were told to pick up a roll of tape (which acted as a control), hold it in their hand for thirty seconds, and rate their urge to smoke. Then, participants in each group were asked to indicate the minimum amount of money that they would require to delay smoking by five minutes in a second session a week later (before which both groups were to abstain from smoking for twelve hours). In the second session both groups were given the same instructions that the hot group had received in the first session and were asked to rate their urge to smoke and to indicate the minimum amount they would accept then to delay smoking. Those in the original cold group demanded a lot more money in the second session than in the first, whereas those in the hot group demanded slightly less. That is, the smokers who were not craving cigarettes in the first session significantly underestimated how much they would crave cigarettes in the second session. In their article, the researchers pose the question, "If even individuals who are addicted to cigarettes cannot appreciate their own craving when they are not in a craving state, how likely is it that, for example, a teenager who has never experienced cigarette craving can imagine what it is like to crave a cigarette?" (p. 930).

Let's now turn to good habits and discuss how behavioral economics can explain the difficulty that people have in acquiring and maintaining good habits. Perhaps not surprisingly, there is a lot less research on this topic than on bad habits. In some sense, it may appear that good habits are driven by System 2, analytic thinking, which is not as enticing to researchers as System 1, experiential thinking. But that's the point. Eat plenty of fruit and vegetables, wear your seat belt, cross only at the light, be faithful to your spouse, take your medications, get your work done on time. We know that if we do these things, we will maximize our satisfaction and long-term well-being. Why don't we do them? After all, System 2 will be controlling our behavior because there are few, if any, visceral factors involved and certainly no affect. This is not exactly true. Consider the model that Ted O'Donoghue and Matt Rabin developed, which we discussed earlier. In situations in which the costs are immediate and the rewards delayed (as is the case with most good habits), naïve decision makers (who combine hyperbolic discounting with a lack of awareness of their self-control problems) will procrastinate. When the rewards for what was supposed to be their good behavior should have started (such as enjoying a healthy and vigorous old age or the companionship of a loving spouse), the naïves will be regretting their nondecisions but will have little recourse. The sophisticates (who still exhibit hyperbolic discounting but at least realize their self-control problems) will do somewhat better but still not as well as the über-rational decision makers envisioned by mainstream economists.

SO WHAT? CAN PATIENT BEHAVIOR BE IMPROVED—AND SHOULD IT?

Return to the beginning of this chapter. Apparently, elite soccer goalkeepers are making a mistake by moving on penalty kicks; the statistics indicate that their odds of success are much better if they remain in the middle. The solution would seem to be pretty obvious. However, if it were truly obvious—or easy—these professionals would already have done it. They have strong incentives for correct behavior: greater success for the team and greater glory and compensation for them. That the goalkeepers have not adopted this practice suggests that several forces may be stopping them. First, they may not know the statistics, or they do not believe them. If this is the case, then the solution is obvious— show them the statistics and demonstrate how the practice will benefit them directly. More likely, the resistance is more deep seated than that. Their success is dependent on both their game intelligence (a System 2 skill) and their reflexes (a System 1 skill). As we have seen in this chapter, there are many instances in which System 1 thinking overwhelms System 2, even when it is detrimental to do so. Overcoming those visceral forces inherent in System 1 may be the key to changing the behavior of professional goalkeepers.

But advising soccer players on their tactics is not the purpose of this book. Analyzing the behavior of patients, providers, and the system and offering recommendations for improvements are. In this chapter, we have discovered that patients often do not act in their best interests— they demand that their physician write a prescription or order a test, when watchful waiting is more appropriate; then they are not adherent with their medication about one-quarter of the time; they make different choices about treatment, depending on how the choices are presented to them; and they engage in bad behaviors that jeopardize their health and avoid good behaviors to improve their health. The question is, How can "we" (however defined) encourage/nudge/incentivize/force people to do what is right for them?

We have discovered in this chapter that, contrary to the predilections of mainstream economists, appealing to logic alone will not work. Part of the problem is that System 2 is not the exclusive, or even dominant, decision-making structure that patients use. Suppose that a cardiologist presents her patient with a series of neutrally framed options for treating ischemic heart disease; these options are complete with quantitative probabilities of success and side effects, which have been developed by her specialty through a consensus conference. (We will be discussing the use of decision analysis and decision aids in more depth in Chapter 6.) The cardiologist should not be surprised when the patient makes the "wrong" choice, asks the physician what she would do, or fails to make any choice at all. As George Loewenstein and his colleagues report (Loewenstein et al. 2001), nonprofessionals evaluate risks and benefits in much different ways than do experts, largely because they place much more weight on emotions. Loewenstein and his coauthors suggest that optimal policy would be to mitigate the real risks and irrational fears that individuals (in this case, patients) have. However, as they point out, there is very little research on the effectiveness of such fear-reduction strategies.

To amplify this point, let's use the work of Neil Weinstein that we discussed earlier in this chapter. If his analysis is correct, then those individuals who are sick or are experiencing the deleterious effects of their bad habits will express more interest in prevention. Ironically, they will not necessarily believe that the ill effects of their bad habits can be prevented. If they do decide to change their ways or engage in preventive activities, Weinstein showed that they have only a short window of time to take action, and the action had better require a single act (for example, bariatric surgery) rather than repeated ones (such as going to the gym three times a week). Otherwise, the opportunity will be lost.

To add to the difficulty of changing the behavior of patients, most objective analyses of potential interventions to improve patient decision making and behavior have found only limited success. For example, in 2008 the Cochrane Collaboration, an international network of health professionals, policy makers, and patients, issued its latest assessment of interventions for enhancing medication adherence (Haynes et al. 2008). It found that, of the ninety-three interventions it reviewed, only forty-one resulted in statistically significant increases in medication adherence and only twenty-nine reported statistically significant improvements in treatment outcomes. Perhaps as importantly, it found that "even the most effective interventions did not lead to large improvements in adherence and treatment outcomes" (p. 17).

Given the uneven record of interventions to change patients' behavior, it would be foolhardy to recommend here a slew of interventions based on behavioral economics and psychology to assist patients in correcting their decision biases. Policy makers should not engage in action bias any more than goalkeepers or patients. Nevertheless, I would like to consider two categories of interventions that have the potential to make positive changes to patient behavior: benevolent framing and commitment devices. If the framing of a decision can significantly influence what a patient chooses, then one remedy is to accept the reality of framing and take advantage of it. This can be done in two ways. One is to show a patient his choices using multiple frames. If the patient makes the same choice regardless of the frame, then he and his physician can be confident that he has made the right choice for himself. If, on the other hand, the patient makes contradictory choices, the physician can then address the inconsistencies and work with the patient to reach a final decision. Admittedly, this process will require more time and skill in presentation by the physician (which, given our reimbursement system, may not be adequately compensated), but it is more likely to result in a better decision, a more confident patient, and a better outcome.

Another approach is for the physician to present the issue in a way that guides the patient to the "right" answer, using Cass Sunstein and Richard Thaler's idea of *libertarian paternalism* (2003). The idea recognizes that since there often can be no neutral frame for patient decision making, the physician—as the patient's agent—has the responsibility to present the information in such a way to lead the patient to make the decision that the patient would have made had he had complete information and objectivity. This approach conveys significant power to the physician (although less than was the case before informed consent became the norm), and we would need to rely on the physician to follow professional standards and ethics and use this power purely for the benefit of the patient.

If this delegation of responsibility carries too many risks, there are other, less invasive defaults that can be applied to improve patient behavior. For instance, to improve adherence to medication regimens, physician prescriptions can be entered directly into an ordering system that automatically sends the medication to the patient (along with periodic refills as appropriate). Periodic tests (such as colonoscopies) can be scheduled, and patients prompted to reschedule if the default appointment is inconvenient. Healthy food could be highlighted in supermarkets and restaurants, with unhealthy food relegated to a separate section or menu.

The second category of intervention in patient decision making and behavior to discuss is *commitment devices*. These are voluntary programs in which patients in a cold state can use their analytical/System 2 thinking to prepare for the situations in which they are in a hot state and will make less than optimal decisions. The model for commitment devices is what were known as "Christmas Clubs," popular in the first half of the twentieth century. People would deposit money on a regular basis in a separate, low- (or no-) interest-bearing savings account and would not be able to withdraw their money until December 1 when they could use it to buy Christmas presents. Those who used them said that the programs gave them the discipline they needed to save. A contemporary version of the Christmas Club is stickK.com, a website created by three professors at Yale University—Dean Karlan (in the economics department), Barry Nalebuff (in the business school), and Ian Ayres (in the law school). People interested in achieving a goal develop a commitment contract on the site, which specifies the goals (for example, weight loss, regular exercise), the stakes for not achieving the goals (such as money, reputation, and the recipient of the stakes), a designated referee, and a support group. The website reports a number of success stories, although I have not seen any formal research to measure the program's effectiveness.

Commitment devices to modify patient behavior could have any number of forms and purposes:

- A medical savings account in which an insurer adds money when the patient reaches—and maintains—specified medication adherence rates.
- Contributions by an employer to the employee's account at a retailer when an employee meets—and maintains—a specified BMI (body mass index) level.
- An account in which the patient automatically contributes funds, which can be withdrawn only if he refrains from smoking cigarettes for a designated amount of time. (Thaler and Sunstein [2008] report a particularly insidious version of this device, in which the participant's failure to reach the target triggers contributions from the fund to a political action committee or an advocacy organization that the participant despises.)
- A fund set up by individuals who want to lose a large amount of weight, in which those who lose weight share in the pool of nonrefundable contributions.

To be effective, the commitment device needs to have four characteristics: It must provide sufficient rewards and/or penalties to overcome the patient's System 1 decision making when he is in the hot state; it must be impervious to "gaming" (for example, the patient should not be able to back out of the arrangement while in the hot state); the device should distinguish between naïve and sophisticated patients; and the device needs to maintain its salience (for example, by varying the commitment amount or payout period) to ensure that the patient continues to pay attention. Even so, as the research has shown, we cannot expect that any commitment device will be the magic solution to overcome the biases and System 1 thinking of patients.

UNDERSTANDING THE BEHAVIOR
OF PATIENTS: TRY THIS AT HOME

Now that you understand some more tenets of behavioral economics and psychology literature, you can relate them to everyday behavior that you observe in your family, among your friends, and in your community.

So try the following:

1. There are plenty of reasons why obesity has become such a problem in the United States. Use the behavioral economics principles in this chapter to consider the following questions:
   a. Why has obesity grown in the United States over the past decade?
   b. Why do diets fail?
   c. What defaults could you devise to reduce overeating and promote exercise?
   d. What creative commitment devices can you develop that might work? How could you test whether they would work?
2. Conduct some behavioral economics research on your own:
   a. Go to fast-food restaurants and ask a random selection of patrons:
      i. How low would the price of the healthy food sold at this restaurant (such as salads) have to be to entice you away from your usual order (such as cheeseburgers or fried chicken)?
      ii. What would be the impact if calorie totals were posted next to the prices, as well as on your receipt? (For instance, would you order only those items that would keep you under a preset calorie count?)
      iii. Would you be in favor of a higher price on high-calorie food items?
      iv. Would you be in favor of a lower price on low-calorie food items?
   b. Poll people at your work, or at parties:
      i. Suppose that you found that you had adopted a bad habit (for instance, overeating or overconsumption of alcohol).

How hard do you think it would be to break yourself of that habit?

ii. What reward, if any, would you want if you broke the habit? For instance: money, a better job, more friends, love.

5

UNDERSTANDING
THE STUBBORNLY
INCONSISTENT CONSUMER

In the previous chapter we found that patients often exhibit some curious and inconsistent behavior. They demand that their physician do something—a pill, a shot, a test—to rid them of their ailments, yet they often do not adhere to the treatment regimen that they had demanded. They want information and autonomy in making their health care decisions (as they should) but make different decisions if information and options are presented in different ways. Sometimes, despite their best efforts, patients find that they cannot develop or maintain those good habits that they and their physicians want (exercise, eating fresh fruits and vegetables) and backslide into behaviors they know are not good for them (smoking, drinking, overeating).

It is not surprising, then, that this inconsistent and puzzling behavior continues when people shift from the role of patient to that of health care consumer and sometimes to that of supplier. In this chapter we will analyze these instances and explain why they occur using the concepts of behavioral economics. Fortunately, we have already introduced and discussed many of the core concepts we will need for this analysis, although we will introduce a few new ones. To preview what we will be about in this chapter, we will be considering:

- Why people are oblivious to the real price of their health care.
- Why people buy health insurance that covers small and predictable losses.
- Why people buy a lot of health care when it's "free."
- Why people sometimes shun health care when it's "free."
- Why people give away a valuable asset that they would not sell.

Of course, as with other chapters, we will consider the "so what?" question—that is, how can we make people more cognizant of the true cost of health care, so that they can be more intelligent consumers and better stewards of scarce health resources?

VIVIDNESS, SALIENCE, AND AFFECT: EXPLAINING CONSUMERS' CASUAL RELATIONSHIP WITH HEALTH CARE PRICES

In Chapter 4 we introduced and used the concept known as *affect*, which is "the specific quality of 'goodness' or 'badness' experienced as a feeling state . . . and demarcating a positive or negative quality of a stimulus" (Slovic et al. 2007). We saw that high-affect situations (such as falling in love or natural disasters) can cause System 1 thinking to overwhelm System 2 thinking. For our discussion in this chapter, we need to introduce two complementary concepts: *vividness* and *salience*. Adapting the definition that Richard Nisbett and Lee Ross (Nisbett and Ross 1980) created, vividness is those qualities of information, ideas, or objects that are "likely to attract and hold our attention and to excite the imagination to the extent that [they are] (a) emotionally interesting, (b) concrete and imagery-provoking, and (c) proximate in a sensory, temporal, or spatial way" (p. 45). For example, it is one thing to describe the statistics of early mortality attributable to cigarette smoking; it is quite another to print a picture of a diseased lung on a pack of cigarettes. It is one thing for health policy experts to present to a congressional committee their analysis of the quantitative impact of a reduction of Medicaid coverage; there is something palpably different—and presumably more powerful—for an affected family (who lives in the district of the committee chair) to describe how they will not be able to get a life-saving transplant for their adorable nine-year-old daughter, who will die in the next six months. The presumption is that vividness will often trump more prosaic and abstract information.

As an example of the impact of vividness, two researchers (Borgida and Nisbett 1977) asked three sets of prospective psychology majors at the University of Michigan to indicate the five to ten psychology courses they thought they would likely or definitely take. The groups were given different information about future courses: One group was shown actual course evaluations by previous students; the second group heard several students rate courses they had taken and discuss their ratings; and the third group was just given the course catalog. The students who heard the face-to-face recommendations from former students were more likely to indicate that they would take the recommended courses and not take the nonrecommended courses than those who just read the catalog or were given the course evaluations. That is, the vivid (and potentially nonrepresentative) information discussed by the former students was more persuasive than the more objective, but colorless, catalog and course evaluation statistics.

Vividness seems like such a self-evident concept that these results do not seem very surprising. However, an extensive review of the literature discovered that experiments largely failed to find that vividly presented information was more influential than more pallid information (Taylor and Thompson 1982). The reviewers concluded that the laboratory setting was, in fact, too successful in focusing the participants' attention on things that they might ordinarily ignore in real life and thus underestimated the impact of vividness in real life. Nevertheless, it does appear that a patently obvious effect such as vividness may not be so patently obvious.

Such is not the case with salience, the other concept we need to introduce here. Salience can be defined as a prominent, conspicuous, or striking attribute of a person, idea, or object. One scholar (Plous 1993) distinguishes between vividness and salience by suggesting that the more vivid something is, the more likely it is to be recalled and convincing, whereas the more salient something is, the more likely it is to be considered a cause of whatever phenomenon is being considered. Think about the statement, "Before Benjamin had a chance to install new brake pads on his recently purchased 1986 Guard Red Porsche 911 Cabriolet, the car collided with a tractor-trailer on I-95 in the snow and was totaled." "1986 Guard Red Porsche 911 Cabriolet" and "I-95" are vivid, but "brake pads" and "the snow" are salient.

Where salience—or, more exactly, its absence—becomes interesting in an economics context is in what Drazen Prelec and George Loewenstein (1998) and Richard Thaler (1999) call *payment decoupling*. In many cases, when you buy something such as groceries or gasoline or a taxi ride, you receive the good or service proximate to the time that you make the payment. As a result, the price is salient to your consumption— and it can be salient in different ways depending on the payment arrangement. When you go to the grocery store, you see the price of each item on the shelf below it, but you don't see the total until you go through the checkout line. (It used to be that a price sticker was on the product itself, which made price even more salient.) When you go to buy gasoline, you can see the unit price several hundred yards away; in fact, gasoline is the only product I know of in which you can comparison shop not by stopping at every vendor and searching for the price but just by driving down the street. In addition, as you are filling up your tank, you see the payment increasing continuously, which adds to the salience. With a taxi ride you know (at least if you are a local) what the unit price will be regardless of which taxi you take, and you see the meter running continuously (even when you are in a traffic jam and making no progress to your destination). Again, there is very high salience between purchase and consumption.

In other cases, payment and consumption are decoupled in time and consumer attention. You may buy an airline ticket with cash, but you go on the flight in the future ("buy now, fly later"); or you purchase the ticket with a credit card ("fly now, pay later"). In still other cases, such as in resorts like Sandals, you make a single payment ahead of time, and all aspects of your consumption at the resort—room, food, drinks, excursions—are covered. Or you join a health club in which monthly payments are automatically charged to your checking account or credit card, and you pay nothing when you use any of the club's services. Or you buy three rooms of furniture, and your first interest-free payment is not due for twelve months. In each of these cases, the decoupling of payment and consumption reduces the salience of the payment, and here's the interesting part: People make different purchase and consumption decisions than when payment and consumption are coupled (something that standard, mainstream economics fails to explain).

Drazen Prelec and George Loewenstein (1998) developed a model, which they corroborated with surveys and experiments, that explained the attractiveness of these kinds of arrangements. First, they distinguished between what they call "decision efficiency" and "hedonic efficiency." Decision efficiency is what economists are typically concerned with: What are the most efficient ways to organize (primarily, in time) the purchase and consumption of goods and services? Mainstream economists use the tools of discounted present value and opportunity costs to argue that to maximize their level of satisfaction, consumers should weigh all the additional (or what economists call "marginal") benefits of any purchase against all the additional/marginal costs of doing so. Using this methodology, these economists determine that, everything else held constant, people should:

- Rent or lease rather than buy (to free up capital).
- Delay payment as long as possible (to be consistent with a universal preference for consumption in the present than in the future).
- Choose the per-use fee, rather than the flat fee, option (to recognize the real cost of consumption).
- Choose among more, instead of fewer, options (to ensure that only the most preferred are chosen).

Thus, the decision efficiency approach creates a tight linkage between payment and consumption.

Prelec and Loewenstein argue that this approach ignores what they call "the pain of paying," and the quest of consumers for hedonic efficiency. That is, consumers do not want to always be thinking about how much they paid (or are continuing to pay, or will pay in the future) for a good or service. They argue that hedonic efficiency is achieved when consumers:

- Buy, rather than rent or lease.
- Pay ahead of time and be done with it.
- Pay flat fees for continuing or bundled goods and services, instead of on a per-use or per-feature basis.
- Prefer a "fully loaded" product to choosing among an array of options.

Under hedonic efficiency consumers want to decouple the opportunity and monetary costs as much as possible when they are consuming a good, in effect creating the illusion that consumption is free (at least at the time of consumption). One estimate, generated by manipulating a number of payment methods with an experimental group, found that the pain of paying can be as high as the equivalent of a 44 percent increase in actual price (Ariely and Silva 2002). Thus, hedonic efficiency and the avoidance of the pain of paying carry significant weight in consumer decision making.

Figure 5.1 presents the trade-off between hedonic and decision efficiency. As Prelec and Loewenstein point out, the countervailing forces of decision and hedonic efficiency create several dilemmas: Should a consumer pay once-and-done or pay over time? Should she pay now or pay later? Should she time her payment to coincide with consumption, or should that connection be broken? Should she buy herself a guilty pleasure or hope that her husband will buy it for her birthday? These dilemmas create some seemingly contradictory behavior. People use debit cards to pay up front, but they also use credit cards to delay payment. They select flat-rate service (say, for telephone service) even though they would save money by choosing a per-call payment option. Couples who share all expenses buy each other expensive gifts.

As with most economic decisions in a world in which the tenets of behavioral economics prevail, consumers make a wide range of decisions regarding coupling and decoupling of payment and consumption. We can predict which direction they will choose. Decision efficiency will prevail when System 2 dominates System 1 thinking. That will occur

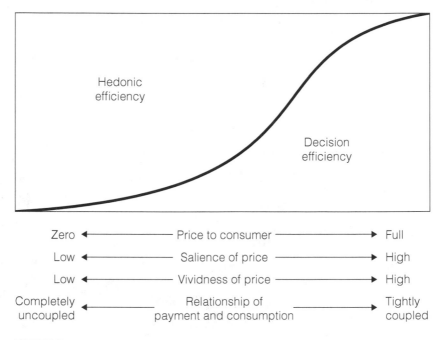

FIGURE 5.1
The trade-off between hedonic and decision efficiency.

with purchases that have low affect, such as washer/dryers, furniture, and business trips. It will occur with purchases for which the benefits are spread out over time (and, thus, consumers will still think that they are getting something in return for their current expenditures). On the other hand, hedonic efficiency will prevail for those goods and services that generate high affect, and those that generate benefits only in the short term (including vacations to exotic locations, coveted luxury items, dinners at fancy restaurants, and Lady Gaga concerts).

With the concepts of vividness, salience, affect, and decision and hedonic efficiency, we can begin to explore—and begin to understand—the behavior of the stubbornly inconsistent health consumer.

ANOMALY 11: *Why are patients oblivious of the "real" price of their health care—and why does this lack of attention promote price inflation?*

In 2009 most Americans (253 million out of 304 million) had at least part of their health care paid for through insurance: 170 million through their employers, 27 million through private insurance purchased directly, 43 million through Medicare (the federal government program for the elderly), 48 million through Medicaid (the state/federal government program for the poor), and 12 million through the military (active duty and discharged) (DeNavas-Walt, Proctor, and Smith 2010). (Some have coverage from multiple sources.) It makes sense that insurance covers some health care expenses. After all, the purpose of insurance is to protect people from the full consequences of significant adverse events that occur with low probability and little predictability. However, there are aspects of insurance that can distort economic decision making. Let's see how.

People buy insurance to cushion catastrophic events, such as their house burning down or their car being stolen—or, in the case of health care, having a massive heart attack that requires a transplant. Companies sell insurance because they can convince enough people to pay premiums that cover the cost of the small expected number of catastrophic claims that are made, plus administrative costs and profit. Insurers are always concerned about "adverse selection," that those who buy insurance will be those most likely to incur losses. They are also concerned that the insureds engage in "moral hazard," that those who are insured can trigger the insured event or that they will modify their behavior because of the presence of insurance. For example, auto insurers are worried that car owners insured by them will be more careless with their car keys (thus increasing the probability of car theft) or that they will drive less carefully (knowing that the insurer will pay for damages if an accident occurs). As a result, insurers put in place practices to inhibit moral hazard. They include in their policies "deductibles" (which require the insured to pay the first portion of any loss), "copayments" (which require the insured to pay a certain dollar amount of any loss above the deductible), and/or "coinsurance" (which requires the insured to pay a percentage of any loss above the deductible). These mechanisms forestall people from filing small claims and, more importantly, temper incentives for moral hazard. The behavior of both buyers and sellers of insurance can be explained by mainstream, neoclassical economics, relying primarily on the price mechanism to incentivize all parties.

But let's return to health insurance. Five out of six Americans pay for their health care through insurance, and let's suppose that our friend Benjamin from previous chapters has finally decided to enroll in his employer's health insurance plan. Nothing wrong with insurance; that's what it's for, except . . . Health insurance creates a number of perverse effects on people's behavior, which can be explained by behavioral economics better than by neoclassical economics. Most significantly, it decouples payment from consumption, and it does so in a number of significant ways. First, health insurance premiums typically are paid on a schedule (for example, annually, quarterly, or monthly) that has no connection to the insured's actual consumption of health services. As Drazen Prelec and George Loewenstein demonstrate, this prepayment improves Benjamin's hedonic efficiency (if not his decision efficiency) when he decides to use health care services. Second, much of the insurance premium is often paid by someone other than the insured. Benjamin's employer is like those surveyed by the Kaiser Family Foundation (Claxton et al. 2010); it pays between 70 and 75 percent of the total premium. (By the way, Benjamin's grandmother is a Medicare beneficiary. The premium she pays covers only 25 percent of the costs of services covered under Part B, and she pays no premium for Part A services. She is subject to a deductible, copayments, and coinsurance, however, when she uses Part A services.) This subsidy paid by Benjamin's employer reduces the salience of the premium to Benjamin even more, as he is oblivious of the actual premium cost and his "pain of paying" is beginning to vanish. Third, because Benjamin gets his insurance through his employer the premium is deducted from his paycheck instead of Benjamin having to write a check every pay period. Benjamin's employer no longer distributes physical pay stubs, so Benjamin no longer even sees the amount that is deducted for health insurance; if he were interested, he would need to log on to his employer's website and search for his pay stub. The convenience of automatic deduction, combined with the decline of paper pay stubs, reduces the salience of the premium yet again, which further decouples the premium from consumption and reduces the pain of paying. Fourth, unlike auto or home insurance, health insurance (except perhaps for coverage that is bought as an individual) is not experience rated. If Benjamin has a number of auto accidents, he will most likely see his insurance premiums increase dramatically at the next renewal date (or even be cancelled). However, if Benjamin has unusually high health expenses this year, his employer or health insurer will not increase his premiums proportionately for next year or cancel his coverage (although he may have difficulty finding a policy if he tries to switch insurers). This peculiarity of health insurance leads to a phenomenon best described by a student in one of my medical economics courses: "We are unperturbed by the idea that we may need to use our health insurance but hope fervently that we never need to use our homeowner's insurance."

So, unlike goods with more salient prices (such as gasoline), people are not continually aware of the cost to them—or the total cost—of their health insurance premiums. In addition, they are not aware of the true costs of the health care that they seek. Of course, most policies have deductibles, so those who are insured will be aware (at least in the first part of the year) of the costs of the first $250 or $500 of their care. Once they have met the annual deductible, then they will be cognizant of only the copayment or coinsurance (typically, 20 percent of the allowed price, and then only until they reach the annual out-of-pocket maximum). Let's consider Benjamin again, who has a typical employer-based health insurance program (Claxton et al. 2010). The price of health care will have full salience to him only for the first $675 of his deductible. Once he reaches that threshold, the salience will be reduced dramatically, as Benjamin is liable for only 20 percent of allowable charges, or the copayment. So, his prescription for a ninety-day supply of 20 mg Lipitor will appear to cost his $70 copayment, not the $284 retail price. Finally, once Benjamin spends a total of $2,500 for health care in a year, he will have reached his out-of-pocket limit and the actual price of care will have no salience to him whatsoever.

Because Benjamin will be less aware of the full price of his health care most of the time, he also will be less aware of any price increases. The reduced salience will lessen the pressure on physicians, hospitals, and other providers to hold down their prices. So we should expect to see that the prices of health care rising faster than they would have otherwise and to be higher than in other markets in which price salience is higher. Although the evidence of the latter is abundant, it is much more difficult to prove the former. One indirect piece of evidence comes from a clever article by Amy Finkelstein, "E-ZTax: Tax Salience and Tax Rates" (2009). Professor Finkelstein found that she no longer knew what the rates were on toll roads once she installed an E-Z Pass transponder on her windshield that allowed her to avoid the long lines at toll booths. The E-Z Pass acts as a kind of "electronic wallet," which the highway authority periodically fills from a driver's specified credit card and withdraws when the driver uses a toll road. Finkelstein speculated that this reduction in salience might allow states to raise the rates (effectively, a tax) without drivers/taxpayers noticing. Sure enough, her careful econometrics revealed that in states with electronic toll collection tolls were 20 to 40 percent higher than they would have been without the E-Z Pass. Hedonic efficiency was trumping decision efficiency. The analogy between the E-Z Pass and health insurance should be clear (if not perfect). The reduced salience caused by health insurance and copayments/coinsurance, however well intentioned, limits the ability of patients to act like normal consumers and balance the value of consumption of health care services with the real price.

The impact of reduced salience is amplified by a tenet of behavioral economics discussed in Chapter 4: the lack of hot–cold empathy. Remember the finding by George Loewenstein and his colleagues (Sayette et al. 2008) that those in a cold decision state often underestimate the impact on decision making when they are in a hot state (and vice versa). In the case of health care, this phenomenon translates to our friend Benjamin in the following way. Suppose that Benjamin is a conscientious health consumer who tries to keep prices in full view when he is choosing a physician, hospital, or pharmacy. However, if he wrenches his knee while playing pickup basketball at the Y, Benjamin will find that deliberate decision making evaporates, and price no longer matters when what is salient are the pain and the anxiety surrounding the injury. Now, it doesn't matter if the orthopedic surgeon charges more than others in the area, and the hospital she admits him to is the most expensive, and the drugs she prescribes are not cheap generics. Price? What price? Insurance will cover most of it, anyway. Let them pay.

ANOMALY 12: *Why do people buy health insurance that covers small dollar "losses" (for example, physician office visits)?*

Insurance is intended to protect the insureds from catastrophic losses while minimizing moral hazard. Yet health insurance does not seem to work that way. According to the Kaiser Family Foundation's annual survey of employer health benefits (Claxton et al. 2010), 30 percent of such plans have no deductibles at all; in addition, over 70 percent of plans cover office visits to a primary care physician, over 90 percent cover preventive visits, and over 90 percent pay for prescription drugs—all before the employee or his family reach the deductible limit. And, for a physician office visit (with a retail price of around $100), the average copayment is only $22, and the average coinsurance is 18 percent.

That is, health insurance is paying most of the cost for a relative low-cost, highly predictable event largely under control of the insured. As noted earlier in this chapter, these attributes violate many of the principles of insurance. If auto insurance were structured like health insurance, the insurer would pay for oil changes and new tires. If home insurance were structured like health insurance, the insurer would pay for periodic termite inspections and treatment and for new appliances when the old ones wore out. What seems ludicrous for these traditional forms of insurance is standard operating procedure for health insurance. Why the difference?

We can appeal to the tenets of behavioral economics for explanations. Let's start with loss aversion, one of the most fundamental principles of behavioral economics (which we discussed in Chapter 2). People hate losses much more than they like gains; in fact, a loss of, say, $100 in value is equivalent to a gain of $200 in value. So people will sometimes do extraordinary things to avoid losses; they will keep stocks that are tanking and continue projects that should be abandoned. In addition, as Kahneman and Tverksy (1979) demonstrate, people will prefer one large loss to multiple smaller losses that are equivalent in total; they would rather pay $100 once than $20 five times. Translating these preferences and loss aversion to field of health care, people will prefer to buy health insurance that covers everything (or close to everything) for a set and periodic premium, instead of having to pay for each health care service. Loss aversion, in turn, is complemented by the decoupling of payment and consumption that health insurance provides. Health insurance assuages the pain of paying for the relatively small, but predictable, visits to the physician or purchase of prescription drugs, by lowering the salience of the full price. Instead of paying $100 for each physician visit, the consumer only has to pay $22 (and not even that if the consumer has reached his annual out-of-pocket limit).

This behavior raises a potentially disquieting question as to whether health insurance is still *insurance* anymore or whether it has evolved into an elaborate prepayment plan. As we have discussed in this chapter, people love the hedonic efficiency created by prepayment plans, and the subsidy of health insurance premiums (by employers through their pretax contributions to employee health plans and by the federal government through Medicare and Medicaid) certainly lowers the pain of paying. It is not surprising, then, that health insurance has moved away from the standard format of insurance policies.

One example of the evolution of health insurance is the growth of high-deductible health plans or "consumer-directed health plans" (which combine a high-deductible health plan with a tax-deductible flexible spending account to help pay for deductibles and copayments). The Kaiser Family Foundation survey (Claxton et al. 2010) found that 27 percent of workers enrolled in an employer-sponsored health benefits plan in 2010 had a deductible of at least $1,000, and 10 percent had a deductible of $2,000 or more. These plans hew more to the fundamental principles of insurance than typical health insurance plans. Perhaps what is happening is that rapidly rising health insurance premiums for standard policies are driving the balance away from hedonic efficiency toward decision efficiency. After all, according to the Kaiser Family Foundation, annual premiums for employer-based health insurance have increased 104 percent over the past decade for single coverage (from \$2,471 to \$5,049) and 139 percent for family coverage (from \$5,791 to \$13,770).

Mainstream economists might object that Anomalies 11 and 12 are not anomalies at all but simply the workings of an active market for health insurance and health care services. Consumers are responding to the prices that they face at the time of consumption. If they have to pay only \$22 for a physician office visit, they will go to the physician more often than if the price was \$100. If this rational behavior engenders higher total costs, then insurers (or employers) will raise premiums and/or restructure policies to accommodate consumer behavior. In fact, mainstream economists will argue, that is what we are seeing, with the introduction of high-deductible health plans and the increasingly limited plans and increased employee contributions that many employers are instituting. What mainstream economists argue may be true, but the issue is more complicated than they portray, and the market adjustments so far do not yet address the fundamental nature of consumer behavior in health care. The behavior that the market is responding to is caused—at least in part—by the response of health consumers to vividness and salience and their desire to decouple payment and consumption to enhance hedonic efficiency. By doing so, health consumers minimize decision efficiency, which is one of the prime tenets of mainstream economics. So the mechanisms of the health insurance and health services markets may be working, but they are reacting to the less-than-rational behavior of consumers. That is not the mark of an efficiently run market envisioned by mainstream economists but rather one better characterized by behavioral economics.

THE SPECIAL VALUE OF ZERO: WHY PRICE IS MORE THAN JUST A NUMBER

In Chapter 1 we discussed a series of experiments conducted by Kristina Shampanier, Nina Mazar, and Dan Ariely (2007) that identified the special value of a zero price. If you recall, when they lowered the price of two similar products (\$10 and \$20 Amazon gift certificates), demand moved in predictable ways; however, when the price of the \$10 gift certificate was lowered from \$1 to \$0 (and the price of the \$20 certificate from $8 to $7) demand for the $10 certificate went from 36 percent to 100 percent. After offering several potential explanations, the researchers concluded that a zero price produces an affect that the $10 Amazon gift certificate is a good that has no costs, no downsides; in effect, sheer happiness. Any reservations that the consumer would have about loss aversion are completely assuaged because she thinks that there can be no losses with a free good.

It turns out that the value of zero is more complicated than that, as the research of a number of behavioral economists, psychologists, and marketing experts has revealed. For instance, Daniel Kahneman and Amos Tversky (1979), in the article that presented the original theory of behavioral economics, noted the remarkable attractiveness of zero (compared to low) risk and people's willingness to pay to obtain it. They conducted an experiment in which the participants were compelled (hypothetically) to play Russian roulette but were given the opportunity to buy the removal of one bullet from a loaded gun. Participants were willing to pay much more for removing the last bullet (and reducing the risk of death to zero) than for going from four bullets to three (even though the decrease in probability was the same). Kahneman and Tversky cited this result as an example of the overweighting of small probabilities, which is a core tenet of behavioral economics.

Conversely, a variety of mainstream economists through the years have shown that consumers perceive high prices as a signal of quality. One group, for example, argued that producers of new, high-quality "experience goods" (that is, goods for which consumers can determine their quality only by using them) can set a high initial price to distinguish their product from inferior competitors (Milgrom and Roberts 1986). However, another showed more generally that "the most efficient way for [a] firm to signal high quality is to charge a price too high to be profitable if the product were in fact of lower quality" and cited examples as diverse as car wax, vodka, skis, and TV sets (Bagwell and Riordan 1991). Although not a direct refutation of the zero-price results of Kristina Shampanier and her colleagues, this research suggests that the role of a low or zero price in determining behavior may be complicated.

ANOMALY 13: *Why did health care utilization and spending jump in the Rand Health Insurance Experiment when price went to zero—with no improvement in health outcomes?*

In 1974 the Rand Corporation undertook a major study sponsored by the federal government. The study was specifically intended to analyze how health insurance affected the demand and expenditures for health care services. At the time there was serious discussion (within a Republican administration, mind you) about creating a national health insurance program, and the policy makers wanted a better idea of the impact of expanded coverage on the federal budget. Rand conducted one of the few true controlled trials in health economics. It enrolled 7,700 people at six sites and randomly assigned them to one of fourteen different fee-for-service plans or to a prepaid health maintenance organization (HMO) plan. The fee-for-service plans differed by coinsurance rate (0, 25, 50, or 95 percent) and annual out-of-pocket expenses (5, 10, or 15 percent of income). Rand then followed the participants' health care utilization and expenditures for three to five years.

Some of the results were as expected; others were pretty startling (Manning et al. 1987). For our purposes here, the most interesting findings were the responses of those who had the zero coinsurance rate (which means that they had no out-of-pocket costs for the duration of the experiment). By any metric, those who faced a zero price were more likely to use health care services—number of physician office visits, number of hospital admissions, probability of using any medical service, probability of being admitted to a hospital—and to incur many more expenses—outpatient, inpatient, total—than any of the other categories. Those who had free care generated 45 percent greater total health care expenses than did those with the 95 percent coinsurance plan. As to particulars, those with free care went to the physician's office 67 percent more than those who had the 95 percent coinsurance plan. By contrast, those who had the 25 percent coinsurance plan went to the doctor only 22 percent more than those with 95 percent coinsurance. That is, the biggest increase in usage and expenses occurred in going from 25 percent to zero percent coinsurance (a 37 percent increase for physician office visits, for example). Even the probability of being admitted to a hospital (which you would imagine to be least in the control of the consumer) was sensitive to the zero price effect; 10.3 percent of those with free care were inpatients, compared to only 8.4 percent of those with 25 percent coinsurance and 7.9 percent of those with 95 percent coinsurance.

Now, this increased utilization might have been worth it, if those with free care had better outcomes, but that was not the case. The researchers (Brook et al. 1983) found that "for the average person enrolled in the experiment, the only significant positive effect of free care was that for corrected far vision" (1430). That is, those with free care and those who had to pay at least something for their care were no different in terms of improvement in physical or role functioning, mental health status, risk of dying, health behaviors (such as smoking, overweight, or hypertension), or perceived health. The researchers recognized that the three-to-five-year time span of the experiment may have been too short for major differences in health to have been realized, but it nonetheless is disquieting that no differences were found.

For our purposes, it would have been nice if the Rand experiment had been able to divide the sample into finer gradations of coinsurance rates, so that we could see how demand for health care increased as coinsurance decreased gradually from 25 to zero percent. On the other hand, I suspect that the Rand researchers did not fully anticipate the behavior of those who had free access to health care. As it was, they made a series of careful calculations to estimate the price elasticity of demand for health care, which is the standard measure in economics of the responsiveness of demand to price changes. They calculated this elasticity to be between -0.1 and -0.2, which means that the participants in the experiment did not change their demand for health care very much when price changed (this, despite the seemingly large impact of free care on the demand for health care).

One of the purposes of the Health Insurance Experiment was to estimate the extent to which health insurance had enabled the rapid increase in health care expenditures in the United States. The Rand research team was concerned that free care could propel expenditures even faster. In fact, they estimated that moving from a 95 percent coinsurance program (which would be an almost pure catastrophic plan) to a free care program would generate a "welfare loss" (when spending on the margin yields little, if any, benefit) of between 18 and 30 percent of total health care expenditures. This finding suggests that health insurance needs safeguards to deter moral hazard to avoid unnecessary expenditures on health care.

Given the standard economic tools that they had, the world-class Rand researchers did not go much further in trying to explain the consumer behavior behind their somewhat surprising results, but these results would be understandable to behavioral economists. The work of Drazen Prelec and George Loewenstein can be used to show that the inherent structure of health insurance decouples payment from consumption; by so doing, insurance improves the insured consumer's hedonic efficiency at the expense of decision efficiency. As a result, most of the participants in the Health Insurance Experiment were cognizant of only part of the incremental cost associated with their care. Price had little salience in their decision to obtain health care. (An exception must be made for those in the 95 percent coinsurance plan, which is a catastrophic insurance program much like auto or home insurance. This group, in effect, acts as the control group to measure the true demand for health care if consumers had to pay the full cost [up to the out-of-pocket limit].)

In addition, the research of Kristina Shampanier and her colleagues suggests that zero coinsurance creates an affect for health care consumers that consumption of health care has no downsides or costs. It is not surprising, then, that utilization of health care for those with free care in the Health Insurance Experiment was dramatically higher than for those participants facing a nonzero price. Because of the structure of the Rand experiment, we cannot be certain that the behavior was caused by the "special value of zero" rather than the usual response of consumers to lower prices. However, because the Rand researchers estimated that the price elasticity of demand for those in the experiment was quite low, it is likely that something other than standard economic behavior was occurring when the effective price of health care went to zero. What we need is research to test the demand for health care at zero and near-zero prices to determine which line of reasoning is correct.

ANOMALY 14: *Why do patients/consumers shun free or low-priced health care products (for example, generic drugs) and services (for example, community health) that have the same efficacy as higher-priced products and services? Why do they think that more expensive is better?*

When I began to give presentations about behavioral economics and health care, I would describe the special value of zero and apply it to health insurance, and the audience would nod their heads in recognition. Occasionally, I would get a question from a physician, nurse, or other health professional who reported a different experience. They would say that their patients resist being prescribed a generic form of a medication because they think that the lower price meant that it was not as good quality as the brand name version. Or a clinician who worked in a community health center (which often offers its services to patients with little or no charge) said that it was sometimes difficult to get patients to come for care because they thought that the service could not be as good as in a private practitioner's office or even the emergency department. If this behavior is common, then the special value of zero may also work in the opposite direction than we just discussed.

Three recent studies in health care illustrate how complicated this zero/low-price issue really is. The first (Waber et al. 2008) involved a pain study on eighty-two adult volunteers. The study participants were given a series of electric shocks and asked to rate the level of pain that they felt; this was followed by their ingestion of a pill they were told was a new analgesic. (In reality, the pill was a placebo.) Half of the group was told that the price of the pill was $2.50, while the other half was told that the price had been discounted to $0.10. The volunteers were then subjected to another series of equivalent electric shocks and were asked to rate their pain. In the regular-price group, 85 percent reported a reduction in pain versus 61 percent of the discounted-price group. This difference occurred regardless of the volunteer's age or gender or the number or intensity of shocks received. So, this study revealed the power of price as an implicit measure of quality (in addition to the well-documented power of the placebo).

The second study (Ashraf, Berry, and Shapiro 2010) involved a field experiment in Zambia, in which the researchers examined the impact of different prices on the demand for, and use of, a home water purification solution. The researchers first conducted a door-to-door survey of 1,260 households in Lusaka, Zambia, gathering information about demographics and health behaviors (including malaria prevention and water purification). Two weeks later, a different team went back to these households and offered to sell them a single bottle of Clorin, a well-known and popular drinking water disinfectant, at different, nonzero prices (which were lower than the retail price); if the respondent agreed to buy the product, she was informed that she might be eligible for a discount, which for 40 percent of the households was a 100 percent discount (that is, the Clorin was free). Two weeks later, the original survey team returned to test the water and measure the amount of Clorin that was used. They found some interesting relationships between price and usage. Willingness to buy was inversely related to the initial offer price, so that a higher price did not act as an indicator of quality (for what was, admittedly, a well-known product). Those who were willing to pay the higher (initial) price were more likely to actually use the product. However, there was no relationship between the final (discounted) price and the likelihood of using the product, meaning that the 40 percent who paid nothing for the product did not use it more than those who paid something; in effect, consumers were neither inordinately attracted to—nor repelled by—a zero price.

Finally, to make the issue of a zero price even more complicated, let's look at one other field experiment in Africa. The researchers (Cohen and Dupas 2010) followed a similar methodology to examine the impact of different prices on demand for, and use of, insecticide-treated bed nets in Kenya. They offered these nets to pregnant women at twenty prenatal clinics, with prices ranging from zero to 40 Kenyan shillings (equivalent to $0.60). The highest price was still a 90 percent subsidy of the real costs of the nets. The researchers found that a price of zero increased consumers' valuation of the product itself, consistent with the findings of Shampanier, Mazar, and Ariely. Contrary to the findings of the second study discussed in the preceding paragraphs, they found that usage of the nets was not related to the price that the women paid; in fact, usage dropped slightly when the price increased from zero to 10 Kenyan shillings, then increased after that.

So, given all the evidence we have reviewed, we are left with a lot of unresolved issues regarding the special value of zero—anomalies within anomalies, if you will. We have found in the Rand Health Insurance Experiment and the malaria prevention project in Kenya that a zero price for health care services or products can generate an extraordinarily large increase in demand. On the other hand, we have found in the Zambian water purification experiment that a higher price results in greater use of a public health product. Finally, we have found in the pain analgesic experiment that people think that a higher-priced drug is a better drug. It is at this point that the omniscient author is supposed to reconcile these discrepancies and reveal the truth to the reader. I am afraid that I must disappoint you. All of the studies we discussed were well designed and executed; none made any glaring error or ignored some key variable. Instead, what we have here is what happens at the early stages of the scientific enterprise, when scientists of different perspectives address an issue in different ways. The results will be contradictory until someone can devise a theory that can incorporate and explain the seemingly disparate behaviors that we have seen. What favors behavioral economics is that—by its nature—it seeks an interdisciplinary approach in all of its work.

SOCIAL VERSUS ECONOMIC NORMS: WHAT HAPPENS WHEN CONSUMERS ARE PRODUCERS

There is one other aspect of a zero price that we need to discuss, one that may be the most profound. This behavior occurs when people are providers of a good or service, rather than consumers. Suppose there was a big storm in your community, and an old oak tree fell in your neighbor's yard. Your neighbor calls and asks if you will bring over your chain saw and help him cut up the tree. You agree, and the two of you spend the next five hours working in his backyard. What would you do if the neighbor then pulls out his wallet and offers to pay you $50? You would refuse, right? After all, you're neighbors, and anyway it gave you a chance to play with your chain saw. But suppose someone you don't know called you and asked you to bring over your chain saw and help him cut down a fallen tree in his backyard, which would probably take about five hours. He said he would pay you $50. In this case, you would probably say "no," but not for the same reason as with your neighbor; this time the reason is that it is not worth your time for just $50.

What's the difference between these two seemingly similar situations (at least to a mainstream economist)? In the second case, you are using an *economic norm*, in which you are making a rational calculation about the best use of your time. In the first case, you are using a *social norm*, that guides your behavior; helping your neighbor is simply the right thing to do. Social norms have been defined as "standards of behavior that are based on widely shared beliefs how individual group members ought to behave in a given situation" (Fehr and Fischbacher 2004). One political scientist (Elster 1989) has cataloged a variety of such norms, including: consumption norms (how you speak, how you dress, what movies you see); norms against behavior contrary to nature (incest, cannibalism, polygamy); norms of reciprocity (how to repay favors); norms of cooperation (how you act with others); and norms of distribution (how income and wealth should be allocated). He noted that norms can be explicit or implicit, are subject to change, and may not always lead to improved welfare for everyone. To this point, social scientists have not been able to determine the mechanisms by which social norms are formed, maintained, and changed. However, we can see their implications for economic actions.

In Chapter 1 we discussed some research by Uri Gneezy and Aldo Rustichini (2000a), in which they found that parents left their children at a day-care center after hours more often when they had to pay a small fine than when there was no fine. They argued that the introduction of a fine changed the environment from one ruled by social norms (in which parents felt guilty for abusing the teachers' generosity in staying beyond their scheduled quitting time) to one ruled by economic norms (in which the parents felt as if they were paying for babysitting services). In a sense, the environment changed from being a relationship (a social contract, if you will) to a transaction. Perhaps as interesting, the parents' behavior did not revert when the fine system was eliminated; the economic norm prevailed even when the impetus disappeared.

Two other researchers (Heyman and Ariely 2004) conducted a series of experiments with students at Berkeley and MIT that yielded some interesting insights into the distinction between economic and social norms. Two of the experiments dealt with activities that the students might be willing to do without pay—one to help a friend (move a sofa) and the other to solve math puzzles (this being MIT and Berkeley, after all). The researchers found that the students were as willing to perform the tasks for either a candy bar, a box of chocolates, or $5 in cash as they were for free, but were less willing if they were given $0.50 or a candy bar that they were told cost $0.50. The third experiment involved a task that the researchers characterized as "utterly uninteresting and without any redeemable value," in particular, repeatedly dragging a light gray circle on the left side of a computer screen onto a dark gray square on the right side for three minutes. Those who were paid nothing dragged an average of 168 circles, about the same as those who were given five Jelly Bellies (162 circles) or a half pound of Jelly Bellies (169 circles). However, those who were paid ten cents dragged an average of only 101 circles, and those paid $4 dragged 159 circles. Their conclusion: People are willing to do a lot of things for free (even boring things) or for gifts (such as the candy), but once price enters the picture the calculus changes dramatically. Their perspective goes from social norm to an economic norm, like a lightbulb switching off.

All of these studies suggest that moving from a zero price to even a small positive price creates a dramatic tipping point, as people shift their thinking from providing a good or service for social reasons to one that provides purely economic benefits to the individual. When that shift occurs, an individual's thought process changes to "Pay me enough, or don't pay at all" (as Gneezy and Rustichini [2000b] say in the title of an article). And, as the research seems to indicate, once the perspective shifts from social to economic norms, it is very difficult to go back. A relationship may become a transaction, but a transaction may never be able to become a relationship.

ANOMALY 15: *Why will some people give away a valuable asset (such as their blood or a kidney) that they would not sell?*

When I was an economics graduate student in the early 1970s, I was searching around for a suitable PhD dissertation topic. I stumbled across a book by an eccentric Englishman, Richard Titmuss, called *The Gift Relationship* (1970). In it, Titmuss extolled the virtues of the British system of collecting and distributing blood for therapeutic purposes and castigated the United States for allowing people to sell their blood. What really set me off was his assertion that banning the sale of blood would increase the amount of blood that was donated, a heresy to me as a novitiate into the economics priesthood. I then pursued a quest to prove him wrong, by doing my research on the market for human blood. I think that I succeeded.

Recent research indicates that Titmuss may have been right, after all. One study (Mellstrom and Johannessen 2008) was similar to the ones described in this section. Undergraduates at a university in Sweden were asked if they were willing to donate blood, under three regimes: no payment, 50 Swedish kroner, and 50 Swedish kroner donated to a charity. The results were remarkably similarly to the studies described earlier: Forty-three percent agreed to donate blood with no payment, whereas only 33 percent of those offered the direct payment were willing, and the number bounced back up to 44 percent for those given the charity option.

On the other hand, Mario Macis, a colleague of mine at Johns Hopkins University, has done an extensive study of American Red Cross blood drives. Although the Red Cross steadfastly refuses to pay people for their blood, they often provide gifts or nonmonetary incentives. Mario and his research team (Lacetera, Macis, and Slonim 2012) studied the effect of different incentives on turnout at 14,000 blood drives in the Midwest. The incentives ranged in value from a $2.95 T-shirt to a jacket worth $9.50. They found that the presence of incentives significantly increased both turnout and number of units of blood collected;

higher-value incentives significantly increased both turnout and units collected; and donors apparently "shopped around" for those drives that provided higher-value incentives. Because the Red Cross does not explicitly pay money for blood donations, the incentives might be considered more like the candy and chocolates given out by James Heyman and Dan Ariely in their experiments. To test the impact of cash (or, more accurately, "near cash"), Mario and his team conducted a natural field experiment in which they randomly selected eighteen blood drives in the area and randomly allocated the incentives among the drives: gift cards from local merchants worth $5, $10, and $15 (as well as a control group with no incentives). The gift cards would be similar to the "monetized" candy and chocolates used by Heyman and Ariely. They found that the higher the face value of the gift card, the higher the turnout and units collected. So my colleague found that economic norms seem to work for what has traditionally been a field governed by social norms.

Giving blood is one thing; after all, the body replenishes a pint of donated blood within two months. The debate over the impact of an economic market is even more intense when the issue is the contribution of nonreplaceable body parts for organ transplantation, especially from live donors. The "market" for kidney transplants has shown a persistent shortage since the development of the procedure. In 2000, 13,450 patients received a kidney transplant, but at the end of the year there were still almost 37,000 eligible patients on the waiting list. In 2010, 16,521 received a kidney transplant (a 26 percent increase from 2000); however, the waiting list at the end of the year contained over 80,000 patients. Between 35 and 40 percent of kidneys are obtained from live donors, a percentage that has not changed much over the past two decades (Health Resources and Services Administration 2009; Organ Procurement and Transplantation Network 2011). Of course, mainstream economists have a ready solution to this mismatch—create a real market, in which the price will rise until enough live people with two healthy kidneys (or relatives of recently deceased people with healthy kidneys) are willing and able to meet the demand. However, the National Organ and Transplant Act passed in 1984 prohibits "valuable consideration" in exchange for kidney donations, so such a market cannot form.

The classic promarket argument has been articulated by Gary Becker and Julio Elias (Becker and Elías 2007). They argued that the prohibition against the sale of kidneys leads to a worse situation, as those eligible for transplants are unable to receive them (even though at least some would be willing and able to pay the additional cost) and continue to suffer, with between 10,000 and 16,000 on the waiting list dying each year. Becker and Elias contended that more potential donors would make their kidneys available if they were offered suitable compensation. They then calculated that the likely market-clearing price for a kidney would be $15,200, based on compensation to the supplier for increased risk of death, time lost during recovery from the surgery, and risk of reduced quality of life postsurgery, which would increase the total cost of a kidney transplant by less than 10 percent.

Becker and Elias dismissed the arguments against allowing a market for organs. To the criticism that such a market would be a "commodification" of body parts, they cited the compensation given to surrogate mothers who carry the eggs of other women and even to the voluntary army that allows "the commodification of the whole body" by putting a soldier in harm's way in exchange for money. To the argument that the poor will be the ones most likely to give up a kidney, they responded, "Should poor individuals be deprived of revenue that could be highly useful to them?" Finally, to the argument that payment will crowd out those who donate a kidney for altruistic reasons, they replied that a purely altruistic system has failed to produce the number of organs needed to meet the demand. To my mind, Becker and Elias's line of reasoning encapsulates the best and worst of mainstream economics. The argument demonstrates the power of analytics and makes explicit the trade-offs that society makes when it prohibits a market from functioning. On the other hand, Becker and Elias have a tin ear to the concerns of society that there are values and norms not captured by the economist's fixation with efficiency as the primary goal.

Economist Alvin Roth has provided the most effective counterargument to the market approach of neoclassical economics (Roth 2007). Although he never used the term *social norms*, his argument was predicated on this concept. Roth contended that society from time to time refuses to allow a market mechanism to allocate resources. He noted that the incidence of this "repugnance" is difficult to predict, in part because some things that used to be repugnant no longer are (for example, interest on loans, a paid standing army) whereas others have become repugnant over time (for example, the sale [slavery] or long-term leasing [indentured servitude] of human beings). Roth made a point that harkens back to the work of James Heyman and Dan Ariely: Payments in kind often vitiate the level of repugnance compared to payments in cash. In that sense, the exchange becomes more like a gift relationship than an economic transaction. Richard Titmuss may have been onto something, after all.

So, we are left with a conundrum for which behavioral economics can provide more assistance than mainstream economics. Mainstream economics maintains that a positive and rising price will always induce more supply, whether it's automobiles or kidneys. Behavioral economics, by explicitly incorporating concepts from psychology, recognizes that social norms strongly influence how individuals will behave and what society will tolerate. It is not surprising, then, that a market for a good like a kidney will not generate as much supply as a mainstream economist would predict. However, as Alvin Roth noted, repugnance can wax and wane, so eventually an economic market may arise. Once it does, it is highly likely that altruistic donors will be "crowded out" of the market, as an economic norm supplants a social one and will be unlikely to return for quite some time.

SO WHAT? HOW CAN PATIENTS AND CONSUMERS BE MADE MORE AWARE OF THE TRUE COST OF HEALTH CARE?

All economists—mainstream and behavioral—believe that people respond to incentives. One thing that sets behavioral economists apart is that we incorporate factors that mainstream economists either ignore or think are of minor significance: the impact of the salience and vividness of a price or characteristic of a good on a consumer's demand for that good; the effect of decoupling payment and consumption; the inordinately large impact of a zero price on demand; and the significance of social norms in driving economic behavior. Sometimes, this perspective yields unique recommendations; other times, the recommendations are the same as those of mainstream economists (which, ironically, should be reassuring, as it demonstrates the robustness of the recommendations). With that in mind, let's consider what behavioral economics offers in terms of a "so what?" regarding the stubbornly inconsistent health consumer.

If, as we found, consumers are largely oblivious to the real cost of their health care, then we need to increase the salience and vividness of that cost to them if they are to become more effective consumers. Behavioral economics provides a number of mechanisms to do this. First, what is now called "health insurance" can be converted into real insurance— policies to cover low-probability, high-expense events such as major acute care episodes, rather than highly predictable, low-expense items such as physician office visits. These high-deductible plans are already available, in the guise of "consumer-driven health plans." Many health economists are strong supporters of the concept, for the same reasons that we have discussed here (Robinson and Ginsburg 2009). If health consumers have more of a financial stake in their health care, they will be more cognizant of the appropriateness and cost of their care.

That consumer-driven health care plans are still a minor part of the health insurance industry is testimony to the power of payment/ consumption decoupling—and of the endowment effect. As we saw in Chapter 2, people are reluctant to make a change unless they are certain that the change is demonstrably better than the status quo. So how do we convince consumers to switch to "real" health insurance? Of course, there is always force; employers faced with ever-increasing premiums could abandon standard health benefit plans in favor of consumer-driven health plans. But, as we discussed in Chapter 4, people strongly desire at least some choice, even if they choose the one option that the employer would have offered. In a more choice-friendly environment, we could encourage consumers to adopt a variation of high-deductible plans known as "value-based health plans" (Fendrick and Chernew 2007). In these plans, the consumer has a high deductible for most services but faces a zero price for services that yield very high benefits to both the consumer and the insurer. A value-based health plan takes advantage of the special value of zero, as well as salience, to nudge consumers to demand health care that is tailored to their current and long-term needs. For example, if a disease management program to monitor policy holders with Type II diabetes can prevent acute care episodes at relatively low cost, it should be offered at no cost to the patient.

A challenge created by standard health insurance is that consumers rarely see the full price of their care. To them, the price is the deductible or copayment that they pay either at time of service or when the provider sends a bill (the latter a further decoupling of consumption and payment). A way to increase the salience of the cost of care is to follow the method used in France's compulsory, universal health insurance program. When visiting a physician, the French consumer must pay the full price, then get reimbursed (typically, 70 percent of the fee) by the insurer (Lundy and Finder 2009). The initial coupling of consumption and payment, combined with the delay between the service and the reimbursement, makes the French consumer of health care directly aware of the price of care.

Another way to elevate the salience of health care prices is to indicate the retail price of health care goods and services on every transaction. So receipts for prescription drugs—or, better yet, the labels on the bottles—would indicate the full price of the drug. In addition to increasing the salience, seeing the full price might generate a placebo effect similar to that found by Rebecca Waber and her colleagues that we discussed earlier. On the other hand, a physician office visit that lasted only five minutes and resulted in a $200 bill that the patient had to pay when she checked out (even though she is ultimately responsible for only $40) might elicit some interesting push-back to the office staff and the physician. This kind of push-back is part of what makes a market an efficient allocator of scarce resources.

Those who worry about the high and rising costs of health care in the United States need to be greatly concerned by the findings of Gneezy and Rustichini and others that when a social norm changes to an economic norm it is difficult to change it back. One recently conducted survey found that people may not be as repulsed by paying organ donors as once thought (Halpern et al. 2010). There are proposals to pay relatives of early Alzheimer's patients to be caregivers, so these patients can stay in their homes longer. Each of these ideas has merit on its own. However, in total they are hastening society along a path to monetize activities that heretofore had been provided for "free." Of course, as sociologists have demonstrated, "free" transactions are not really free; instead, they are exchanges that build the trust, relationships, and interdependence that make communities work.

As strange as it might seem for an economist to say, the big "so what?" here is for us to find ways to encourage the preservation of social norms at the expense of economic norms. Pandora's box may already have been opened, but there are at least some intermediate steps that we can take to retard the monetization of all transactions and relationships in health care. One lesson comes directly from the various experiments that were discussed in this chapter: In-kind payments may be a sufficient tool to give people incentives while preserving social norms. (So, T-shirts and jackets can attract blood donors as well as—or better than—cash, but without damaging the social contract.) For the preceding examples, kidney donors could be publicly acknowledged as heroes, and they and their immediate relatives could be given preferential treatment if they needed replacement organs. Those relatives providing extensive care for loved ones with Alzheimer's could be eligible for respite care, including a cruise or a long weekend at a desired location. None of these ideas is earth shattering, but each might get us to get closer to our goals of affordable and compassionate health care.

INTERVIEW WITH GEORGE LOEWENSTEIN, PHD
Herbert A. Simon Chair of Economics and Psychology,
Carnegie Mellon University
George Loewenstein is one of the small number of economists who have transformed behavioral economics from a niche into an integral part of economics. The reader of this book will quickly realize how his research has advanced behavioral economics, in such areas as intertemporal choice, preferences, emotions and taste prediction, policy, and health issues. Educated at Brandeis (BA, 1977) and Yale (PhD, 1985), Professor Loewenstein was on the faculty at the University of Chicago Graduate

School of Business before settling into Carnegie Mellon in 1990. In recognition of his contributions to the field, he was elected president of the Judgment/Decision Making Society in 2001–2002, and is a fellow of the American Psychological Society and a member of the American Academy of Arts and Sciences.

From your standpoint, to what extent has behavioral economics established itself as a legitimate field of economic study?
The placement of behavioral economists in top economics departments and the placement of their work in top journals show that it has established itself as a central area within economics. Behavioral economics has, I believe, come of age.

Do you think that behavioral economists have established a unified, coherent theory, compared to neoclassical economics?
In my own view, the coherence and unification of standard theory is dramatically overblown. Sure, economists have the utility maximization rational choice model. But, depending on a specific domain that economics is applied to, the model looks completely different. The utility functions have different arguments. Sometimes you're dealing with expected utility or discounted utility. Sometimes leisure might enter into the utility function, and other times just consumption and sometimes people are maximizing wealth, sometimes consumption.

At the same time, there is a lot of coherence to behavioral economics. Behavioral economists also tend to assume utility maximization but make some slightly different assumptions from those made in conventional economics: prospect theory instead of expected utility, present-biased preferences, loss aversion, projection bias, etc. And, in many of our models, the standard model is a special case. Behavioral economics may be somewhat more flexible, but I don't think it is really less coherent than conventional economics.

Given that neoclassical economics has had well over a century to reach its current level of development, I would say behavioral economics is doing spectacularly. Behavioral economics began about twenty years ago; it's actually quite impressive how far it has come in such a short period of time.

Behavioral economics began by importing ideas from other fields, but by now it's an export industry. At this point, we have behavioral law and economics, behavioral labor economics, behavioral finance, and many other applications. So, I suppose it's a glass half-empty/half-full story, but, to me, given how young the field is, it's amazing how many subfields it has infiltrated and influenced.

What has been the singular contribution of behavioral economics to the analysis of economic behavior?
I would say that loss aversion is probably the most robust phenomenon, the one that is probably best understood at this point, has been applied to the widest range of phenomena and subjected to the most exhaustive testing. There have been so many different field studies showing the impact of loss aversion—in the housing market, labor supply, the behavior of unions after they win or lose negotiations—that it has really proved to be an exceptionally fertile and robust idea.

What has been the most prominent failure of behavioral economics to date?
I wouldn't call it a failure, but I think the biggest limitation is that we have barely made inroads into macroeconomics. We have all these macroeconomic crises unfolding, and behavioral economists haven't been very visible in the public discussion, and that's unfortunate.

What do you see as the trajectory of behavioral economics?
I hope and believe that eventually there will be no such thing as behavioral economics because all economics will be behavioral economics, by which I mean much more psychologically realistic than it was in the past. The distinction between behavioral and nonbehavioral is going to get thinner and thinner, and eventually maybe disappear, and whether you call the end product behavioral or neoclassical—whether you say neoclassical has been influenced by behavioral or whether you say it's behavioral—is just a matter of labeling. Ultimately, behavioral economics and standard economics are on a path to unity as the insights of behavioral economics become widely accepted.

Turning to more specific aspects of behavioral economics,
why do you think that the behavioral economics approach to
addiction is superior to that of neoclassical economics?
Let me answer a broader question first. In traditional economics,
there's basically one major situation in which some kind of regulatory or taxation/subsidy intervention is warranted: externalities, that
is, costs people impose on other people, but don't internalize. A major
insight of behavioral economics is that there's another category of situations that can justify policy intervention, those characterized by what
my coauthors and I have dubbed "internalities." These are situations
in which people impose costs on themselves that they don't internalize.
There are a variety of reasons why people might be subject to internalities, including that sometimes the negative consequences of our behavior are intangible, so they're difficult to notice. In other cases, the
consequences are delayed, and we tend to discount the future steeply.
So, behavioral economics introduces a second category of justifications
for state intervention.

I think that's a major insight that behavioral economics has to offer.
One of the reasons that traditional economics hasn't fared so well in the
health area is because so many of the problems that we observe—like
diabetics who aren't doing the first thing that they need to do to avoid
having horrible complications, or grossly obese people who are suffering terrible health consequences but can't mobilize themselves to lose
weight, or cigarette smokers who desperately want to quit but can't—
involve self-destructive behaviors. Economists are not going to get very
far analyzing these types of self-destructive behaviors with a model that
assumes that people are maximizing their long-term well-being.

I remember when the Chicago economist Kevin Murphy gave the
opening address at a conference on childhood obesity, the theme of
which was something to the effect of: "I don't even know why this conference is happening. If children are obese, it must be that the pleasure
they derive from eating outweighs the negative effects of being obese.
So why are we here?" That kind of attitude is not going to strike a responsive chord in people who are concerned about public health.

*What evidence do you think is needed for behavioral economics
to gain acceptance, in general and in health care?*
I suppose there are two possible types of evidence. One is empirical
evidence that is consistent with the behavioral perspective and inconsistent with the standard perspective. Let me give an example from my
own work, and it's specifically work on addiction. You take an addict
who is coming in for a treatment with Buprenorphine (a methadone-
like maintenance drug). You ask them, "Five days from now, you are
going to come in for your next treatment, and we're giving you a choice
to make now between getting an extra dose of Buprenorphine five days
from now or getting money." The thing you manipulate is whether you
ask them to make this decision *before* they get their current treatment
or *after* they get the dose. What you find is that before they get the
dose, they value the extra dose of Buprenorphine five days later about
twice as much as they value it after they get their dose. It's a real decision; it really affects them five days later. Normatively, whether they
make this decision a few minutes earlier (before getting their dose) or
a few minutes later (after getting their dose) should not affect the decision they make for five days later, but it does; it has an enormous effect.

This result was predicted by a behavioral effect—projection
bias—but it's completely inconsistent with standard economic models.
So that's an example of evidence showing a pattern of behavior that
doesn't fit the standard model.

But I would say the more compelling research would be showing
that policy interventions that are based on behavioral ideas are more
effective than interventions that don't take account of these behavioral ideas. An example, again from my own research, comes from
the domain of health. My colleagues and I were asked by a company
headquartered in Pittsburgh to help it motivate its workers to complete
health risk assessments (a survey about health that helps companies
to give workers the services they need). The company was paying $25
to every worker who completed one, and it was willing to increase the
amount to $50. We compared two interventions. One group continued
to get $25; for a second, experimental, group we increased the effective

amount to $50. For a third group, we incorporated ideas from behavioral economics, like regret aversion and overweighting of small probabilities. We found that doubling the reward from $25 to $50 had pretty much zero impact on the number of workers who completed the HRA, but the behavioral intervention (which also had an expected value of $25 so it cost exactly the same amount per worker) was dramatically more effective in increasing HRA completion.

What this intervention shows is that a dollar is not equal to a dollar; the motivational impact of a dollar depends critically on how you deliver it. Instead of effectively burning money, using ideas from behavioral economics, you can have a dramatic impact on behavior. So, I would say that's pretty strong evidence supporting the utility of applying behavioral economics to public health.

Why have most interventions to overcome
bad or suboptimal behavior failed?
Informational interventions have failed for a number of reasons. First, the reason that people engage in bad behavior is not usually because they lack information. We all know what it takes to lose weight, and it is not a lack of information that prevents us from achieving that goal. It's more an issue of self-control than of information.

Second, people tend to be overwhelmed by information. Give people more, good information, and it tends to displace other existing good information because they have limited attention. Third, very often people are already biased in a direction that is, if anything, helping them to achieve self-control. People probably exaggerate the calories in food, and people overestimate the health risks of smoking and so on. So these are all situations in which, if you give them more accurate information, you are going to, if anything, exacerbate the problem.

Why, in general, is it so difficult to change people's behaviors? Well, the American public got fat for a variety of overlapping reasons having to do with diminished exercise, increased portion sizes, lower prices of processed foods, higher premium on time, and greater convenience from processed foods. So there is just an incredible array of forces pushing people in unhealthy directions. And it's not really surprising that the relatively small attempts to change behavior that are attempted in field studies are often not very effective, because the forces going in the other direction are so overwhelming.

In that case, what is the answer?
To my mind, these are public health problems, and behavioral economic interventions—the types of intervention that have gotten a lot of play in the press like nudges—that can help on the margin. Behavioral economics interventions are usually very low cost, so they can be quite cost effective, and they can have a substantial impact in some situations (such as default contribution rates on retirement plans). But they're certainly not going to solve our public health problems. If we want to solve the public health problems, we need to kind of take a public health perspective, and we need to think about how to modify all of these different forces that are leading people to engage in unhealthy behaviors. So, I think behavioral economics is great, and interventions that play on behavioral economics ideas tend to be more effective and cost effective than those that don't. But at the same time, if we really want to solve these public health problems, it's going to take much more dramatic social change.

It seems a shame that now that economists have been able to get public health folks to take us seriously, that the best we can say is that we can affect behavior on the margin.
Unfortunately, there are people who don't want to think about larger changes, who are using behavioral economics interventions to substitute for the types of more fundamental intervention that we need. In my opinion, those people were never going to be open to the kind of public health initiatives that are needed in any case. They just found behavioral economics to be a kind of convenient false ally.

Perhaps the prime example is David Cameron (prime minister of Great Britain). He wants people to reduce their electricity usage. We know the best way to get people to reduce their electricity use is to charge them a price that reflects the true cost of generating the electricity, the true social cost. But being in the conservative party and of a somewhat libertarian bent, he is loath to do something like that. So, instead, he is a big advocate of showing people their neighbors' electricity bills. It's fine to show people their neighbors' electricity bills, and most of the research shows that it has a small impact, something between a 1.5 and 2.0 percent reduction in the electricity use. But it's not the best and most effective way to get somebody to cut down on their electricity use. To the extent that Cameron is using these ideas as an excuse for not using the proven method of an excise tax, that's unfortunate.

How, then, do you effect this fundamental change?
I'm a big advocate of testing almost any policy on a small scale before you implement it on a large scale, because almost all traditional economics and behavioral economics research suggests that it's very difficult to predict, not only the individual level of response, but also the aggregate response to any kind of change in policy. Certainly, there needs to be more field testing of interventions, and it's a huge mistake to trot out some kind of new intervention without testing it. A good example is calorie labeling, where there was one flawed study done at Subway that was picked up on and used to justify calorie labeling in New York City. All of the research except for one study has shown that calorie labeling in New York has not had a beneficial effect, and, yet, it's now being implemented nationally. We are implementing calorie labeling at a mass scale with almost no evidence that it is effective. We need to proceed boldly when it comes to theory and research but timidly when it comes to turning our ideas and research findings into policy.

6 UNDERSTANDING THE MEDICAL DECISION-MAKING PROCESS, OR WHY A PHYSICIAN CAN MAKE THE SAME MISTAKES AS A PATIENT

In episode 33 of *House*, the brilliant, egomaniacal, misanthropic, charismatic Dr. Gregory House and his medical team are presented with the case of Margo Dalton, a "supermom" with a twinge in her arm followed by a series of uncontrollable muscle spasms and a psychotic breakdown. In the course of the episode, House and his team consider and test an amazing array of potential diagnoses—pregnancy, Huntington disease, spontaneous schizophrenia, cocaine use, protein C deficiency, endometrial cancer—and finally discover a benign liver tumor caused by the patient's taking Ritalin and birth control pills (at the same time she is undergoing fertility treatments). In the course of the episode, House uses straight analytics, aphorisms ("Nothing explains everything"), and just plain hunches to arrive at the final diagnosis. Just a day's work at Princeton-Plainsboro Teaching Hospital, but certainly not how we remember Marcus Welby, MD, practicing medicine or, more significantly, how patients see their physicians acting during a typical office visit.

Much has been written about how physicians make diagnosis and treatment decisions, from those intended for clinicians (Elstein, Shulman, and Sprafka 1978; Sox 1988; Kassirer, Wong, and Kopelman 2010) to those written for a lay audience (Groopman 2007). Some of these implore physicians to use all of their diagnostic skills (Epstein 1999), whereas others urge them to be more quantitative and analytical (Pauker and Kassirer 1980; 1987). A growing line of research is examining how nonclinical factors are affecting physician decision making, including the sociological environment (Eisenberg 1979) and economic incentive structures (Frølich et al. 2007).

In addition, there is a mounting debate within the medical profession about the proper balance between the science and art of medicine. Those of a more scientific bent are calling for more standardization in the field, to reduce what they see as unnecessary variations in the amount and outcomes of care and to eliminate easily avoided errors. For their part, most clinicians acknowledge the critical role of science in medicine but note that many individual cases require that the clinician go beyond the standard approaches. As such, they decry what they see as the potential devolution of clinical practice into "cookbook medicine."

It should not be surprising that the tenets of behavioral psychology and behavioral economics are beginning to be applied to medical decision making, including framing (Christensen et al. 1995), hindsight bias (Arkes et al. 1981), outcome bias (Caplan, Posner, and Cheney 1991), action bias (Ayanian and Berwick 1991), and the paradox of choice (Schwartz and Chapman 1999). The challenge is that, despite the publication of such research in the top medical journals, the lessons of behavioral psychology/economics have not been inculcated into formal medical education or everyday clinical decision making. For his part, Dr. House has yet to diagnose that he or his colleagues have fallen victim to the many biases discussed so far in this book.

In this chapter we will discuss how physicians are as susceptible to the findings of behavioral economics and psychology as are their patients. In addition, we will introduce some concepts that expand on the theories of System 1/System 2 thinking discussed in Chapter 4 and show how they apply to how physicians make decisions in diagnosing and treating illness. As in our earlier discussion about society, patients, and consumers, we will not argue that behavioral economics/psychology provides the silver bullet that explains all of physician behavior. Rather, we will contend that this field does yield unique insights that can help physicians to improve their clinical judgment and help patients to understand how their physicians work.

HEURISTICS: WHY PHYSICIANS
MAY NOT ALWAYS BE SCIENTISTS

We live our lives through rules of thumb. These enable us to make decisions and take actions without having to deliberate every single detail. Among the more common and interesting rules of thumb (courtesy of Tom Parker [2008]) are:

- You can support a mortgage that is no more than three times your income.
- You should follow another car no closer than the distance you will drive in two seconds.
- Use ammonia for a bee sting and vinegar for a wasp sting.
- Zigzag to outrun a crocodile.
- To predict final adult height, double a child's height on his or her second birthday.

In some cases, these rules of thumb are based on facts and reality; in others, they come from unsubstantiated folk wisdom.

Behavioral psychologists and economists (Kahneman, Slovic, and Tversky 1982; Gilovich, Griffin, and Kahneman 2002) have been exploring the nature of a broader set of decision tools known as *heuristics*. Heuristics are strategies for decision making that use a relatively small number of simple and readily accessible rules rather than engaging the full gamut of possibilities. Heuristics can be as simple as the rules of thumb given in the preceding paragraph or as complex as multilevel decision trees. Over fifty years ago Herbert Simon (Simon 1955; 1956; 1957) introduced the concept of *bounded rationality* to explain why people use heuristics. According to Simon, rational decision making can be bounded in three ways: the presence of risk and uncertainty, which replace precision with probabilities; the absence of complete information about alternatives, which prevents a person from knowing all the characteristics and consequences of each choice; and the inherent complexity of reality, which impedes a decision maker from understanding all the interactions and possible consequences of each choice. Faced with the realities of bounded rationality, our friend Benjamin from earlier chapters would no longer try to maximize his level of satisfaction, happiness, or utility. Instead, he would—in Simon's felicitous terms—*satisfice*; that is, he would make a choice that achieves some threshold of satisfaction instead of searching for the absolute highest alternative.

The concept of satisficing harkens back to the discussion we had in Chapter 3 about the work of Sheena Iyengar and Barry Schwartz, showing that consumers often did not prefer more choices to fewer. They demonstrated that choice overload could make decision makers frustrated, unhappy, and prone to inaction. Although we saw in Chapter 4 that neutralizing action bias might not be such a bad thing, in many cases action paralysis may be detrimental to the decision maker's well-being. Benjamin has to make some decisions sometime and get on with his life.

Behavioral psychologists have explored the nature of heuristics and bounded rationality along two tracks. The first, known as the "heuristics and biases" program, has investigated when heuristics lead decision makers astray; the second, known as "fast and frugal," argues that heuristics are largely efficient and accurate mechanisms for decision making in a complex world. We shall examine both, to set the stage for a discussion of how physicians make their clinical decisions.

Amos Tversky and Daniel Kahneman were the early champions of the heuristics and biases camp. In an early article (Tversky and Kahneman 1974), they identified three kinds of heuristics that could produce biased decision making. The first, anchoring, we discussed in some detail in Chapter 2, in the context of the controversy over the new guidelines for mammography screening. The second kind of heuristic was "availability." People estimate the probability that something will occur based on the ease with which they can think of examples. For instance, people using the availability heuristic will believe that unemployment is high if they can think of people they know who are out of work, or they will think that there is an outbreak of prostate cancer if they hear that friends (or friends of friends) have recently contracted the disease. To test the availability heuristic, Tversky and Kahneman (1973) conducted an experiment in which they recorded four audio lists of names: two lists of entertainers and two of other public figures. Two of the lists (one each of entertainers and public figures) consisted of one-half famous women and one-half not-so-famous men; the other two lists consisted of one-half not-so-famous women and one-half famous men. The experimental participants listened to one recording; half of them were then asked to write down as many names as they could remember from the list, and the other half were asked whether the list contained more names of men or of women. In both cases the participants remembered more famous than not-so-famous names, confirming that they recalled the more familiar—the more readily available—names.

The third kind of heuristic identified by Kahneman and Tverksy was "representativeness," in which people determine whether A is related to B based on the extent to which A resembles (or is "representative" of) B. So, we would use the representativeness heuristic to predict that our friend Benjamin would be a database analyst if he seems to have the characteristics of a database analyst. Nothing surprising or controversial here, except that people tend to make some odd, and incorrect, choices when they apply probabilities. Tversky and Kahneman, in yet another study (Tversky and Kahneman 1971), showed that people seem to believe in "the law of small numbers." That is, they often draw unwarranted inferences from a very small sample; for example, many people will conclude that a coin flip sequence of HHHHTTTT demonstrates that the coin is not true, whereas they think that a sequence of HTHTHTHT reflects true randomness. Where this leads to trouble is in the gambler's fallacy we discussed in Chapter 2, in which the gambler believes that long shots have to win sometime or that a particular roll of the dice is "due" if it has not occurred in awhile. Another common mistake is the "hot hand" fallacy, in which we perceive that basketball or baseball players seem at times to get "in the zone" and can't miss. It doesn't matter that these streaks are nothing more than a manifestation of statistical distributions; we continue to believe (Gilovich, Vallone, and Tversky 1985; Camerer 1989). Kahneman and Tversky conclude that:

The notion that sampling variance decreases in proportion to sample size is apparently not part of man's repertoire of intuitions. . . . On the one hand, people are often willing to take seriously a result stated in percentages, with no concern for the number of observations, which may be ridiculously small. On the other hand, people often remain skeptical in the face of solid evidence from a large sample. (Kahneman and Tversky 1972: 444)

Given this reasoning, it is not difficult to conclude that heuristics are poor substitutes for more deliberate, logical decision making. However, even the leaders of the heuristics and biases program do not go that far. In fact, Daniel Kahneman, with Barbara Fredrickson (Fredrickson and Kahneman 1993), suggest their own heuristic—the peak-end rule—that says that a "good first approximation" of the value to a person of an experience is the simple average of the most extreme affect during the episode and the affect experienced near its end. So, we could measure Benjamin's enjoyment of a Madonna concert by what he thought was the best part of the show (say, the tribute to Michael Jackson) plus the encore (which may be why performers have encores and save their best songs for last).

Gerd Gigerenzer and his team make an even stronger argument—that heuristics are efficient ways to make decisions and in certain situations can lead to more accurate decisions than when decision makers have more information at their disposal (Gigerenzer and Gaissmaier 2011). They advocate the use of what they call "fast and frugal" methods to make decisions quickly and accurately. Examples of fast and frugal heuristics are "Take the first," meaning choose the first thing that comes into your mind about the issue at hand; and "Take the best," meaning choose based on the single best reason you can think of (regardless of the number of reasons—or their relative importance—on either side of the issue) (Gigerenzer, Todd, and ABC Research Group 1999).

How do heuristics work? How can we make better decisions with less information? Gigerenzer argues that there is an inverse-U-shaped relationship between decision accuracy and the amount of information, time, or computational power available. We would all do a better job in decision making if we went from a situation of no information, no time, and no ability to calculate to one with some information, some time to consider it, and a way to do so. However, at some point more

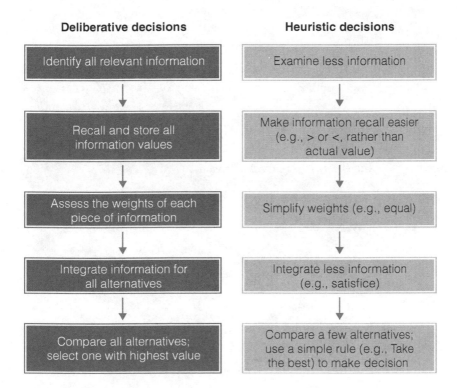

FIGURE 6.1

Comparing decision algorithms.

SOURCE: Shah, A. K., & Oppenheimer, D. M. (2008). Heuristics made easy: An effort-reduction framework. *Psychological Bulletin*, 134(2), 207–222.

information overwhelms us, more time just gives us more opportunity to consider more options, and computational power becomes an enabler (in the worst sense of the word). The result is analysis paralysis, frustration, fear of making the wrong decision, and probably a wrong decision.

Two psychologists at Princeton recently developed a framework for understanding heuristics, which is summarized in Figure 6.1 (Shah and Oppenheimer 2008). They contrast deliberative decisions (in particular, what is known as the "weighted additive rule") with heuristic decisions. In a deliberative decision, decision makers must identify and consider all information relevant to the issue at hand, then give a weight to each piece of information (based on its importance in making the decision), aggregate the weighted values of the information, compare all the alternatives, and make a decision. They contend that all heuristics use at least one of the methods shown on the right-hand side of the figure to reduce the amount of effort required to make a decision. As a result, heuristics save us information, time, and/or computational power to make decisions that may be as good as those that employ the entire armamentarium of decision analysis. Finally, they point out that there is a direct connection between the heuristic/deliberative decision making algorithms and System 1/System 2 thinking that we discussed in Chapter 4.

ANOMALY 16: *How can a physician diagnose a problem by spending only a short time with a patient, often without lab work or images? And why is this so unnerving to patients?*

There are too many [heuristics] to count, but many of them are so ingrained that we hardly think of them. Examples: fever + stiff neck = meningitis until proven otherwise. Amenorrhea in a woman = pregnancy until proven otherwise. Pleuritic chest pain + hemoptysis + dyspnea = pulmonary embolus until proven otherwise etc. . . . There are hundreds of them that we go through, often without thinking, when taking a history, examining a patient, and otherwise generating a management plan. (Stephen D. Sisson, MD, associate professor, internal medicine, Johns Hopkins University School of Medicine)

One day I naïvely asked Steve Sisson, my internist, whether he ever used heuristics in his clinical practice. His reply revealed that, in some sense, practicing medicine is all about using heuristics. When I later asked him how he learned these heuristics, he said that for him only 10 percent was from formal medical training or reading, 60 percent came from other health professionals and "being on the wards and watching things play out," and 30 percent was from his personal experience. To understand why Dr. Sisson and other physicians use heuristics, consider this story that he told me about one of his first nights as an intern. He had diagnosed and admitted a patient with community-acquired pneumonia, then "spent like forty-five minutes trying to think through what was the appropriate antibiotic coverage." He then called the senior resident to report on the case and discuss a management plan. "And before I even said anything, she said, 'So you put the patient on cefuroxime and erythromycin, right? Because that's what we do for everybody with community-acquired pneumonia.' And, you know, she said it without batting an eye. I can tell you that the next hundred patients I admitted with community-acquired pneumonia I spent microseconds thinking about antibiotic selection because I had a heuristic for management of that."

Dr. Sisson did say that there were several books that he relied on for heuristics. For abdominal pain, his bible is *Cope's Early Diagnosis of the Acute Abdomen* (Silen and Cope 2010). On page 76 we are told that the symptoms for appendicitis "almost always occur" in the following order: pain (usually epigastric or umbilical); anorexia, nausea, or vomiting; tenderness in the abdomen or pelvis; fever; and raised white blood count. On page 29 we learn that "the attitude [of the patient] in bed is noteworthy. . . . With extensive peritonitis, the knees are frequently drawn up to relax the abdominal tension. . . . Patients with pain of pancreatic or retroperitoneal origin often prefer the sitting to the recumbent position."

This approach to diagnosis was confirmed to me by Dr. Edward Bessman, chairman of the Department of Emergency Medicine at Johns Hopkins Bayview Medical Center. As Dr. Bessman put it, "We see the first ten minutes of everything," so the clinicians need to diagnose and treat the 60,000 patients who come through the emergency department quickly and accurately. He cited the "Ottawa Ankle Rules" (OHRI Emergency Medicine Research n.d.), which were created to help emergency physicians determine whether to order an X-ray for a patient with an ankle injury. He also said that he does something similar to what *Cope's* suggests regarding the attitude of the patient. In fact, he says that he can pick up "a whole lot of cues" the instant he enters an exam room: the look and smell of the patient, the sound of the patient's respiration, even what the other people in the room are doing (for example, if the nurse looks calm or anxious). He learned none of these cues in medical school but rather "around the campfire" and—more significantly—during the first six months of postresident clinical practice. When he started, he thought that "everything was important" but quickly learned that "you can't think of everything at once"; you have to decide what to think of first, and heuristics allowed him to do that. Dr. Bessman pointed out, though, that the sign of a good clinician is to push the less important information aside but not remove it entirely (in case the original diagnosis is not correct). After all, with 60,000 patient visits in a given year, some are bound to have uncommon ailments.

If heuristics are effective at Johns Hopkins, one would think that they should not be controversial. Not so. The medical profession has debated the usefulness of heuristics for decades. One of the most famous examples of the untoward effects of heuristics was reported in 1945 (Bakwin 1945). At that time the rule of thumb was that about half of children need their tonsils removed. A national child health organization surveyed a group of 1,000 eleven-year-olds in New York City; 61 percent had had their tonsils removed. The remaining 39 percent were examined by a group of physicians, who recommended 45 percent of the children for tonsillectomy; the remainder were examined by yet another group of physicians, who recommended that 46 percent of this smaller group have their tonsils removed; finally, the 116 remaining children were examined by a third group of physicians, who recommended that 43 percent undergo the surgery, so that, in the end, all but 65 of the 1,000 original children were recommended to have their tonsils removed. Clearly, this was a case of heuristics gone wild.

The benefits of heuristics and bounded rationality to a busy clinician in primary care or the emergency department are obvious. How else can a primary care physician see the twenty-five to thirty patient visits per day the practice needs to stay financially viable, and how else can an emergency department process the 200 patients who can come through its doors on a given day? As Dr. Sisson told me, a general internist sees "a lot of the same things over and over again," so heuristics are a natural device to use. Nevertheless, the use of heuristics can be unsettling to the patient. Let's return to our friend Benjamin, who has been drinking a lot of water these days, and getting up to go to the bathroom three and four times a night. At first, he thought the thirst was the result of his new vigorous exercise routine, but it has continued even though he has slacked off the exercise the past couple of weeks. Good news, though:

He has been losing weight, even though he has been eating more. His girlfriend, Elaine, convinces him to call his doctor, although he doesn't like to complain or to bother his family physician, who seems to be very busy. He dutifully makes the appointment, takes time off from work, and drives to the medical office building; after checking in at registration, he waits fifteen minutes, is called into an exam room and waits another ten minutes. His anxiety level is growing by the time his physician enters the room. After twenty seconds of chitchat, she asks him what's wrong. He tells her of his symptoms. She lets him continue talking for a minute, then examines him for another minute, then declares that he has Type II diabetes and presents her recommended treatment plan. Total encounter time: four minutes, thirty seconds. Benjamin is both amazed, and a little put off, that a diagnosis of such import can be made in such a short time—and without a battery of tests.

If Benjamin were to ask his physician why she suspects Type II diabetes, she would probably reply that she has seen numerous cases like this. If he were to persist and ask her to show him the medical evidence that these symptoms always mean diabetes, she would admit that she does not have the evidence at her fingertips but reassures him that she is very confident that her diagnosis is correct. As it turns out, there really are no formal studies that demonstrate definitively the sensitivity and specificity of the relationship among thirst, frequent urination, and weight loss, but the heuristic is listed in one of her (and Dr. Sisson's) key references, *Sapira's Art & Science of Bedside Diagnosis* (Orient and Sapira 2000). And, as Dr. Sisson told me, the connection is "just so obvious," and he estimates that one-third of his patients have adult-onset diabetes.

In a sense, the different perspectives of physician and patient to heuristics can be explained by the behavioral economics concept of framing. The physician views the patient visit as one of twenty-five that she will have on a given day, one of 5,000 in a year. As Steve Sisson indicated, this physician will see largely the same array of symptoms day in, day out, so that there are few surprises. Not that it is boring per se, but the cases are mostly ordinary. If she is like Dr. Sisson, "one of the things I really enjoy is when I see something that's a little bit off," but for the most part the patient presentations will be as expected. In these circumstances, using System 1 and a set of heuristics is an efficient and accurate mechanism. In Gerd Gigerenzer's terms, fast and frugal wins the day.

But consider the encounter from the patient's perspective. Benjamin has never been around anyone who was developing diabetes and certainly is not expecting that he would contract it. To him, his symptoms before seeing the physician are worrisome and unexplained. He does not want to be a case study in a medical journal, but he anticipates that the physician will need to work a bit to find the right diagnosis. After all, doesn't it take Gregory House and his medical team hours of discussion and tests and patient encounters before reaching the final—and correct—diagnosis? In fact, experiments in behavioral economics have demonstrated that consumers often suffer from input bias, in which they systematically associate the quantity of resources used to produce a good or service with the quality of that good or service, especially when it is hard to measure actual quality (Chinander and Schweitzer 2003). So when his physician spends less than five minutes with him, Benjamin suspects that she is just too busy and says the first thing that comes into her mind (which, in a way, is what she does). What he does not realize is that his physician's training and experience are what allow her to internalize and apply hundreds of heuristics almost without thinking (at least, System 2 thinking). It is not that she is shortchanging Benjamin or minimizing his condition; the "work" of diagnosis has been done long before Benjamin or his physician entered the exam room.

Admittedly, this is an idealized depiction of a physician–patient encounter. A physician in a busy practice may be an outstanding diagnostician, but the explosion of medical knowledge is so daunting for even the most well-meaning clinician that she might be led astray by outdated heuristics. An editorial in the *Journal of the American Medical Association* (Shaneyfelt 2001) estimated that a general internist would need to read twenty medical journal articles per day to maintain her current level of knowledge, and that two-thirds of internists could not pass board certification exams fifteen years after their certifications. Combine these grim statistics with patient input bias, and you have a situation where "fast and frugal" is no longer the best way to practice.

ANOMALY 17: *Why do many physicians take a long time to adopt a new procedure, drug regimen, or treatment protocol that has demonstrated efficacy? In particular, why don't physicians wash their hands as frequently as they should?*

In 1847 Ignaz Semmelweis was a twenty-nine-year-old physician who had recently been appointed as an assistant to the director of the maternity clinic at the prestigious Vienna General Hospital. Dr. Semmelweis was disturbed by the persistently high incidence of puerperal fever among the patients who had just given birth. At the time obstetricians had a variety of explanations for the disease: inadequate ventilation, too much blood, "stagnation of the circulation," protracted labor, and death of the fetus. Spurred by the death of a colleague with similar symptoms as in puerperal fever, Semmelweis hypothesized that there was a singular cause of the disease, which physicians in the clinic transmitted when they failed to wash their hands properly as they went from dissecting cadavers to examining patients. He had all the physicians wash their hands thoroughly in a solution of chloride of lime before treating patients. Almost immediately, the patient mortality rate dropped by over 80 percent. Surprisingly (at least to us in the twenty-first century), his findings were largely criticized or ignored by the clinicians at the General Hospital and elsewhere for decades, despite replication in other hospitals. It was not that physicians were ignorant of the benefits of washing their hands as they moved between tasks; the issue was whether washing more diligently, and with the chlorine solution, was that important in preventing the spread of disease (Carter and Carter 1994).

Hospital, and even national, politics certainly played a role in the professional rejection of Semmelweis's findings. However, the real reason was that his hypothesis, that decaying organic matter was either the cause or the carrier of the disease, contradicted the prevailing theory of disease propagation, which focused on "dangerous vapors" or "miasma" in the air. It was only after this theory was supplanted by the germ theory of disease that Semmelweis's results were truly accepted by the medical profession. The initial reactions of physicians to Semmelweis's findings can be explained, at least in part, by some concepts of behavioral economics that we have already discussed. Physicians at the time were heavily invested in the existing medical paradigm, so the endowment effect was very powerful; to dislodge the paradigm would require a lot more than the contradictory results of a single, albeit dramatic, experiment. As a result, clinicians used a heuristic that not only worked (from their perspective) but was superior to earlier treatment methods: Because disease is caused by environmental factors, they should focus on improving ventilation and reducing patient density in hospitals.

Now, fast-forward to the present time. The germ theory of disease in general, and Dr. Semmelweis's findings about clinician hand washing in particular, have been the reigning medical paradigm for over 140 years. Yet physicians wash their hands, on average, less than half of the time when they should. For instance, a systematic review by the World Health Organization of seventy-six studies conducted between 1981 and 2008 found hand-washing adherence among health care workers to be 38 percent (World Health Organization 2009). Over the past several decades there have been major initiatives to increase adherence rates, most recently by the Centers for Disease Control and Prevention (Centers for Disease Control and Prevention 2002), the Joint Commission (The Joint Commission 2009), and the World Health Organization (World Health Organization 2009). None of these has generated sustainable results.

Why have health professionals not been adherent to what is widely recognized as "the simplest, most effective measure for preventing nosocomial infections" (Pittet 2001: 234)? Multiple studies have revealed that objectively observed nonadherence is positively related to whether the health professional is a physician (rather than a nurse); male; working in intensive care, surgery, or the emergency department; engaged in activities with high risk of cross-transmission of disease; working in an understaffed or overcrowded unit; and having a high number of opportunities for good high hygiene (World Health Organization 2009). Many of these factors suggest that nonadherence is highest in those situations in which it is most critical. Clinicians themselves report that they do not always adhere to hand-washing guidelines because of the irritation or dryness of hand-washing agents, inconveniently located sinks, lack of time, lack of knowledge of hand-washing guidelines or protocols, forgetfulness, the priority of patient needs, lack of institutional promotion, lack of sanctions to nonadherents, and lack of institutional safety climate.

What are we to make of this behavior? Certainly physicians and other health professionals care about their patients and do not wish to harm them. Why would they ignore 140 years of history and evidence? Would forgetfulness or concern about dry, chapped hands be sufficient reason to not adhere to widely recognized hand-washing regimens? The answer, as you might imagine, is not so simple. As we saw early in this chapter, physicians employ heuristics that work for them and will maintain those heuristics until they have compelling reasons to change. So they have positive attitudes toward hand hygiene after contact with patients, before using intravenous devices, even after contact with different sites on the same patient (Pittet et al. 2004). They do wash their hands before and after significant encounters with patients, but not as much as they think they do. (One study found that physicians estimated their hand-washing rates to be 73 percent, when the observed frequency was really 9 percent [Handwashing Liaison Group 1999]).

The lack of salience of the consequences of nonadherence adds to the problem. That is, it is not immediately obvious to a physician that he will be transmitting disease if he fails to wash his hands after every single patient encounter. After an encounter in which he has handled hazardous material or come into contact with bodily fluids, yes; after an ordinary, uneventful follow-up visit with minimal physical contact, not so much. And with the severe time constraints that many physicians practice under, hand washing after each patient encounter will only add to the late hours he is already keeping. So if he can engage in a little optimism or overconfidence bias and get through the day without major incident, then so be it. After all, he can think, there are so many different ways in which patients can contract hospital-acquired infections, his hand washing after every two or three patients cannot make that much of a difference.

Thus, the lack of full compliance with hand-washing regimens can be explained not by physician callousness, arrogance, or ignorance, but by the natural working of behavioral economics—heuristics, salience, and bias. We will consider ways to ameliorate this behavior later in this chapter.

FRAMING, BIASES, AND AFFECT: WHY PHYSICIANS MAY BE AS SUSCEPTIBLE AS PATIENTS

The public stereotype of physicians (albeit not exclusively) has been either brilliant scientists or humanitarian healers. (Think of the real Michael DeBakey, Jonas Salk, and Benjamin Carson or the fictitious Martin Arrowsmith, James Kildare, and Hawkeye Pierce.) They might be dismayed to discover that physicians are as vulnerable as patients are to the forces identified by behavioral psychology and economics. We shall consider here some salient examples of seemingly anomalous behavior of physicians.

ANOMALY 18: *Why do physicians' clinical decisions depend on how the options are framed?*

We start with framing. In Chapter 4, we discussed the study by Barbara McNeil and her colleagues that looked at how study participants made hypothetical choices for the treatment of lung cancer. As you will recall, each of the participant categories—middle-aged men with chronic health conditions, Stanford MBA students, and practicing radiologists—made significantly different choices between radiation and surgery depending on whether the outcomes were presented in a survival frame or a mortality frame. That radiologists, trained to be objective, dispassionate professionals, were no better than chronic care patients or bright students in interpreting the data suggests the universality of the power of framing.

Let's turn to another study that specifically examined physician behavior in a potentially more realistic setting. In perhaps the most famous study (Redelmeier and Shafir 1995), 287 family physicians in Ontario were presented with a medical scenario involving a hypothetical patient of theirs: a sixty-seven-year-old farmer with chronic right hip pain. The physicians were told that the diagnosis was osteoarthritis and that they had been treating the patient with a variety of nonsteroidal anti-inflammatory agents (such as aspirin and naproxen), none of which had worked sufficiently. The physicians had decided to refer the patient to an orthopedic consultant for possible hip replacement surgery. Half of the physicians were told that just before making the referral they checked the drug formulary and found that there was one medication that had not yet been tried, ibuprofen. The other half were told that they had found two medications that had not yet been tried, ibuprofen and piroxicam. The question to the physicians: What do you do? The researchers found that many more physicians (72 percent compared to 53 percent) chose to continue referring to the orthopedist without starting any medication when the option was two new medications rather than one. Let's look at it another way. When faced with a choice of referring the patient to the orthopedic surgeon with or without prescribing ibuprofen, 47 percent of physicians chose to prescribe ibuprofen, but when faced with a choice of prescribing nothing, ibuprofen, or piroxicam only 28 percent choose to prescribe ibuprofen or piroxicam. That is, the availability of more options led the physicians to make no choice.

As with much of what we have discussed in this book, mainstream economists would have a hard time explaining this behavior. After all, why would the addition of an alternative (that is, piroxicam) change a physician's choice of the one medication—if the physician were not going to choose piroxicam (what economists call the "irrelevance of independent alternatives")? Behavioral economists know better, because what we have here is the confluence of a number of powerful behavioral psychology/economics forces. We have the "fewer choices are better than more choices" work of Sheena Iyengar combined with the bounded rationality of Herbert Simon. The physicians in this study clearly made different choices when their treatment alternatives were more limited. We have the endowment effect of Kahneman, Knetsch, and Thaler, in which most of the physicians chose the status quo option of no new medications. Finally, we have the loss aversion of Kahneman and Tversky, in which the physicians were reluctant to make a decision that had both positive and negative aspects.

The most disquieting aspect of the study of Ontario physicians is that physicians face multiple—and growing numbers of—medical options in their practice. New drugs (both branded and generic), new and improved diagnostic tests, and alternative treatment modalities confront practitioners who must make dozens of medical decisions every day. It is not surprising, then, that they turn to heuristics to guide their actions. The challenge will be for them (and us as patients) to ensure that their heuristics are "fast and frugal"—and correct.

ANOMALY 19: *Why do physicians keep practicing defensive medicine even in states with malpractice reform?*

For decades physicians in the United States have been plagued by worries that each encounter that they might have with a patient could result in a lawsuit for malpractice. The physician fails to diagnose a cancer soon enough for treatment, and the patient dies; he does not correctly interpret a lab result and prescribe the right medication for high blood pressure, and the patient dies of heart failure; she accidentally cuts an artery during surgery, and the patient suffers an inordinate loss of blood. Physicians have seen waves of malpractice crises throughout their careers, as both the number of lawsuits and the amount of premiums have skyrocketed, especially for high-risk specialties. Calls are regularly made for reform, and many states have enacted changes to the system (such as monetary caps on damages or creation of a statewide patient compensation fund) (Studdert, Mello, and Brennan 2004).

In the absence of malpractice reform, many physicians engage in (or say they engage in) "defensive medicine." That is, they order tests or perform procedures that may have no real benefit to the patient but will protect the physician if her judgment and actions are questioned when a patient suffers an adverse outcome. Physicians argue that defensive medicine only increases the cost of health care and that one of the key elements of comprehensive health reform must be malpractice reform. (The Patient Protection and Affordable Care Act passed in 2010 did little in this regard.) One would expect, then, that defensive medicine—or, at least, physician fears of malpractice lawsuits—should be lower in those states that have enacted meaningful tort reform. As a recent article in *Health Affairs* demonstrates, this is not the case (Carrier et al. 2010). Using a well-validated national survey of 4,700 practicing physicians, the researchers found a pervasive concern about malpractice risk among physicians: Seventy-eight percent agreed with the statement, "Relying on clinical judgment rather than on technology to make a diagnosis is becoming risky because of the threat of malpractice suits," and over 60 percent agreed that they ordered tests or second opinions to reduce the risk of being sued. The researchers noted that the one-third of the states with the lowest malpractice risk for physicians had only 38 percent of the paid claims per 1,000 physicians, 44 percent of the average payment per paid claim, and 34 percent of the malpractice premiums as the one-third of the states with the highest malpractice risk. Yet the malpractice concerns of those physicians in the low-malpractice-risk states were remarkably similar to those in the high-malpractice-risk states: a composite malpractice concern score of 63.5 percent versus 67.8 percent.

To a mainstream economist, these results are puzzling: Physicians should be adjusting their own probabilities of being sued to those in their local environment; to do otherwise is nonrational. To a behavioral economist, the results are perfectly understandable. The first concepts that come to mind are affect and salience. Recall from Chapter 4 the hypothetical electric shock experiments (Rottenstreich and Hsee 2001) in which the study participants drastically overweighted low probability events that were especially vivid. Clearly, malpractice risk holds the same kind of affect and salience for physicians. They are trying to do their best for every patient, and a malpractice suit can be interpreted as an assault on their professionalism and their identity. It is no wonder, then, that even a malpractice premium that is two-thirds lower fails to assuage a physician's fear of malpractice suits.

We can appeal to other behavioral economics concepts to explain physician concerns about malpractice lawsuits. Take the availability heuristic, for example. For the most part, a physician will not be measuring malpractice risk by the actual statistics but from the experiences of colleagues in her practice, the medical staff at the hospital, and in her specialty nationwide. One study (Lawthers et al. 1992) found that physicians overestimate their colleagues' probability of being sued by a factor of three. So an obstetrician-gynecologist, even in a low-malpractice-risk state, will know and work with other obstetrician-gynecologists who have been sued for malpractice. And she will have colleagues nationwide, many in high-risk states, whose experiences she will hear about at professional conferences. Despite the fact that 70 percent of claims will be closed with no payment, the anticipated pain of the suit itself will be enough to trigger her behavior.

Finally, we can appeal to the concepts of the "chagrin factor" or regret bias to explain physician behavior. Renowned epidemiologist Alvan Feinstein criticized the advocacy of quantitative decision analysis in medicine, arguing that it failed to account for the fact that many clinicians use a much simpler, qualitative decision mechanism that seems to serve them well. That is, they identify the clinical alternative that would lead to the most chagrin if it occurred and avoid that option (Feinstein 1985). In effect, he was saying that the System 2 thinking inherent in quantitative medical decision making was an incomplete picture of how clinicians actually work. The chagrin factor, or what others (Hozo and Djulbegovic 2008) have called "acceptable regret," is nothing more than a heuristic, with all the pluses and minuses of a heuristic. In the case of physician fear of malpractice suits, chagrin also explains why physicians practice defensive medicine, even in states for which the legal risk is relatively low.

ANOMALY 20: *Why does physician adherence to clinical guidelines decline when financial incentives are removed?*

Health policy makers in the United States have been frustrated by the significant variability in health care expenditures in different communities and the apparent reluctance of the medical profession to address this unevenness. (There will be more on this in Chapter 7.) In addition, they (and physicians themselves) have been frustrated that physicians who deliver higher-quality care are not paid any more than those who provide lower-quality care. In part, payers have paid physicians the same amount because they lacked the metrics to measure clinical and service quality. These problems have led to two major initiatives in the past decade, the development of "pay-for-performance" compensation systems to incentivize physicians to provide better service and clinical quality, and the creation and dissemination of clinical guidelines to reduce the unnecessary variability in care.

Several health care organizations have combined these initiatives into one. Over the past decade, the Kaiser Permanente organization has created dozens of quality indicators. It has experimented with adding, and then dropping, financial incentives directed at medical facilities (but not specifically to individual physicians). A recent article (Lester et al. 2010) explored the impact of adding and removing financial incentives for four clinical quality indicators at thirty-five medical facilities in Kaiser's Northern California region from 1999 to 2007. When an incentive was added for the control of hypertension, the percentage of patients with systolic blood pressure below 140 mm Hg increased from 58 to 78 percent. (The incentive was not switched off during the study period.) Incentives were added in 2001 for the control of HbA1c levels for diabetic patients; patient adherence jumped from 47 to 70 percent. Medical facilities were incentivized to screen for diabetic retinopathy for adults at the beginning of the period and removed in 2004; adherence rates increased from 85 to 88 percent during the incentivized period but declined gradually to 80 percent after the incentives ended. Finally, financial incentives for cervical cancer screening were in place at the beginning of the period, removed for five years, and then reinstituted for the last two years of the study. Consistent with the other findings, screening rates rose slightly during the incentive period (from 77 to 78 percent), gradually declined to 74 percent when there were no financial incentives, and increased slightly (to 75 percent) when financial incentives returned.

These findings are similar to others that have found that financial incentives have at best a modest, and only short-term, impact on quality of health care (Scott et al. 2011). The questions are why, and why does removal of the incentives lead to a reduction in clinical quality (a reduction that sometimes leads to lower clinical quality than before the introduction of the incentive system)? The behavioral economics answer lies in the discussion we introduced in Chapter 3 about intrinsic and extrinsic motivation and the crowding out phenomenon. As Edward Deci has shown throughout his extensive career (Deci and Ryan 1985; Deci, Koestner, and Ryan 1999), both intrinsic motivation and extrinsic motivation are important in influencing human behavior. Professionals (such as physicians) are primarily motivated by intrinsic factors; however, they can also be motivated by extrinsic factors (such as money). Deci's primary insights for our purposes are that once extrinsic motivation is introduced, it may crowd out intrinsic motivation; in addition, if the extrinsic motivation is removed, the intrinsic motivation will not return to the previous level, and behavior may actually be worse than before the extrinsic motivation was introduced.

Such behavior makes little or no sense to the mainstream economist. Incentives are incentives, and people and organizations will respond to achieve their own interests. Behavioral economists argue that people and organizations are not calculating machines. Not only do they need time to adjust to changing circumstances, they likely will not return to their original behavior when incentives are removed. We can appeal to the concept of heuristics to explain the behavior of the physicians at Kaiser Permanente. Prior to the implementation of the financial incentives for each of the four quality indicators, physicians most likely were using heuristics to determine which patients needed intervention to meet the target values. However, once the financial incentives were put in place, they found that those heuristics were no longer applicable and had to use System 2 thinking to determine a new treatment protocol. Once that protocol was in place, physicians would most likely reach a new plateau for the quality metric and stay there. However, if the extrinsic motivator—the financial incentive—were removed before the physicians could internalize it as a heuristic, they might return to their prior heuristic. In this case, the intervention would not become ingrained into the physicians' System 1 decision-making process.

SO WHAT? WHAT CAN BE DONE TO INFLUENCE HOW PRACTITIONERS MAKE DECISIONS?

So far in this chapter, we have found that physicians do not always conform to the stereotype of brilliant scientists or compassionate healers. Although it is not surprising that the reality does not match the ideal, it is concerning that physicians are as vulnerable to decision biases as the rest of us. At the same time, it is also clear that physicians make lots of good medical decisions, using what Dr. Hilliard Jason has called "the process of making adequate decisions with inadequate information" (Elstein, Shulman, and Sprafka 1978: vii). In fact, they can diagnose many patient problems in a remarkably short amount of time—almost too short for some patients.

That leads us to the question: What can be done to improve the decision making of physicians, so that they make fewer mistakes and provide better care? One immediate answer is that physicians need to be more deliberate and use System 2/analytical thinking instead of System 1/ heuristics. This advice is at the heart of many books (for example, Sox 1988; Kassirer, Wong, and Kopelman 2010) and journal articles (for example, Pauker and Kassirer 1980; 1987) on medical decision making. Nevertheless, there is growing awareness that the pressures of clinical practice and the seemingly inherent limitations on cognitive processes make such advice moot. Physicians cannot afford—from either a patient-care or a financial perspective—to use only System 2; they must use System 1. In that regard, Dr. Pat Croskerry, who has investigated the pitfalls of heuristic thinking in medicine, has proposed what he calls "a universal model of diagnostic reasoning" (Croskerry 2009). In this model, a physician engages both System 1 and System 2 reasoning. If a patient presents with symptoms that the physician recognizes, he uses the "fast and frugal" System 1 process; if the physician does not recognize the symptoms, then System 2 is used. Over time, through experience, System 2 processing defaults to System 1 for most patient presentations. A key element of Croskerry's model is that physicians must allow either system to override the other. Thus, the physician might use System 1 to diagnose shingles from a presentation of rash, but the physician needs to be alert to aberrant or atypical features that would indicate another issue. (Remember Ed Bessman's dictum of putting aside less important information but still keeping the information available if needed.) By integrating heuristics and System 1 thinking into recognized physician decision making, Dr. Croskerry legitimizes what physicians already do and—perhaps more importantly—sanctions research to improve this side of physician thinking.

So, instead of fighting a futile battle against a virtually unstoppable force, we can accept that biases will occur. In fact, we can embrace decision-making biases and help physicians to work around them. For example, physicians bring into play the status quo bias when they continue to use diagnostic and treatment heuristics that have become outdated. As we noted earlier, practicing physicians have a difficult time in keeping up with the burgeoning medical literature. Researchers need to make new scientific findings more salient to the individual practitioner. For example, when the U.S. Preventive Services Task Force released its recommendations regarding screening mammographies, it could have created a series of short videos that showed a physician discussing the new guidelines with different kinds of patients (for example, a forty-six-year-old with no family history of breast cancer, a forty-year-old whose mother and aunt contracted breast cancer, and a seventy-year-old who had been getting biennial mammograms for decades). By making the scientific information more salient and relevant to the clinician, the Task Force would improve the chances that its recommendations break through the physician's entrenched heuristics.

Likewise, because physicians are susceptible to framing effects it is possible that their behavior can be steered in the right direction. A recent article (Grant and Hofmann 2011) found that physicians improved their adherence to hand hygiene in the hospital from 37 percent to 54 percent if the messaging focused on the impact of hand washing on patients ("Hand hygiene prevents patients from catching diseases") rather than on the physicians themselves ("Hand hygiene prevents you from catching diseases"). That is, the framing of the issue away from physicians and onto their patients performed a bit of psychological jujitsu by taking advantage of physicians' intrinsic concern for their patients while avoiding having to confront physicians about their overconfidence regarding their invulnerability to disease.

Most physicians recognize the value of System 2 thinking and the use of decision analysis tools. Many do not use these tools because they are awkward to use, especially during a patient encounter, which means that either physicians will not use them at all or they will use them by memory. (In a speech I heard Don Berwick give several years ago, he said, "Expecting physicians to practice the way they do now is like expecting travel agents to memorize the Official Airline Guide.") The answer is to create easy-to-use, unobtrusive decision support systems for physicians to use on a tablet computer or other handheld device. A large number of studies have demonstrated that computer-based decision support systems perform better than physicians. Unfortunately, under the category of "No good deed goes unpunished," several research studies have shown that patients rate the diagnostic ability of physicians who use such systems as significantly lower than those physicians who use no decision aids (Arkes, Shaffer, and Medow 2007). Professor James Wolf at Illinois State University, who studies physician adoption of technology, suggests a reason: "Patients object when they ask their doctor a question and then she or he immediately types in the question into their laptop and then reads back the answer. It gives patients the feeling that they just paid a $25 copay to have someone Google something for them" (Shaw 2011: 42). So we will need to overcome patients' input bias and demonstrate the value of decision support systems in their own care.

A final strategy for improving physicians' decision making comes from a systematic review of 235 analyses of strategies to disseminate and implement clinical guidelines for physician practices (Grol and Grimshaw 2003). The researchers found that interventions that focused on a single intervention—education, information, reminders, performance feedback, financial reward—had, at best, only short-term effects. However, most of the multifaceted interventions that they reviewed had "pronounced" effects on physician practice patterns and patient outcomes. The trick, then, is to find those combinations of strategies that can effect significant and long-term improvements in physician decision making. This is not an easy task, but it is likely to be more successful than trying to debias the medical profession.

UNDERSTANDING THE BEHAVIOR
OF PHYSICIANS: TRY THIS AT HOME
This chapter has described how physicians use System 1 and System 2 thinking to make diagnostic and treatment decisions. We have shown that physicians are subject to cognitive biases but that many of the heuristics that they employ are useful and accurate.

The following scenarios are taken from research studies on physician behavior. For each scenario, predict how the physicians behaved. (Note: The study subjects don't always succumb to a bias.)

1. Physicians were asked to consider two alternative surgical treatments for colon cancer (shown below). Half were asked what treatment they would recommend for one of their patients; the other half were asked what treatment they would choose for themselves. Which treatment would they choose, and would they choose differently for their patients and themselves (Ubel, Angott, and Zikmund-Fisher 2011)?

    a. Surgery 1 cures colon cancer without any complications in 80 percent of patients. It does not cure the cancer in 16 percent of patients, and these patients die of colon cancer within two years. In addition, 1 percent of patients are cured of their cancer but must undergo a colostomy; 1 percent are cured of their cancer but experience chronic diarrhea; 1 percent are cured of their cancer but experience intermittent bowel obstruction; and 1 percent are cured of their cancer but experience a wound infection.

    b. Surgery 2 cures cancer without any complications in 80 percent of patients. It does not cure the cancer in 20 percent of patients, and these patients die of colon cancer within two years.

2. Anesthesiologists were asked to rate the appropriateness of care in twenty-one cases involving adverse anesthetic outcomes, such as airway obstruction, aspiration of gastric contents, convulsion, difficult intubation, eye injury, and ulnar nerve injury. The anesthesiologists were given a detailed six-page abstract for each case. Half of the anesthesiologists were told that adverse outcome was temporary; half were told it was permanent. Did the anesthesiologists rate the appropriateness differently based on outcome, and, if so, by how much (Caplan, Posner, and Cheney 1991)?

3. Resident physicians in primary care were asked to recommend decisions in four medical and four nonmedical scenarios. Each scenario was varied by the amount of resources already invested in the current plan and whether the current plan had been initiated by the

current decision maker or someone else. To what extent—if any—
would the residents' decisions depend on how many resources had
already been used and who was making the current decision (Bornstein, Emler, and Chapman 1999)?

a. *Medical scenario (with variations in parentheses)*: Ms. S., a
fifty-four-year-old female with a history of heartburn, comes
to Dr. Gordon's office. Ms. S. had an upper GI series done six
weeks ago that showed that she had gastroesophageal reflux.
(Ms. S. states that six weeks earlier her daughter's doctor ordered an upper GI series on her daughter that showed that she
had gastroesophageal reflux.) Dr. Gordon (her daughter's doctor) gave her a prescription for Stopcid, an antisecretory medicine, which she has to take twice a day and is associated with
some drowsiness. She purchased a four-month supply for $40
($400). Ms. S. has been taking the medicine for two months and
returns to Dr. Gordon's office because she still has heartburn
symptoms and is tired all the time. What should Dr. Gordon do?

b. *Nonmedical scenario (with variations in parentheses)*: Agatha
decides that she wants to take cello lessons (Agatha's husband
decides to give Agatha a cello and cello lessons for her birthday.) She (He) spends $100 ($1,000) on a beginner cello and an
additional $40 ($200) on the first month (three months) of cello
lessons. After one month (three months) of lessons, Agatha real-
izes that she no longer enjoys the cello and wants to stop taking
lessons. That is, it is almost certain that if Agatha signs up for
more lessons, she will not enjoy them and will never enjoy playing the cello. What should Agatha do?

4. Physicians were divided into five groups and asked to review the
same medical case. One group was asked to make an estimate of the
probability of four possible diagnoses. The other four groups were
asked to do the same thing, but each of these groups was told that a
different diagnosis was correct. The question to the reader is as follows: Would knowing the "correct" diagnosis affect the physicians'
probabilities of each diagnosis (Arkes et al. 1981)?

The case: A thirty-seven-year-old male bartender had been well until he developed increasing pain in his left knee, which became hot and swollen. A few days later, pain, swelling, and heat developed in his left wrist and right knee. Examination revealed swelling, heat, and effusion in both knees and left wrist. There were no deformities. His liver was enlarged 2 cm below the costal margin. CBC was normal. ESR was 30 mm (westergren). Latex test was negative. SMA 12 was not back yet. Joint fluid contains 20,000 WBC; 80 percent polys: viscosity low. There were excess pus cells in urine. Fever was 100° F.

Possibly diagnoses: Reiter's syndrome (incomplete); poststreptococcal arthritis in an adult (rheumatic fever); gout; serum hepatitis in pre-icteric phase.

7 EXPLAINING THE CUMULATIVE IMPACT OF PHYSICIANS' DECISIONS

A joke that I have heard—and told—for decades is that the most expensive piece of medical equipment—more expensive than CT scanners or MRIs or gamma knives—is the physician's pen. With this pen, physicians trigger most of the spending in health care. In most cases, physicians use their pens to good effect, to diagnose and treat their patients and to return them to good health. But, as we saw in previous chapters, sometimes physicians prescribe drugs or order tests because patients demand them or because they use a heuristic learned long ago. Whatever the reason, the individual decisions by physicians can have a massive impact on the health care system.

In this chapter, we shall explore the interaction between what Nobel laureate Thomas Schelling has called *micromotives and macrobehavior* (Schelling 1978). Although not a behavioral economist per se, Schelling and his ideas fit nicely within the field. In particular, he advanced the notion that aggregate behavior is not simply a summation of the behavior of individuals. Rather, "people are responding to an environment that consists of other people responding to *their* environment, which consists of people responding to an environment of people's responses" (p. 14). In such a complex environment, the end result of individual micromotives may be macrobehavior that the individuals themselves would not have predicted or preferred. So, when a physician uses a heuristic in his practice to treat a patient, the result may be appropriate for the patient but have unexpected consequences for the health care system. Given the physician's fealty to the Hippocratic oath to do all he can on behalf of his patient, we should not expect that the physician will consider the macro-effects of his microbehavior. Nevertheless, as a society we need to ad-dress the macrobehavior. For example, many Americans are concerned about the millions of people in the United States without health insur-ance and (presumably) health care. Yet a recent survey of primary care physicians (Sirovich, Woloshin, and Schwartz 2011) found that 42 per-cent of respondents believed that patients within their own practice were receiving too much medical care, with only 6 percent believing that they were receiving too little care. And over a quarter of these physicians said that they were practicing more aggressively than they would like to. As we saw in Chapters 2 and 3, too much care can cause as many problems as too little care. That physicians, who have substantial influence over the amount of care provided, believe that they are providing too much care is an indication of the power of micromotives over macrobehavior.

In this chapter we will focus on two aspects of physician micro-motives that drive some curious macrobehavior: the fact that physicians in different communities practice in much different ways (despite the universality of medical knowledge and technology) and the fact that tens of thousands of patients die each year in the United States from blood-stream infections attributable to central lines—even though most of these could be avoided by the use of a simple checklist. We will also look at how some macrobehavior can influence micromotives—the power of recommendations from the U.S. Preventive Services Task Force on phy-sician behavior, despite the Task Force's lack of formal authority. With these examples we will show how the decisions and actions of individu-als are influenced by the forces explained by behavioral economics and roll up into consequences for the U.S. health care system.

THE POWER OF HEURISTICS AND BIASES TO DRIVE THE PRACTICE OF MEDICINE IN A COMMUNITY

ANOMALY 21: *Why do physicians practice differently in different communities, even though the communities may be similar?*

In the June 1, 2009, issue of *The New Yorker*, Dr. Atul Gawande (Gawande 2009) published an article, "The Cost Conundrum," which compared the costs of health care in two cities in Texas, McAllen and El Paso. He found that per capita health care costs for Medicare patients in McAllen were twice the national average and also twice what Medicare was spending for elderly patients in El Paso. In fact, per capita Medicare costs were the highest in the country, except for Miami. In one sense, this was old news. In the 1970s, Jack Wennberg and Alan Gittelsohn (Wennberg and Gittelsohn 1973) published the first study showing the wide variations in health care costs from one area of the country to another, in their case among small areas in Vermont. This effort grew into *The Dartmouth Atlas of Health Care*, created and maintained by the Dartmouth Institute for Health Policy and Clinical Practice (Dartmouth Institute for Health Policy and Clinical Practice 2011).

But three things were different in 2009. First, the article was written by an articulate physician who could explain complicated issues in an engaging way. Second, the article was published in a popular magazine, not an academic journal. Third, the election of Barack Obama in 2008 had propelled the issue of health care reform back into the public conversation, after a fifteen-year hiatus. President Obama reportedly carried Gawande's article from meeting to meeting, declaring that the problems described there were among the major reasons that comprehensive health reform was needed.

Table 7.1 shows data from the Dartmouth Atlas for selected areas in 2008 (the latest year for which data are available and two years later than the data that Dr. Gawande used for his article). There's Miami and McAllen at the top, 73 and 61 percent (respectively) above the national average. But there are other high-expenditure areas as well, such as Dearborn, MI, and St. Petersburg, FL. A number of areas cluster close to the national average: Muncie, IN (known as Middletown, USA), and Baltimore, MD (home of Johns Hopkins Medical Institutions). Almost as remarkable as the high-expenditure are the low-expenditure areas, like Dubuque, IA, and Grand Junction, CO, whose per capita Medicare costs are just three-quarters of the national average and less than half of that in Miami or McAllen. (To counter objections that are often raised with numbers such as these, the data have already been adjusted

TABLE 7.1
Medicare spending per enrollee in selected areas, 2008.

Area	Total spending	Inpatient services	Physician services
Miami, FL	$15,571	$5,008	$3,547
McAllen, TX	14,529	5,864	3,288
Monroe, LA	12,027	5,583	2,337
St. Petersburg, FL	11,341	5,400	3,600
Dearborn, MI	11,085	5,695	3,040
Munster, IN	10,906	5,709	2,908
Little Rock, AR	9,048	4,792	2,277
Muncie, IN	9,025	4,486	2,428
National average	$9,021	$4,419	$2,467
Baltimore, MD	9,016	4,403	2,562
New Haven, CT	8,963	4,567	2,662
El Paso, TX	7,868	3,585	2,139
Boise, ID	7,105	3,237	1,547
Sacramento, CA	7,056	3,478	2,101
Dubuque, IA	6,738	3,325	1,749
San Mateo County, CA	6,723	3,051	2,085
Grand Junction, CO	6,694	3,254	1,395

SOURCE: Dartmouth Institute for Health Policy and Clinical Practice 2011.

for differences in health care prices and demographics [age, sex, race] among the different areas.)

Several researchers have drilled down into the *Dartmouth Atlas* data to try to explain the disparities in expenditures. One major study published several years ago (Fisher et al. 2003a,b) compared the kinds of expenditures undertaken in those communities that were in the lowest and highest quintiles of Medicare per capita expenditures. The researchers found many more physician office visits, tests (for example, MRIs and EEGs), minor procedures (such as skin biopsies and laryngoscopies), inpatient and intensive care unit (ICU) days, and end-of-life care in the highest quintile areas compared to the lowest quintile areas. However, the areas had almost identical per capita rates of major surgery, such as coronary bypass, total hip replacement, and hernia repair.

Unfortunately, quality of care—whether calculated by process measures (such as the number of patients with acute myocardial infarction receiving reperfusion within twelve hours of hospital admission or receiving ACE inhibitors at discharge) or outcome measures (for example, risk of death or functional status)—was no different in the communities with the lowest or highest quintiles of expenditures. Finally, there were no differences between the quintiles in patient satisfaction scores, whether measured by general satisfaction with care (overall quality and accessibility) or satisfaction with the patient's usual physician (technical skills, interpersonal manner, and information giving).

Other surveys of physicians and patients reveal that these key stakeholders perceive no real differences in access or quality of care in their communities, either. One survey of over 10,000 physicians asked the respondents about their ability to obtain medically necessary services in their community for their patients (Sirovich et al. 2006). Those physicians in the highest quintile areas of Medicare expenditures were no more likely than those in the lowest quintile to report access to high-quality mental health services for their patients (32 percent compared to 33 percent) and were significantly less likely to report that they had satisfactory access to high-quality specialist referrals (66 percent compared to 79 percent) or diagnostic imaging services (70 percent compared to 83 percent). About the same proportion of physicians in high- and low-expenditure areas reported having adequate time to spend with their patients (65 percent) and being able to provide high-quality care (73 percent versus 77 percent). However, physicians in high-expenditure areas were less likely to agree that they had "the freedom to make clinical decisions that meet my patients' needs" (77 percent compared to 82 percent), the ability to maintain continuing relationships with patients "that promote the delivery of high-quality care" (62 percent versus 71 percent), and a level of communications with other physicians sufficient to ensure high-quality care (73 percent versus 83 percent).

The patient perspective is no more encouraging. A survey conducted in 2005 of 2,500 Medicare beneficiaries (Fowler et al. 2008) found that respondents in the highest per capita Medicare expenditure quintile areas reported no better perceived quality of care (on seven of ten measures) than those in the lowest quintile. The seven included receiving the medical care that they wanted, receiving the right number of tests, having physicians spend enough time with them, having physicians explain the purposes of new medications, having physicians who knew about the side effects they experienced on medications, receiving the quality of care that "most people your age get," and people in their community receiving a quality of care comparable to that of the rest of the country. Respondents in the highest quintile did report having an easier time in seeing specialists and having their physicians know about pain that they were experiencing. But, perhaps most disturbing, only 55 percent of survey respondents in the highest quintile communities rated their overall health care as either a 9 or a 10 (on a 0 to 10 scale), compared to 63 percent of those in the lowest quintile.

There are any number of reasons that have been raised to explain the disparity in Medicare spending among areas of the country—and the consequent absence of impact on access or quality of care. Dr. Gawande reported that a hospital administrator in McAllen cited the local physicians' "entrepreneurial spirit" reflected in their investments in ventures both in health care (imaging centers, outpatient surgery centers) and in the general economy (shopping malls, orange groves). "There's no lack of work ethic," he said. Gawande offered a more sinister motive, what he called "the culture of money," fostered by physicians "who see their practice primarily as a revenue stream," and as a result a medical community that "came to treat patients the way subprime-mortgage lenders treated home buyers: as profit centers." He cited one physician who said, "We took a wrong turn when doctors stopped being doctors and became businessmen." As you might imagine, the story and his argument were not well received among the physicians of McAllen.

Health economics in the neoclassical tradition has its own take on this issue. In 1974, Robert Evans (Evans 1984) articulated the theory known as "supplier-induced demand." The essence of the theory is (as we discussed in earlier chapters) that a physician acts as both a patient's agent in negotiating the health care system and as a provider of care in that system. Given the inherent asymmetry of information between physician and patient and the power of a physician to direct care, a physician has the ability to "induce demand" and, thus, to provide care that may not be necessary. So, many health economists would attribute the wide variation in practice patterns throughout the United States as a manifestation of supplier-induced demand, in which those physicians in McAllen, Texas, have just been more aggressive than those in El Paso in inducing demand. The health economics literature is replete with tests of this theory. (See, for instance, the work by Victor Fuchs [1978], Jerry Cromwell and Janet Mitchell [1986], David Dranove and Paul Wehner [1994], and Jonathan Gruber and Maria Owings [1996].) The research results have been mixed, with some strong evidence in favor but also a number of null or contrary findings.

We can use the principles of behavioral economics to shed a different light on the situation in McAllen and other communities. As Dr. Gawande pointed out, there is something different in the medical communities of McAllen and Grand Junction. The questions from a behavioral economics perspective are, how did that happen and why has it stayed that way? The renowned physician, Arnold Epstein, provides our first clue. In an editorial in the *New England Journal of Medicine* (Epstein 2010) he reflected back on his training:

In my third and fourth years of medical school at Duke University, I was totally engaged in learning clinical strategies and algorithms. . . . I learned them as an apprentice, trailing fellows and attending physicians on ward rounds and in the clinic, since the level of detail needed to guide these decisions never seemed to be in the scientific literature. After finishing medical school, I moved to Boston for house-staff training. To my great surprise, I encountered a whole new set of protocols for exactly the same conditions. Their proponents espoused them with equal vigor and certainty as my mentors at Duke, yet the strategies were often substantially different.

What the young Dr. Epstein discovered was the power of heuristics in medical decision making. Medical communities develop their own rules of thumb and practice patterns over time, even in academic medical communities supposedly driven by science and evidence-based medicine. Dr. Epstein concludes his reminiscence with the observation, "It was then that I realized the scary truth: the science behind medicine is sorely lacking, and often there is no clearly right answer." And in the absence of a right answer, a medical community finds its own answers. In Grand Junction, the answer is, "Do what is medically necessary, and no more." In McAllen, it is, "Do whatever can be done." This is not to say that there are not aggressive clinicians in Grand Junction and conservative ones in McAllen. Rather, the medical communities over time have developed—and come to accept—a style of care that allows them to achieve their goals. Remembering what we learned about heuristics in the prior chapter, good heuristics enable a physician to go through her day caring for as many patients as she can. She primarily employs System 1 thinking—supported by heuristics that she learned on the job, in the community—because it works. She finds through hallway conversations, departmental meetings at the hospital, and "curbside consults" that she is practicing a style of medicine typical in her community. The salience of observing each other's behavior is much more powerful in influencing practice decisions than reading journal articles or listening to someone from the outside come in and question their clinical habits. The retort, "You don't understand. We're different here," is not a declaration of willful ignorance, but a recognition of the power of heuristics. It suggests that utilization patterns—when to order tests, when to admit a patient to a hospital, when to choose surgery over medical treatment—will be difficult to change without compelling reasons.

Despite the power of heuristics in a medical community, there are clinical areas in which national standards prevail. Note the research described in the preceding pages that found no differences between the highest and lowest quintile communities in terms of rates of major surgery. In effect, a national standard appears to prevail for these procedures. In addition, a recent study (Sirovich et al. 2008) surveyed 1,275 primary care physicians about the "intensity" of their practice, as measured by their stated treatment response to a series of clinical vignettes. The researchers found, as expected, a wide variation in practice intensity across geographic areas, with practice intensity highly correlated with overall health care spending in the area. However, for clinical decisions for which there is definitive evidence or practice guidelines (such as screening mammography and standard exercise tolerance testing), the variations among areas largely disappeared. In these cases, the strong evidence trumped local custom.

The power of heuristics in medical care also demonstrates how the practice of medicine in a community is not simply a summation of the practices of all the clinicians in that community. Through their individual actions physicians create a style of practice, but that style is highly influenced by the other practitioners. It is the rare physician who will order many more tests, admit many more patients, or choose surgical more frequently than medical treatment than his colleagues. Over time, the practice style of the community, that is, the heuristics inherent in the "standard of practice," will sway the individual physician's decision making. In Schelling's terms, the macrobehavior of the particular medical community will drive the micromotives of the individual practitioner.

THE POWER OF HEURISTICS AND BIASES TO RETARD—OR ADVANCE—MEDICAL PROGRESS

In the past decade there has been a flurry of interest in creating medical checklists. Dr. Peter Pronovost of Johns Hopkins University has led a major effort to use a simple checklist to reduce what are called central line-associated bloodstream infections (CLABSIs) (Pronovost and Vohr 2010). Dr. Atul Gawande has led an effort through the World Health Organization to reduce complications and deaths associated with surgery, using an extensive checklist (Gawande 2010). The impetus for these efforts has been concern over the unexplained variations in practices from hospital to hospital and the worry that clinicians and hospitals are too accepting of infections and related deaths as an unavoidable "fact of life" of modern medicine. Both Pronovost and Gawande argue that many deaths in hospitals are preventable and are caused by a culture of professional autonomy and undercommunication. They see checklists as a way to overcome these barriers to care. We shall see that the principles of behavioral economics may be at work, as well.

ANOMALY 22: *Why do tens of thousands of patients die each year in the United States from central line-associated bloodstream infections—even though a simple five-step checklist used by physicians and nurses could reduce that number by two-thirds?*

Health professionals have long known that hospital-acquired infections (HAIs) have been a problem. Recall Ignaz Semmelweis and his work in the 1840s demonstrating the transmission of infection to women after delivery. Unfortunately, the problem of HAIs persists. No one really had undertaken a systematic, nationwide investigation of the magnitude of the problem in the United States until a 2007 report from the Centers for Disease Control and Prevention (CDC) (Klevens et al. 2007). That report estimated that 1.7 million HAIs occurred in hospitals in 2002, meaning that one of every twenty patients acquired an infection caused by the hospitalization itself. These infections led to 99,000 deaths. According to the report, "The number of HAIs exceeded the number of cases of any currently notifiable disease, and deaths associated with HAIs in hospitals exceeded the number attributable to several of the top ten leading causes of death reported" in the United States.

In 2001 Dr. Peter Pronovost began to focus his professional life to eliminating at least one form of hospital-acquired infection: central line–associated bloodstream infections. He was inspired by the tragic case of Josie King, an eighteen-month-old who died of CLABSI in the pediatric intensive care unit at Johns Hopkins Children's Center, her death caused in large part by a series of medical errors. As the CDC report revealed, 82,000 CLABSIs occurred in ICUs in the United States in 2002, leading to 20,000 deaths. (Another 133,000 CLABSIs occurred in other settings, with an additional 10,000 deaths.) So Dr. Pronovost chose to work on a critical, but at the time little recognized, problem in the U.S. health care system.

Pronovost and his team used and adapted guidelines that had already been developed by the CDC to produce a simple, five-step checklist for clinicians to use when they placed central lines into a patient:

• Wash your hands using soap or alcohol prior to inserting the catheter.

- Wear sterile gloves, hat, mask, and gown and completely cover the patient with sterile drapes.
- Avoid placing the catheter in the groin.
- Clean the insertion site on the patient's skin with chlorhexidine antiseptic solution.
- Remove catheters when they are no longer needed.

To a nonmedical person, these steps seem like common sense. In fact, one wonders why clinicians would even have to be reminded to do these things.

Dr. Pronovost's research demonstrates how hard it is to implement such a checklist despite the astonishing results once it is used. He and his team started with Hopkins, and, after much travail and resistance, managed to reduce infection rates in the ICU to near zero. They then applied the checklist to 103 hospitals in Michigan in 2004 and 2005. Again, they had to overcome obstacles ranging from poor and inconsistent data collection to resistance from clinicians and indifference from administrators. The results, reported in 2006 (Pronovost et al. 2006), were indeed startling: The median rate of CLABSIs per 1,000 catheter-days decreased from 2.7 before the checklist to zero (that's right, 0) after three months. These results persisted through the eighteen months of the study, and a follow-up study of ninety of the participating hospitals (Pronovost et al. 2010) confirmed that these results were sustained. In effect, the use of the five-step checklist became part of the everyday operation of ICUs in the state.

It would be heartening to report that hospitals throughout the United States have adopted the CLABSI checklist and that these infections are going the way of smallpox or polio, but that would be an overstatement. There has been some progress. The number of states that mandate reporting of HAIs by hospitals has grown from seven in 2006 to twenty-one. A number of health care organizations, such as the Joint Commission, are creating national patient safety goals related to HAIs. Most encouraging, the CDC has been documenting significant drops in CLABSIs among patients hospitalized in ICUs.

Nevertheless, the response of physicians and administrators to the CLABSI checklist has been discouragingly slow, given the severity of the issue and the dramatic results found in the Michigan initiative. In particular, in his book Dr. Pronovost described two failed attempts (in New Jersey and Maryland) to replicate the Michigan experience. Reflecting on these failures and the other struggles to disseminate the checklist, he mentioned a variety of causes: the complexity of health care, in which an individual practitioner is no longer able to remember all the possible options for diagnosis and treatment but does not have an environment that supports a team approach to care; a health care hierarchy in which the physician is the unquestioned leader (what he calls "a private club of self-styled deities"); and a "toxic" culture in which "doctors are not allowed to make errors."

In a separate effort, Michael Cabana and his colleagues at Johns Hopkins undertook a formal examination of why physicians do not follow clinical practice guidelines (which often form the basis of checklists) (Cabana et al. 1999). They reviewed the literature on guidelines and used the seventy-six articles that they found to develop a framework for understanding the barriers to physician adherence. They identified two barriers related to physician knowledge: lack of familiarity and lack of awareness (related to the volume of published information and the lack of time to stay informed). There were five barriers related to physician attitude: lack of agreement with specific guidelines (such as applicability to patient), lack of agreement with guidelines in general (concerns about "cookbook medicine" and guidelines' challenge to professional autonomy), lack of confidence that the guidelines will work, lack of confidence that the physician can perform all the steps in the guidelines, and lack of motivation (due to habit and routines). Finally, there were three external barriers related to behavior: patient factors (such as the inability to reconcile patient preferences with a guideline), guideline factors (such as the presence of contradictory guidelines), and environmental factors (for example, lack of time or resources, organizational constraints).

Against this array of barriers and seeming dysfunction is the reality of a medical community committed to providing the best care for patients. How can we resolve this anomaly? It should not be surprising at this point that behavioral economics can supply some of the answers. In fact, Dr. Pronovost's book hints at some of these explanations. Early on, he describes his struggle to convince physicians at Johns Hopkins to accept the checklist: "What was striking was that nobody debated the evidence, nobody challenged the items on the checklist, and nobody questioned whether we should do them. But everyone objected to the change in culture. *The doctors saw it as a loss*—a loss of power and respect" (p. 49, emphasis added). We can recognize that phenomenon as loss aversion, or the endowment effect. Even though physicians knew the right thing to do—and wanted to do it—the sense of loss associated with the change was a formidable challenge to overcome. (It does suggest that changing the frame to a gain might be helpful.) Likewise, Dr. Pronovost describes resistance to his approach from even the quality improvement community: "We were trying to develop more robust methods in quality improvement yet the majority of the field had been doing it the same way for many years and was reluctant to change" (p. 180). If, as we saw in Chapter 2, people are reluctant to give up a coffee mug in their possession for ten minutes, it is not surprising that professionals in the health care quality improvement arena would resist changing the methodologies that they had used successfully for decades.

Given this background, we can use the concept of heuristics to organize our analysis of physician resistance of adopting the five-step checklist to avoid central line–associated bloodstream infections. As we discussed earlier, physicians use heuristics all the time in their practices to guide their actions and improve practice efficiency. Some of these heuristics are based on the results of randomized clinical trials, but most stem from the apprenticeship nature of much of medical education plus the clinician's experience over time. As we have seen, these heuristics usually serve physicians so well that they are reluctant to abandon what they consider to be an effective approach for an alternative (which may be yet another example of overconfidence bias). For example, standard protocol in a hospital for the insertion of central lines might be that clinicians are expected to wash their hands thoroughly, wear sterile gloves, and clean the insertion site with chlorhexidine. But a full drape kit is not always available when the busy clinician arrives to insert the line, and the decision to remove the catheter is left to the attending physician (who learned when to do so during her first year of residency fifteen years ago). Sure, the ICU might have some bloodstream infections, but no more than any other hospital in the area; after all, these are very sick patients who are vulnerable to all sorts of infections. Central supply cannot be expected to have enough drape kits every time a physician wants to insert a line, and physicians cannot be waiting around for the kit if the patient needs a central line immediately. The protocol that all the clinicians use for when to withdraw the central line has been standard practice for years, and no one has offered any evidence (at least, that anyone could remember) to justify earlier removal of central lines. Better to be safe than sorry and keep the lines in an extra day.

Several other concepts in behavioral economics could be relevant here. First, we can appeal to the endowment effect and status quo bias. Introducing a CLABSI checklist has the effect of replacing a clinician's existing heuristic with another heuristic. Without demonstrable and even incontrovertible evidence, most clinicians will naturally resist the change. As a result, proponents of the checklist will have a more formidable task in gaining acceptance than would be the case if logic and reason were the controlling factors. Second, George Loewenstein's hot–cold empathy gap plays a role in the resistance to a checklist. Physicians might agree in concept to the CLABSI checklist when it is presented at a medical conference or a hospital medical staff meeting. The evidence offered makes sense, and it is difficult to object to any of the individual checklist items. (Who would be in favor of keeping a catheter in a patient longer than the patient needed it?) But their behavior could be quite different when they are back in the ICU, in the hot state, faced with a patient who urgently needs a central line. The clinician's System 1 activates the longstanding heuristics for inserting the line. Perhaps after the procedure is completed the physician might contemplate what he had learned at the conference, but most likely he will be off to the next case.

This experience illustrates a third concept of relevance here: System 1 and System 2 thinking. For a clinician to change his way of practice, he will need to consciously disconnect his System 1 thinking about inserting central lines and apply System 2 thinking to perform all of the steps of the checklist. This will require more time (which the clinician rarely has) and the application of processes that will require more coordination among the ICU staff (to make sure that drape kits are available and that they are deployed correctly, as well as to create a system to monitor the length of time that the catheter is in the patient and to alert the physician appropriately). Over time, the processes will become more routine, and the System 2 thinking will evolve to System 1, but in the interim the clinician will feel worse off. And, if the clinician applies hyperbolic discounting, the pain of the interim period will be intense and could overcome the clinician's best intentions of doing the right thing for patients.

Let's integrate these concepts with Schelling's ideas of micromotives and macrobehavior. Most physicians pride themselves on their professionalism and devotion to their patients. They treasure their autonomy to practice medicine as they deem appropriate (at least, within bounds). They bristle at being told what to do, and many dismiss checklists and practice guidelines as "cookbook medicine." In Atul Gawande's words, "It somehow feels beneath us to use a checklist, an embarrassment. It runs counter to deeply held beliefs about how the truly great . . . handle situations of high stakes and complexity. The truly great are daring. They improvise. They do not have protocols and checklists" (Gawande 2010: 173). Yet, in reality, physicians do follow their own protocols and checklists, ones that they have learned and borrowed and created. Many of these heuristics are consonant with what their colleagues at the hospital or in the area are using. Because most of medicine is not "daring," but rather commonplace, physicians can do their work—competently and compassionately—using System 1 methods supplemented by System 2. So the irony is that the mystique of American medicine may be the individual clinician, but the reality is a community of practice. And, as such, the micromotives of physicians lead them to practice in a way consistent with their local peers. In many cases, this process results in good quality care and patient outcomes. However, as the work of Peter Pronovost and Atul Gawande demonstrates, it can also lead to a situation in which local customs retard the optimal—and achievable—level of care. No physician prefers this situation, but, as we have just seen, the forces of behavioral economics (among others) can produce perverse macrobehavior.

THE POWER OF HEURISTICS TO
PERPETUATE MEDICAL ERRORS

Central line-associated bloodstream infections are just one category of adverse outcomes in medicine. In November 1999, the Institute of Medicine (IOM) issued its path-breaking report, *To Err is Human* (Kohn, Corrigan, and Donaldson 2000), decrying the problem of pervasive errors occurring throughout the U.S. health care system. The press release for the report described the situation in stark detail: "Health care in the United States is not as safe as it should be—and can be. At least 44,000 people, and perhaps as many as 98,000 people, die in hospitals each year as a result of medical errors that could have been prevented." (The death toll has taken on a life of its own, with some describing it as "the equivalent of a 747 crashing every other day each year." More on this later.) As the title of the report suggests, the IOM focused on systemic causes of errors, not the behavior of individual practitioners. It identified problems such as a culture within health care organizations that emphasized blame over learning when errors occur and an absence of nationwide systems to track errors and find solutions to problems inherent in the system of care. The report and its successors have driven major changes in how hospitals and other health care organizations have addressed patient safety.

Several years after the IOM report, the actuarial consulting firm Milliman undertook a major project to measure the annual cost of medical errors (Van Den Bos et al. 2011). They reviewed a vast database of medical claims in the United States from 2000 to 2008 and identified 564,000 inpatient injuries and 1.8 million outpatient injuries in 2008. Using a panel of clinical and actuarial experts, they estimated the proportion of different injuries that could be attributable to medical errors. They then calculated total medical costs (inpatient, outpatient, and pharmacy) associated with these medical errors. Their estimate: 1.5 million medical errors, with medical costs of $17.1 billion in 2008. Ten types of errors accounted for 69 percent of total medical costs, including postoperative infections ($3.36 billion); pressure ulcers ($3.27 billion); mechanical complications of noncardiac devices, implants, or grafts

($1.07 billion); and postlaminectomy syndrome $1.00 billion). Combined with the findings of the IOM report, these estimates suggest that the U.S. health care system has failed to prevent numerous errors, which drive up the cost of health care.

ANOMALY 23: *Why do medical errors—many of which would seem to be easily avoided—still exist?*

Mainstream economics has a straightforward explanation for the perpetuation of medical errors. A rational clinician—and, by extension, a rational health care system—will reduce medical errors up to the point where the marginal benefits of reducing errors will just equal the marginal costs. The errors that are easy to fix (for example, a physician's washing his hands as he goes from the dissecting table to the delivery ward) will be fixed, whereas those that would require significant time and/or resources or cause collateral problems (for example, redesigning a surgical procedure that will avoid one error in 100,000 surgeries but add thirty minutes to each surgery and create additional surgical risks) will not.

As we have seen in previous chapters, behavioral economics suggests that other forces are in play. For instance, consider the analogy mentioned earlier that the 44,000 to 98,000 hospital deaths caused each year by preventable errors is equivalent to a 747 crashing every other day. The hundreds of error-related deaths occurring every day in hospitals throughout the country do not have the same salience as the crash of an airplane filled with passengers, but the effect is the same. We tolerate the results of the micromotives of clinicians, even though it leads to macrobehavior that we might find unacceptable.

How many errors are actually caused by clinician behavior that can be explained using the behavioral economics principles we have discussed in this book? The careful work of a team of medical researchers gives us the first answers to this question (Graber, Franklin, and Gordon 2005). They examined 100 internal medicine cases in which diagnostic errors were made. The researchers first developed a taxonomy that distinguished among system-related errors, individual behavior-related errors, and "no-fault" errors (such as patient-related errors or unusual presentations of disease). Applying this taxonomy to the 100 cases, they determined that seven were attributable to no-fault errors, nineteen were caused by system-related errors only, twenty-eight by cognitive errors only, and forty-six by both system-related and cognitive errors. (Thus, seventy-four of the 100 cases were caused, at least to some extent, by cognitive errors.) The researchers identified a total of 228 system-related errors and 320 cognitive errors, averaging 5.9 errors per case. The most common system-related errors were policies and procedures (apparent in thirty-three cases), inefficient processes (thirty-two cases), poor communications or teamwork (twenty-seven cases), patient neglect (twenty-three cases), and failed oversight of system issues (twenty cases).

It is the cognitive errors that are of most interest for our purposes. The researchers found that of the 320 cognitive factors, only eleven were related to insufficient knowledge or diagnostic skill on the part of the clinician. The remainder were due to faulty data gathering, information processing, or verification, and many of these have behavioral economics implications. For example, in thirty-nine of the seventy-four cases caused by cognitive error, one of the causes was "premature closure," that is, the failure of the clinician to consider other potential diagnoses once an initial one had been chosen. The researchers gave as an example a wrong diagnosis of musculoskeletal pain after a car crash, when a ruptured spleen was ultimately found to be the cause. Premature closure is an example of the incorrect use of the satisficing heuristic, in which the physician stops his search for a solution once he has found one that meets some threshold criteria. This problem strikes to the heart of the debate between the "heuristics and biases" and the "fast and frugal" camps of behavioral psychologists and economists. The fast and frugal advocates (led by Gerd Gigerenzer) argue that the benefits of heuristics far outweigh the costs, so that premature closure is a relatively minor problem. On the other hand, the heuristics and biases group (led by Daniel Kahneman) see premature closure as an inherent problem with heuristics and one that deserves attention by clinicians. As to what clinicians need to do, remember Ed Bessman's admonition from the previous chapter, that a good clinician will push less important information aside but will be able to recall it when the original diagnosis does not work. In over half of the cases here with cognitive errors, this important step was not taken.

In twenty-five of the seventy-four cognitive-error cases, the researchers identified "overestimating or underestimating the usefulness or salience of a finding" as a source of error. This error occurs when a clinician is aware of a symptom but either fixates on it (and minimizes other symptoms) or fails to recognize its significance. An example that the researchers gave was a wrong diagnosis of sepsis in a patient who had a stable white blood cell count in the setting of myelodysplastic syndrome. We recognize the concept of salience from Chapter 5, when we discussed how patients are often only vaguely aware of the real price of health care. We can define salience here as a prominent, conspicuous, or striking attribute of a patient's presentation of his symptoms. As behavioral psychologists have demonstrated, the more something is salient, the more likely it is to be considered a cause of whatever phenomenon is being considered (Plous 1993). Thus, this clinical error stems from the same root cause as the tendency of patients to ignore the real price of care when they make their decisions to consume health care.

A third, and final, source of cognitive error to be gleaned from the research on the 100 cases of medical error relates to a common theme in this and the previous chapter. That is, they found that in twenty-three of the seventy-four cases of cognitive error, the clinician either failed to apply the appropriate heuristic or applied it in inappropriate or atypical circumstances. For example, a clinician used a heuristic to diagnose bronchitis in a patient who was later found to have a pulmonary embolism. In fourteen of the cases, the clinician used a heuristic to diagnose a single cause of illness, when the patient had multiple conditions. In seven cases, the clinician chose the most common condition as the diagnosis, although a less common condition was responsible (which we recognize as the representative heuristic). Of course, we have extensively discussed the use of heuristics by physicians and have noted that they can facilitate decision making if used correctly. The research described here, though, illustrates how widespread their misuse is, resulting in one-third of the cognitive errors in diagnosis in a set of internal medicine cases.

So it is clear that the concepts of behavioral economics and psychology can explain how physicians can continue to make clinical errors that could be avoided. Before we leave this discussion, it is important to note one important statistic from the work of Graber, Franklin, and Gordon. They found an average of 5.9 factors that contributed to error in each of the cases they reviewed. Thus, it was not just a misuse of a single heuristic, or a solitary lapse in judgment in applying a salient symptom, or one mistake due to bias. Rather, it was a constellation of errors, similar to J. T. Reason's "Swiss cheese" model of error (Reason 1990), in which harm stems from multiple breakdowns in the system of safeguards set up to prevent injury. This finding echoes a theme throughout this book: that behavioral economics provides some, but not all, of the material explanations for anomalies in the health care sector. The finding also suggests that the prevention of error will require multiple approaches, from the systems perspective of the Institute of Medicine to the focus on individual clinician decision making of behavioral economics.

INTERVIEW WITH PETER PRONOVOST, MD, PHD
Professor, Johns Hopkins University School of Medicine
Director, Armstrong Institute for Patient Safety and Quality
Dr. Peter Pronovost is one of the country's leading experts in patient safety and quality. He has led the effort at Johns Hopkins University and Health System to make medical care safer for patients. His efforts have been widely recognized, including being named one of *Time* magazine's "100 Most Influential People" in 2008 and being awarded a "genius" grant from the MacArthur Foundation. He has been at Hopkins since 1987, where he earned his medical degree, completed residency and fellowship programs, and earned a doctorate in clinical investigation. He has written over 300 peer-reviewed articles and chronicled his efforts to develop effective checklists in *Safe Patients, Smart Hospitals*, published in 2010.

Physicians use heuristics all the time. How do you see
checklists and practice guidelines fitting into that?
One of the really important areas of behavioral economics is how to
address the area of physician overconfidence. Just like we are overconfident about the market for real estate prices, physicians are really
overconfident about our ability to diagnose the patients who will benefit from therapy. Part of what we have is overconfidence about our
cognitive ability to remember the guidelines and the latest evidence-
based therapy. So, checklists are a mechanism to defend against that by
reducing ambiguity and making it clear about the behavioral expectations for treating someone.

   Pattern recognition is Daniel Kahneman's System 1 thinking, but
being able to see when you deviate from the pattern, that is System 2
thinking. We interchange this all the time in medicine. I say, "Yes, it
looks like sepsis, but it's not really, I think it's adrenal insufficiency."
I think that a diagnostic or treatment checklist could really help with
that. But there's, I think, some natural resistance to using a checklist.
It requires that clinicians accept that they are fallible, and, to be honest, that's a pill much of medicine hasn't swallowed yet, because if I am
not fallible, why do I need a cognitive aid?

Do you think the checklists can limit the judgment of physicians?
I think our work with the WHO Checklist suggests that, if the checklist is dictated to clinicians, there are likely going to be antibodies to it,
and rightfully so, because it may not be sensitive to context. So creating one checklist for the world scares me. When people ask to see "the
Michigan checklist," I laugh and I say, "There are 103 ICUs, and there
are 103 checklists." They are 99 percent the same, but that 1 percent is
key for it being right there for them. Everyone believes their checklist is
the best, and it is—for their context.

   One of the things that I have really struggled with in developing
and using checklists or standardizing work is to try to dampen down
mindless variation but encourage mindful variation. What I mean by
that is that we still have resistance that I call mindless, and that is resistance because of my position or collar or ego. "I am the chair of the

department. You are not telling me what to do." We need to dampen down that, because it's harmful to patients.

On the other hand, I don't want to dampen down mindful variation, that is, variation based on a hypothesis or a hunch on how to do something, grounded in either some theory or some preexisting information. We need to encourage mindful variation; that's how innovation advances; that's how we are going to improve productivity and we are going to advance science. Teasing those two out is sometimes really difficult.

Physicians use heuristics, even those not based on strict evidence, because they work. How could you convince them to change and use a checklist?
I have no doubt they are highly efficient, and I need to make so many decisions a day as a doctor that I would be paralyzed if I didn't use them. So heuristics are certainly efficient. But what I would ask you to do is think about efficiency as a continuous variable, rather than a dichotomous variable. Let's take how good they are, and what we know about how good they are. We don't have a really good mechanism of identifying diagnostic errors, so it's pretty hard to tell how good they are. There are several studies, for example, that show that one in ten patients who die in the ICU die from something other than what the clinicians thought they were treating them for. The estimates of outpatient diagnostic errors are probably really even higher. In outpatient care, a third of the people are going to get better no matter what you do, so it's hard to tease out the presence of errors.

One concept I like from behavioral economics is this notion of opting out rather than opting in. I think it applies to compliance with checklists. Of course, you need to allow clinicians to opt out, but if the order set says, "Do you want to use this checklist?" you are going to have low compliance as opposed to, "You are automatically going to use this checklist unless you have a reason not to." Health care has been slow to adopt the opt-out, and I think we really need to.

How much autonomy should physicians have in using checklists?
I think one of the biggest challenges in patient safety is, "When do you trump physician autonomy?" Because we doctors are so socialized that,

"I am the advocate for the patient and I know best. Therefore I should, through professionalism, be allowed to do what's best for the patient." That might have worked well when all of the technologies I had fit into a black bag and half of them were homeopathic. It doesn't work very well when there are exceedingly complex technologies, or when, as we do now, we publish 18,000 clinical trials a year. How on earth could you keep up with everything? So if you are a surgeon and the infectious disease doctor says, "This skin prep is clearly better than another one," should that surgeon really have the ability to say, "No, I want to use this other one?"

Again, if it's mindful resistance, perhaps; if it's mindless, no. They shouldn't be able to opt out. We haven't made clear decision rules of when could we trump someone. It goes both ways. Too often, insurers trump physician autonomy with absolutely no transparency of what evidence they were basing it on. Or hospital managers also said, "No, you have to do it this way," and those efforts have largely failed. What I have seen that has worked is when the community decides what the rules are, but then they have to agree to abide by them.

How do you do that?
My simple heuristic is that, in any industry, there's really only four ways you can change behavior: you can regulate it; you can create economic incentives; you can create hierarchy, so that management will do it; or you can use what are called network approaches (which is a community that works through social norms). Though all are needed to some extent, and all have their own risks and benefits, what has worked in health care, by far, is the network approach, that is, the community sets the rules. The regulatory approaches are only going to get us to a bare minimum, because medicine is too complicated to think you are going to set the rules for everything. Economic incentives have worked some, but the empirical evidence about pay-per-performance shows that it's pretty weak. Hierarchies do not work at all amongst professionals.

What does work well is when the community sets up the rules. What we did in our Michigan work was essentially a network approach; we called it a "clinical community." The communities set up the rules, they created a checklist, and they defined it, but there were some harder tactics to make sure they complied with their own rules, such as we posted their infection rates. What I see is a mixture of top-down environment, where the clinicians cannot opt out, once they have set the rules.

Isn't there a danger that a medical community could set rules that would create a situation such as in McAllen, Texas?
What we have now is a health care environment of completely individual entrepreneurs, so that we have set rules, but every doctor can set his own rules, often not based on evidence. What I am saying is that the tribe of doctors has to set the rules. That is, we have to agree on what we are going to do—what is going to be the standard practice— and then we have to be held accountable for those rules. In McAllen, Texas, essentially there were no rules. When there isn't that evidence, the tribe sets up tacit norms and sometimes they get it wrong, but they set up heuristics to make it work.

I think the amount of overt fraud among physicians is real, but small. I think it's really just human nature—the tribe agreed on a way of doing things because they needed a way to survive. Many of them went to medical school at the same place where there was a way of doing it; there is a Hopkins way and a Maryland way, and you get into the community, and this is how we manage things. Not that it's necessarily malicious. The variation just clusters by, this is our tribe, this is how we do things. This is why I think that is both the risk and the hope, that if you think you are going to change practice, believing the Joint Commission or a regulator is going to solve that, to me it is naïve. We need them to protect against the bad apple; they are never going to give us the kind of health care system that we all want. Instead, you have to work through influencing those social norms.

How do you create the kind of environment that facilitates these changes?
One of the things I have written about the way forward is the equivalent of the Securities and Exchange Commission in health care. When President Roosevelt proposed the SEC, there were no rules of financial

reporting, so you could read a balance sheet or an income statement and have no clue what went into it. The SEC requires public sector auditing, accountability, and penalties for publicly traded companies, and there are organizations (like Bloomberg) that analyze the publicly available data. I think McAllen, Texas, wouldn't have happened if there were private sector agreement on what is good cardiac care, what is good treatment of heart failure, and then there was a way to make that data transparent, because the social norms would self-regulate.

We naïvely assume there is an outcome measure tree that I can go pick these measures from, but the reality is, they don't exist in health care, and we need to create a mechanism to create the thousands of measures. We haven't created the meta-mechanism of saying, how we are going to generate (or let the market generate) all these measures so that they are valid and that the process is transparent? Once we do, you could then influence these norms.

I am not saying that the SEC has served well as the regulator. It has failed pretty miserably as a regulator, but it has done exceedingly well as a transparency truth agency. Right now there are stronger protections on what you say about toothpaste than on what you say about how good your health care is.

SO WHAT? HOW CAN THE MEDICAL PROFESSION TAKE THE LEAD IN EFFECTING CHANGE?

As this chapter has demonstrated, the behavior of the medical profession in total is not just a simple summation of the behavior of individual physicians. Physician behavior is driven by a complex combination of the internal motivation and decision-making processes of the individual physician and the social norms and rules of the medical community. This interaction suggests that a combination of strategies might need to be developed. In Chapter 6 we proposed strategies that might work on the individual level. In this chapter we will consider some on a societal level.

Even these proposals need to be tempered with the reality that the medical profession, including the medical education establishment, has yet to embrace the concept of meta-thinking about clinical decision making. For example, in 2003 Pat Croskerry proposed the implementation of a debiasing technique he called "cognitive forcing strategies" in clinical decision making (Croskerry 2003). Recognizing that clinicians have little awareness of their own cognitive processes and that traditional medical education has done little in this regard, Croskerry proposed the creation of systems of rules that require clinicians to "consciously apply a metacognitive step and cognitively force a necessary consideration of alternatives." Such a system could be similar to computerized order-entry systems that ask the clinician whether a generic could be prescribed or alert the clinician about possible interaction effects of the prescribed drug with others that the patient is taking. More likely, the technique would be taught to physicians in medical school, residency, and continuing medical education.

Based on correspondence with Dr. Croskerry, it appears that few academic medical centers have adopted anything like his approach. He reported to me that his professional home, Dalhousie University in Halifax, Nova Scotia, only recently created a group tasked with developing a curriculum with critical thinking as a cornerstone and are only now conducting faculty development seminars. One indication of the challenges for this approach comes from a recently published exploratory study that applied cognitive forcing strategies to fifty-six students at McMaster University; the experiment found that less than half of the participants used these strategies correctly (Sherbino et al. 2011). In some sense, it is not surprising that a short program could not overcome a lifetime of heuristic thinking, but the experiment did suggest that further attempts are warranted.

Picking up on the experience of clinicians with computerized order-entry systems, a number of authors have advocated for expert systems to augment clinicians' cognitive skills (Hunt et al. 1998; Garg et al. 2005; Graber, Franklin, and Gordon 2005; Chaudhry et al. 2006). These systems may have an impact on clinicians' thinking, at least on the margin. However, as Peter Pronovost has found, imposing a system on professionals is likely to be less successful than expected. Clinicians will insist that their patients are different—and they may be (but probably not much). More significantly, they will contend that the systems are awkward to use, which they will be (even if beautifully designed) because they will force physicians out of their System 1 thinking mode and into System 2. Finally, they will bristle at being told what to do and "forced" to practice "cookbook medicine."

The experiences of Peter Pronovost, Atul Gawande, and others in developing checklists suggest another, perhaps more promising approach. Checklists have real potential, if they adhere to several principles. As Dr. Pronovost pointed out, checklists need to be based on real science and backed by empirical evidence. In addition, they need to be flexible enough that physicians in a community can adapt the checklist to their local circumstances. What may be lost in standardization is more than recovered by greater adherence. In addition, it is critical that the checklist be carefully framed. For example, it should be positioned as simply a formalized heuristic, similar to what physicians use all the time. Thus, the checklist can be framed as an extension of what physicians already do.

The checklists should be deliberately framed as gains, avoiding the perception of loss of professional autonomy or tradition. Clinicians should perceive them as complementing their current practices, not replacing them. For example, Dr. Gawande frames checklists as freeing clinicians, rather than constraining them. "The fear people have about the idea of adherence to protocol is rigidity. . . . But what you find, when a checklist is well made, is exactly the opposite. The checklist gets the dumb stuff out of the way, the routines your brain shouldn't have to occupy itself with" (Gawande 2010: 177). So clinicians do not have to remember the checklist for inserting and managing central lines; they just have to do the work that only they can do. As Dr. Pronovost has found, gaining clinician acceptance of a checklist is not easy, but the rewards can be palpable and long lasting.

Behavioral economics suggests that checklists not be framed as replacing the clinicians' System 2 thinking. As Dr. Pronovost has noted, there are situations in which a checklist is inappropriate. ("If I don't get a central line in this patient *now*, he will die!") In addition, the creators and implementers of the checklists need to anticipate "checklist fatigue," in which clinicians begin to go through the motions of applying the checklist without internalizing it; in these cases, the checklist becomes an administrative burden, not an integral part of clinical practice. One way of avoiding this problem is to engage Pat Croskerry's cognitive forcing strategies at key points in the implementation process, to make clinicians aware of their thought processes and the benefits of using the checklist.

There is a final approach, which might seem patently obvious. As we have found in this book, the thinking and decision-making processes that behavioral economics and psychology can help to explain are deeply ingrained. As a result, there is no magic bullet, no single technique that will free people of their cognitive biases. In a systematic review of the research on the implementation of clinical guidelines, Anneke Francke and her colleagues at the Netherlands Institute for Health Services Research (Francke et al. 2008) concluded that only multiple strategies will be effective in obtaining clinician adherence. It will require a strong evidence base and formal education and clinician engagement and performance feedback. How do we accomplish this task? Perhaps Peter Pronovost's "Health Care SEC" is the answer. It certainly seems to be an interesting way of integrating clinicians' micromotives with the health care system's macrobehavior.

8   CAN WE USE THE CONCEPTS OF BEHAVIORAL ECONOMICS TO TRANSFORM HEALTH CARE?

Once in every show
There comes a song like this
It starts off soft and low
And ends up with a kiss.
—Monty Python's *Spamalot* (Idle 2005)

In books like this, it is typical that the author concludes by delivering sage advice about how to overcome the problems that he has carefully explained. These directives are occasionally helpful; too often, they are bromides to give the reader a stronger sense of control over powerful forces than is realistic. As a result, I am tempted to say that the only sage advice is, "There is no sage advice." I am confident that behavioral economics provides both explanations and predictions that are better than those offered by mainstream, neoclassical economics, especially in health care. However, behavioral economists have demonstrated that there are no simple fixes (at least, so far). There is no "seven-step program." We cannot be easily deprogrammed to identify and avoid overconfidence bias, for instance. Most of us cannot be trained to use Bayesian analysis to internalize the difference between a one in 10,000 risk and a one in 1,000,000 risk. We cannot be turned into calculating machines, to avoid inflating a small, but high-affect, risk. We are what we are, and in some sense the best we can do at this point is to understand how we actually make decisions. For now, perhaps our goal should just be a more honest starting point for understanding. In addition, though, we can recognize the complexity of our individual and collective decisions when it comes to health care and start to undertake the hard work necessary to determine what behaviors we can change. This approach will require an appreciation of nuance, as it requires the incorporation of insights from a range of social sciences, especially psychology.

Nuance often comes at the price of simplicity. Nevertheless, in this chapter I hope to deliver some of both, as an endpoint to what we learned in the previous chapters and as a beginning for interested readers. First, I will summarize major findings for you to bear in mind after you have closed the book, making the case that behavioral economics provides a helpful lens with which to look at health care and health care reform. I will describe the limitations of this new discipline, to temper our collective enthusiasm over its initial success and apparent applicability to the U.S. health care sector. I will consider the extent to which the tenets of behavioral economics can help to modify—or, more likely, accommodate—the behavior of consumers/patients and health professionals and to improve the performance of the system as a whole. Finally, because this is a new discipline, I will suggest what I view as the most promising areas for additional research—to bolster our confidence in the current findings and to apply behavioral economics to the phenomena that my colleagues and I have observed in health care.

WHAT WE KNOW

Although I was trained as a mainstream, neoclassical economist, I have found, increasingly, that the explanations and predictions of human behavior by behavioral economists are more accurate and (despite the lack of advanced mathematics) more elegant than those of mainstream economics, especially when it comes to health care. The tenets of behavioral economics allow for more variability in human behavior in decision making. Yet they are not so elastic that behavioral economists can always find an explanation for what people do and how they act.

Mainstream economics has always had a difficult time explaining how patients and physicians act. Consumers have never purchased health care services the same way they buy groceries, and their preferences have rarely exhibited the kind of consistency that mainstream economics requires. Patients rarely have sufficient information to make truly utility-maximizing decisions in health care, so standard theory introduced the concept of the physician as the patient's agent to preserve a modicum of informed choice. But physicians themselves have a potential conflict of interest because they provide many of the services for which they are advising their patients. Thus, a convoluted argument regarding "supplier-induced demand" had to be devised, which took physician behavior even further from the neoclassical model of supply.

The increasing complexity and lack of intuitive appeal of neoclassical economics in explaining the health care sector have opened the door for alternative, ad hoc theories. A couple of what could be called "folk theories" have arisen. One is what I would term the "idiot patient" theory, which contends that patients are inherently incapable of making rational choices in health care. This theory goes something like this: The consequences of health care decisions are too high; the information needed to make rational decisions is too great and/or too complex for the typical patient to understand; and the existence of health insurance shields patients from the full financial impact of their decisions. All of these problems make standard economic decision making impossible. This theory manifests itself in policies like banning trans fats from restaurant menus, limiting the size of portions in fast-food restaurants, barring TV advertisements for cigarettes, and (now almost a century ago) prohibiting the sale of alcohol.

A second folk theory is the "physician conspiracy" theory, which posits that physicians scheme among themselves (and with drug and medical device firms) to maintain their traditional power and hierarchical position in the field and deliberately limit competition. These actions allegedly subject patients to unneeded and costly therapies. This theory has led to such policies as the prohibition of physician ownership of hospitals and of the routine ordering of tests that are performed on equipment in physicians' offices.

These theories are not altogether wrong, but they require circumstances to align in just the right way. Otherwise, their explanations of behavior become ever more elaborate. In this book I have tried to demonstrate that behavioral economics is more widely applicable to patient and physician behavior in the United States and requires fewer assumptions about human behavior in health care. Patients do not have to act like calculating machines to make sound decisions about their health, but neither are they passive participants in their care. Physicians do not have to be the perfect amalgamation of Marcus Welby and Gregory House, in addition to acting as profit-maximizing businesspeople. Behavioral economics allows people to be reasonably rational (remember the discussions about satisficing, bounded rationality, and the use of heuristics) while stumbling in predictable ways (recall our extensive consideration of the multiple biases that people exhibit). It's the rationality that enables people to pursue and achieve their goals in health care, but it's the foreseeable missteps that explain why they often fail. Thus, the anomalies that we have considered throughout this book demonstrate that it is not necessary to assume patient naïveté or physician mendacity to explain their behavior. Something less dramatic, and more ordinary and forgiving, is going on here. Imperfect people are making imperfect decisions, and behavioral economics does a better job than mainstream economics of explaining and predicting this reality.

We have seen that the forces identified by behavioral economics strongly influence how people make decisions in general and in health care in particular. In part, the power of these forces is that individuals rarely recognize them; if they do, they often believe that the forces influence others but not themselves. This perceptual immunity enables people to repeat the same mistakes, something that mainstream economics rarely predicts. As a result, the opportunities for successful interventions to remedy the missteps are limited.

CAVEATS AND LIMITATIONS

Despite the power of a behavioral economics lens in explaining a wide variety of anomalies in health care, we must be careful not to get overly excited about this relatively new discipline—at least at this stage. While behavioral economics appears to be more useful than neoclassical economics on health care issues, it is not necessarily *the* answer. There are several reasons for us to counsel moderation. First, social science in general is not like the hard sciences. In the words of Nobel laureate Murray Gell-Mann, "Think how hard physics would be if particles could think." People make choices for all sorts of reasons, which social scientists likely will never fully understand. In a sense, we are looking for tendencies of behavior more than unanimity of action. Almost none of the studies discussed in this book reported that every participant exhibited decision bias or even loss aversion, or was vulnerable to framing and anchoring. The experiments found statistically and behaviorally significant results, but there was nothing like the confirmations of Einsteinian physics.

Likewise, we need to be cautious about making inferences from individual research studies, even if they provide results that are attractive for our purposes. For example, the famous Brickman et al. study of happiness (Brickman, Coates, and Janoff-Bulman 1978), reported in Chapter 3, has been cited over 1,400 times, even though the researchers drew their conclusions from a sample of only seventy-three people. We need to be guarded in applying the results of studies that use a pool of experimental subjects who may not be representative of the population in which we are interested. Consider the myriad of experiments that have been conducted using undergraduate students but whose results have been projected onto adults in much different economic and social circumstances (Henrich, Heine, and Norenzayan 2010).

We need to be careful not to rely on the results from studies for which there has been little or no replication. It is well known that editors of academic journals are partial to studies that are new and surprising and less interested in publishing research that replicates prior research (Ioannidis 2005; Moonesinghe et al. 2007; Young, Ioannidis, and Al-Ubaydli 2008). As a result of this bias, a researcher will shun replication studies (unless they are the first step of other research) and seek the novel and unexpected. Unfortunately, we can be confident that what we are seeing in behavioral economics research is real only when studies are reproduced with new samples and methods. Until then, we all may be vulnerable to what has been called *the illusion of explanatory depth*, in which "people feel they understand complex phenomena with far greater precision, coherence, and depth than they really do" (Rozenblit and Keil 2002). In short, the replication process is a necessary step in the natural maturation of the field.

Even though behavioral economics is still maturing, health policy makers will be tempted to apply its findings if the findings meet their needs. In so doing, they need to reckon with another point: their own susceptibility to the biases that we have described. Just as patients and physicians are largely unaware that they make biased decisions, policy makers are likely to succumb to what one scholar has termed *the illusion of regulatory competence* (Tasic 2009). For example, given the pressures of public opinion, elected officials and appointed regulators are likely to suffer from action bias, even though watchful waiting might be the better course for many issues. Similarly, they are apt to engage in confirmation bias and cherry-pick the behavioral economics research that supports their preexisting positions. Because, as we have found, there are contradictory studies in this emerging field, an indiscriminant policy maker can often find some research to support his preconceived notions. So the choice in health policy is not between biased private sector decision making and rational public sector decision making but between biased decisions in both arenas.

A final note of caution for policy making: Efforts so far to debias people and their decision making have not been very successful. Perhaps as we come to better understand the mechanisms of choices and actions, future initiatives may be more successful. Until then, the best we may be able to do is to inform health policy makers of the potential for bias—on everyone's part—and to design programs that mitigate its likelihood. Of course, this opens up the potential for an ethically gray area in which policy makers use people's biases against them. For example, we have seen the power of the default steer choices (through passive acceptance of the default); health policy makers could exploit this tendency to accomplish their own goals (which might be contrary to those of the public). This possibility could be particularly pernicious, as policy makers would be offering the illusion of choice knowing that most people will "choose" the initial choice that is offered.

MODIFYING—OR ACCOMMODATING—PATIENTS' BEHAVIOR: WHAT BENJAMIN CAN DO

Arguably, Daniel Kahneman and Amos Tversky have changed the way that psychologists and economists, and now some health professionals, think about human behavior. People are both simple and complex, although not in the ways that social scientists of the past century have thought. People are simple in the sense that much of their behavior can be accurately predicted by simple models: If the price of a product increases, a consumer will buy less; if a behavior is reinforced, a person will do more of it. However, people are complex in that their decisions often depend on how choices are framed or on how many choices they have. They make decisions in a hot state that they come to regret when they are in a cold state—and vice versa. Sometimes, they make decisions based on intuitive, System 1 thinking, and other times they use deliberative, System 2 thinking.

When people make decisions regarding their health care, it seems that complexity dominates simplicity. Patients often behave differently than predicted by mainstream economics and more like that posited by behavioral economics. How, then, do we use this understanding of the health care sector and our behavior in it? First, we can appreciate how the forces inherent in health care will affect patient decision making and prepare for it. For example, in the past decade there has been a significant growth in the area of end-of-life care. Instead of always employing heroic efforts to save a life, health professionals are encouraging patients and their families to consider palliative and hospice care. In addition, they are advocating that patients prepare formal medical directives, which might include so-called "Do Not Resuscitate" (DNR) orders. Of course, these decisions are usually made in a cold state, when the issues are more theoretical and abstract. The challenge is when patients are in extremis and they and their families are in a hot state. At that point, the deliberative DNR decision may not hold sway, and the family could call on the caregivers to do everything possible to "save grandma." The health professionals then face the dilemma of whether to follow the considered System 2 choice or the immediate System 1 demand. The findings of behavioral economics suggest that health professionals work with patients and their families ahead of time to understand what will be done and not done when the actual DNR event occurs. This preparation could be instrumental in ensuring that end-of-life care will be less chaotic and traumatic.

Second, as George Loewenstein noted, the approach and principles of behavioral economics are much more aligned with those of public health than are those of mainstream economics, and this perspective provides another avenue for modifying or accommodating patient behavior. Unlike neoclassical economics, behavioral economics allows for government intervention for what Professor Loewenstein calls *internalities*, when a person makes a decision without sufficient understanding of the long-term consequences, due to hyperbolic discounting or overconfidence bias. Because of internalities, behavioral economists will support market interventions that would be anathema to mainstream economists. For example, neoclassical economists might admit that obesity is a major social problem but would argue against public involvement in what is primarily an individual decision. Behavioral economists, on the other hand, would note that many obese people express a desire to lose weight but lack the willpower to exercise and limit their calorie intake; in these cases, they would argue that intervention is warranted to provide a nudge, commitment device, or other incentive for the obese person to do what he knows that he needs to do to improve his health.

As a consequence, behavioral economists are much more supportive of public health initiatives that are targeted to individual behavior that affect only themselves, such as diet, drinking, drug use, and other lifestyle choices. This support is especially strong for those programs that focus on information and persuasion (for example, high-affect publicity about the dangers of smoking) rather than on dictates (such as banning smoking in Manhattan). Many of these interventions have been tested in diverse circumstances; they offer valid opportunities for improving individuals' decisions and actions without coercion.

So, what would we advise our friend Benjamin to do? Remember, he is a twenty-seven-year-old database analyst living with his girlfriend on the north side of Chicago. At the risk of violating my contention that there are no easy fixes, no seven-step programs, there are some lessons from behavioral economics and psychology that will serve him well:

- Buy health insurance. It's not really insurance, but a prepayment system. You will need it and use it.

- Appreciate when your physician advises watchful waiting when you have a mild illness. Remember that more care does not mean better care. There are downsides to almost all treatment.

- When your physician develops a treatment protocol and you agree to it, follow it—even when your symptoms appear to subside.

- Recognize that your physician has seen—and treated—almost everything during her career. What is new and puzzling to you is routine for her. As one of my physician students said, "Common things are common." Be glad that your physician has seen your condition many times before and can diagnose most ailments quickly.

- Acknowledge the hot–cold paradox. When you make a health-related decision, pause and ask yourself what decision you would have made had you been in the other decision state. If the decision is the same, great. If not, you have some more thinking to do.

- When your girlfriend Elaine finally convinces you to stop smoking, the two of you should create some commitment devices to help you to follow through. As discussed in Chapter 4, you can use a commitment device to reward yourself for good behavior and/or punish yourself for bad behavior. It can be as ordinary as paying yourself twice the cost of a pack of cigarettes for each day that you don't smoke or as clever (and as painful for a Cubs fan) as wearing a Chicago White Sox cap one day for each cigarette you smoke.

As simple as these recommendations seem, the behavioral economics research presented in this book demonstrates that Benjamin and all of us like him face a significant challenge in adopting them.

MODIFYING—AND ACCOMMODATING—PHYSICIANS' BEHAVIOR

We have demonstrated that physicians are susceptible to many of the same biases and framing effects as patients. We have also found that physicians use heuristics extensively in their clinical practice; heuristics enable them to treat their patients expeditiously and effectively but also leave them open to premature closure of diagnosis and treatment. From my discussions with practicing physicians, it is clear that they picked up their heuristics when they were in training as a part of what is known as the "invisible curriculum," when they were observing attending physicians with patients, making diagnoses, and determining treatment plans. They then developed their own heuristics as they gained experience in their own practice. In effect, they have relied on on-the-job training and just-in-time learning, which is often how adults gain professional skills. Only rarely did practicing physicians learn heuristics formally in medical school or continuing medical education programs.

This reality suggests several approaches for making physicians more aware of how they make decisions and for improving the practice of medicine. First, medical schools must improve the teaching of decision making or at least make students aware of the concept of metacognition and the need to be self-aware as to how they will be making decisions as clinicians. Pat Croskerry has created several interesting proposals in this regard (Croskerry 2003; 2009). As he has noted in conversation, few (if any) medical schools in the United States or Canada have adopted his model (perhaps because it is an involved process and medical schools are hard pressed to add yet another unit to a standard curriculum that still must be completed in four years). As educators at Johns Hopkins School of Medicine have found, offering decision making as an elective has not proved to be effective, either. One solution, then, might be for medical educators to incorporate decision making as a way of teaching rather than as a specific subject. However, this approach has its own challenges, as it would require retooling of faculty—never an easy task. I expect, though, that the effort will be easier for those teaching at the graduate medical education level, as the teaching in these settings is more hands-on and experiential than didactic.

The second approach to improve heuristics and the delivery of care is the development and dissemination of checklists and practice guidelines. As the experiences of Peter Pronovost, Atul Gawande, and others have shown, creating checklists and practice guidelines is difficult work—assembling the right experts, assessing the research literature, and fashioning a final product that is true to the science while being useful and accessible to the practitioner. Drs. Pronovost and Gawande note that the more difficult work is implementation—convincing institutions and health professionals to adopt the checklists and guidelines as an integral part of their clinical practice. Dr. Pronovost, in particular, promotes the use of a flexible, bottom-up approach to this process; he argues that what is lost in terms of uniformity is more than made up for in greater acceptance and deeper commitment by the clinicians. As we showed in our discussion about choice, effective choice generates higher satisfaction with the process and greater dedication to the decision. Even though a grassroots approach takes more time and, as Dr. Pronovost has experienced, results in only minor adjustments to the checklists and guidelines, it creates more ownership among the clinicians within an institution. In Dr. Pronovost's words, "Everyone believes their checklist is the best, and it is—for their context."

Admittedly, these are not "big" ideas designed to transform how physicians practice medicine in one grand experiment. The results of behavioral economics research do not support grand shifts—at least not yet. Rather, the research supports trying to influence physician behavior on the margin: Accept that the biases will occur, but find ways to work around them.

IMPROVING THE HEALTH CARE SYSTEM
Thinking about how physicians and patients behave seems small scale when we set our sights on the health care system. Modesty and "small ball" are rarely the hallmarks of policy. Add to that the likelihood that policy makers suffer from the same biases as patients and physicians—as

well as the illusion of regulatory competence—and we have the prospect for grand experiments. Unfortunately, some of these come from an overambitious application of behavioral economics. For instance, Section 4205 of the Patient Protection and Affordable Care Act (PPACA) requires that restaurants that are part of a chain with twenty or more locations list calorie and other nutritional information on their menus. This provision is likely the result of the one study that George Loewenstein noted in my interview with him. The fact that other studies have contradicted this finding demonstrates the danger of implementing policy based on incomplete research.

In addition, we already discussed the biggest idea in the PPACA—individual mandates to buy health insurance—and why behavioral economics would support it. Nevertheless, it is the most contentious part of the health reform legislation and the one that precipitated the constitutional challenge that was brought to the Supreme Court. Now that the law has been upheld by the Court, the primary task shifts to implementation. The experience in Massachusetts with its individual mandate law suggests that the individual mandate will be less intrusive than many thought. Most Massachusetts residents complied with little rancor. A study found that 400,000 people became insured after the law went into effect in 2007, so that about 98 percent of residents in the state have health insurance (In Massachusetts 2012). By 2009 (the last year for which data are available), only 48,000 people—less than one percent of the state's population—were required to pay a penalty in lieu of buying insurance, even though the penalty was significantly less than the expected insurance premium. A recent study by The Urban Institute (Blumberg, Buettgens, and Feder 2012) estimated that only 6 percent of Americans would be subject to the individual mandate penalty as stipulated in the PPACA. In effect, most Americans would be abiding by the mandate through their own actions (by purchasing health insurance) or would be exempted because either they had low income or the premium for the lowest cost plan that was available was unaffordable (defined as more than 8 percent of their family income). Those few who would have to pay the penalty would do so while filing their annual federal income tax (which would reduce the salience of the penalty).

Given these findings and the tenets of behavioral economics, it is likely that the controversy over the individual mandate will largely disappear by full implementation in 2016. Once insurance coverage becomes the expectation, it will have the same effect as the numerous laws on the books (such as seat belt usage and no-smoking policies) that are maintained more by social norms than legal enforcement. In effect, as we have seen in other contexts, the mandate will act as a default.

As an example of how public policy can promote innovation in health care, Section 2705 of the PPACA allows employers to provide a premium discount, rebate, or other reward of up to 30 percent of the cost of coverage to those employees who participate in corporate wellness programs and satisfy a standard related to health status. This provision differs from the individual mandate because it authorizes small-scale experiments instead of imposing a requirement. Employers are relatively free to try out different approaches and see what works—just the kind of implementation strategy that behavioral economists suggest (Volpp et al. 2011). In addition to using monetary reward or penalties, these initiatives could employ the tools of behavioral economics—loss aversion, framing, salience, defaults, even overconfidence bias—to potentially great effect. To be most useful for health policy, a clearinghouse should be established to catalog and disseminate the results of each initiative's effectiveness (and perhaps to advise on data collection and analysis protocols—so that we can determine what really works). Again, this is not a big idea, but it is one that could advance both the science and application of behavioral economics in health policy.

Finally, we should consider the lessons from the work of the U.S. Preventive Services Task Force that we discussed in Chapter 2. It is clear that framing strongly influences the degree of support for health policy issues. One of the ideas that Ned Calonge, former chairman of the Task Force, proposed during my interview with him was that the Task Force and those opposed to a particular recommendation would engage in an "adversarial collaboration," in which both sides could issue a joint statement that explicitly articulates the points of agreement and disagreement. In effect, the two sides would frame the debate as they would like, so that readers could recognize the frames and consider the issue on their own terms. Obviously, each side would not be limited to that single presentation to make its case, but the adversarial collaboration could set the tone for the debate. Once more, this is a small idea but one that might make a difference.

A RESEARCH AGENDA

As I have noted, behavioral economics is a young discipline, and only recently have researchers considered its application to health care. The academic community needs to strengthen the empirical validity of its theories and propositions. We need to test the concepts of this field in real-world health care situations. In this book, I have applied the principles of behavioral economics to almost two dozen anomalies in health care, but many of my arguments have been based on translating findings from research in other settings. Thus, we need formal studies, either in the lab or in natural experiments, to verify this book's interpretations in the health arena. Based on my research for this book, here are the research questions in health care for which behavioral economics hold the most promise:

1. *The effects of framing and anchoring on patient decision making.* What are the most appropriate ways to present treatment alternatives to patients? For example, should clinicians present the alternatives in a survival or mortality frame; should they present benefits before risks or vice versa; should they present multiple frames, or does this just confuse patients? How can patients be engaged to use both System 1 and System 2 thinking? Is there a way to minimize the hot–cold empathy gap, so that patients can make decisions that they will not regret later?

2. *The optimal choice structure in health care.* How many choices do patients—or physicians—really want and need? At what point do patients and physicians shift from viewing choice as being attractive to being debilitating? Do patients make better decisions regarding their health care when they have all the available options or with a subset? If a subset, how should the subset be selected? Are physicians subject to similar problems as patients in terms of selecting among multiple alternatives? If so, how can these problems be managed to ensure optimal patient care?

3. *Improving patient adherence to treatment regimens.* Are positive frames or negative frames more effective in increasing patient adherence? How can frequency and dosage be manipulated to maintain adherence to medications for chronic (especially asymptomatic) conditions? Why does adherence seem to be low for pain medication, which has high affect?

4. *Promoting good health habits and discouraging bad ones.* How effective are extrinsic—compared to intrinsic—motivators in influencing health behaviors? What is the relative effectiveness of money, near-money, and other economic incentives on health behaviors? What is the role of commitment devices in influencing health behavior? Which devices are more effective: reward or penalty based?

5. *The use of heuristics in medical practice.* Where do physicians learn the heuristics that they use? How do they decide which heuristics to use? What is the role of practice location in determining physicians' application of heuristics? What are the primary factors that lead physicians to discard one heuristic and adopt another? What circumstances lead physicians to go beyond the heuristic and search for alternative explanations of patient conditions?

6. *The relative power of economic versus social norms in influencing patient and physician behavior.* Health care is both an economic service and a social interaction. Which force is more powerful in driving patient—or physician—behavior and under what circumstances? What happens when economic norms replace social norms; can social norms ever be recovered?

7. *The role of internalities in justifying government intervention into health care decisions.* As noted earlier in this chapter, a major point of contention between neoclassical and behavioral economists is the circumstances that justify government intervention. Neoclassical economists limit such involvement to material instances of externalities not addressed in a market transaction, whereas behavioral economists expand the criteria to include internalities that arise from hyperbolic discounting and loss aversion. Are there circumstances in health care (on the patient or provider side) that involve

no externalities in which government intervention would improve the allocation of resources?

8. *The special value of zero.* When is a zero price an attractor and when is it a repellent? Is there really anything "special" about a price of zero, or is it just a price?

As I consider this research agenda, I realize that these questions range far afield from mainstream, neoclassical economics. Most economists from this perspective would consider these questions to be more in the realm of psychology or sociology and would counsel against taking them up. Behavioral economists would counter that that objection is the point: Many health care issues extend beyond the traditional boundaries of economics and require a multidisciplinary approach.

In addition to a vigorous research agenda that is not limited to traditional boundaries, we must find some way to support confirmation and extension research. Many surprising results—even in behavioral economics—are wrong; they cannot be confirmed, or sometimes, in the words of one *New Yorker* article, "The truth wears off" (Lehrer 2010). In addition, mainstream, neoclassical economics has had at least a century head start, with an abundance of independent confirmation (or refutation) of its hypotheses. Behavioral economists have a lot of catching up to do and need the support of journal editors in the discipline to build a body of tested and replicated research. For example, journals in economics should follow the lead of the *Journal of Consumer Research*, which since 2001 has published a section called, "Re-Inquiries," intended to "re-think, re-test, re-interpret, re-analyze, or re-present . . . theories, frameworks, themes, data, findings, and methodologies generated in prior scholarship" (Mick 2001: 1). We must expect that some of the studies cited in this book will be refuted by future research, and the sooner we find that out, the sooner we can make valid inferences and recommendations about health policy.

In addition, we need to resist the temptation (likely driven by overconfidence bias) to embrace and implement the newest, most clever, and most provocative results of behavioral economics in health care. A much more effective approach—in terms of advancing the field and applying its insights—will be to undertake a robust series of small-scale interventions to confirm the usefulness of this discipline in health care and to test the sensitivity of patient and physician behavior to changes in frames, anchors, defaults, and biases. The Robert Wood Johnson Foundation is one of the first private entities to fund such efforts. In its initial call for proposals, the Foundation noted that they "see possibility in unconventional approaches and remain open to untested models, new connections, risk and failure," and that they are "interested in accelerating the rate at which the principles and tools of this discipline are evaluated and, if successful, applied to health and health care" (Robert Wood Johnson Foundation 2011: 1). Other foundations dedicated to health policy issues would do well to follow the lead of this premier organization, if we are to gain a fuller understanding of patient and provider behavior and find ways of increasing the value of the money spent on health care in this country.

THIS IS (NOT) THE END

When I decided to write this book, I did not intend it to be the definitive treatise on the connections between behavioral economics and health care. Rather, I wanted to reveal what I saw as the insights that this new field can bring to the study of health care and health reform and to start a conversation about deepening these insights, expanding the research base, and applying the results to create a more effective health care system. I hoped to show health professionals how their clinical behavior—even honed after years of training and experience—is susceptible to biases that could lead to results that they had not intended. I wanted to expose health policy makers to a new perspective on the forces shaping individual and collective decision making in health care. I aimed to demonstrate to my fellow health economists a whole new world of exciting research possibilities. Finally, I wanted to show those outside the health care industry how intriguing the findings of behavioral economics are and how useful they can be in understanding their own health care decisions as well as the vital functioning of the health care system. If I have succeeded, then we all should have an interesting and vigorous conversation. Let us begin.

WHERE TO GO NEXT: A BRIEF BIBLIOGRAPHY
OF BEHAVIORAL ECONOMICS AND PSYCHOLOGY

Books like this one tend to have three kinds of readers. The first wants an overview of the field. The second wants to become immersed in the field and will devour the bibliography at the end of the book. The third wants to read more but does not have the time, interest, or patience to wade through academic journal articles. The following is my recommended reading list for this last group, starting with what I think is the best book about the field so far, followed by four targeted books in behavioral economics/psychology, and finishing with two expansive books on thinking and the brain. Enjoy.

Daniel Kahneman, *Thinking, Fast and Slow*. New York: Farrar, Straus & Giroux, 2011.

The Nobel Prize winner's intellectual memoir of his professional career especially highlights his work with Amos Tversky. This book presents Kahneman's most extended discussion to date of System 1 and System 2 thinking, as well as a review of his (and others') work in heuristics and biases, and choice. The book is engagingly written, with accessible explanations of his research.

Richard H. Thaler and Cass R. Sunstein, *Nudge*. New Haven, CT: Yale University Press, 2008.

The creators of the concept of "libertarian paternalism" describe the importance of what they call "choice architecture"—organizing the framework within which people make decisions. They discuss the practical and ethical consequences of creating this architecture (including defaults) and present real-life situations (such as the Medicare Part D program that we discussed in Chapter 3).

Barry Schwartz, *The Paradox of Choice*. New York: HarperCollins, 2004.

The first psychologist to thoroughly investigate the downsides of choice, Schwartz presents the results of his and other researchers' studies of how people make decisions and how we can suffer as we make those decisions. He expands on many of the studies that we have considered in this book and puts them into context.

Sheena Iyengar, *The Art of Choosing*. New York: Twelve, 2010.

This is an excellent complement to the Schwartz book. The author of the famous "jam study," Professor Iyengar combines descriptions of her own and others' research on choice, personal memoir, and practical advice. More so than the authors of other books on this list, she makes the research personal and demonstrates why it can make a difference in everyone's lives.

Daniel Gilbert, *Stumbling on Happiness*. New York: Vintage, 2005.

Gilbert, a professor of psychology at Harvard University, describes the multitude of reasons we have difficulty in achieving happiness—our cognitive shortcomings, our faulty memories, our inability to predict future states, you name it. Reading this book is entertaining and enlightening—like spending an evening at your favorite bar with your smartest friend.

Steven Pinker, *How the Mind Works*. New York: Norton, 1997.

A cognitive neuroscientist, Pinker does a masterful job of synthesizing current—and sometimes controversial—research on the human mind. The book gives the reader a renewed appreciation of how the mind does what it does, as well as an appreciation of how Professor Pinker can make this complex science understandable to the rest of us.

Jonathan Baron, *Thinking and Deciding*, 4th ed. Cambridge, UK, and New York: Cambridge University Press, 2008.

Baron does for thinking what Pinker does for the mind—reviews the research in an intelligent and engaging way. He discusses in depth many of the concepts we touched on in this book: the nature of rationality, how people deal with probabilities, choice under certainty and uncertainty, time preferences, moral judgment, and fairness.

Abaluck, Jason T., and Jonathan Gruber. 2011. Choice inconsistencies among the elderly: Evidence from plan choice in the Medicare Part D program. *American Economic Review*. 101 (4): 1180–1210.

Agassi, Andre. 2009. *Open: An autobiography*. New York: Alfred A. Knopf.

Ainslie, George, and Nick Haslam. 1992. Hyperbolic discounting. In *Choice over Time*, eds. George Loewenstein and Jon Elster, 57–92. New York: Russell Sage Foundation.

Alhakami, Ali, and Paul Slovic. 1994. A psychological study of the inverse relationship between perceived risk and perceived benefit. *Risk Analysis* 14 (6): 1085–1096.

Ali, Mukthar M. 1977. Probability and utility estimates for racetrack bettors. *Journal of Political Economy* 85 (4) (08): 803–815.

Allen, Jonathan. 2009. Grayson: GOP wants "you to die." Retrieved on October 29, 2012, from www.politico.com/news/stories/0909/27726.html.

American Cancer Society. 2009. American Cancer Society responds to changes to USPSTF mammography guidelines. In American Cancer

Society [database online]. Retrieved on October 29, 2012, from http://pressroom.cancer.org/index.php?s=43&item=201.

American College of Radiology. 2009. *Press release: USPSTF mammography recommendations will result in countless unnecessary breast cancer deaths each year.* Reston, VA: American College of Radiology.

Amsterlaw, Jennifer, Brian Zikmund-Fisher, Angela Fagerlin, and Peter A. Ubel. 2006. Can avoidance of complications lead to biased healthcare decisions? *Judgment and Decision Making* 1 (1): 64–75.

Anderson Cooper 360 Degrees. 2009. Controversy erupts over new breast cancer screening guidelines. Broadcast November 17 by CNN.

Ariely, Dan, George Loewenstein, and Drazen Prelec. 2003. "Coherent arbitrariness": Stable demand curves without stable preferences. *Quarterly Journal of Economics* 118 (1) (February): 73–105.

Ariely, Dan, and Jose Silva. 2002. Payment method design: Psychological and economic aspects of payments. Working Paper, Center for e-Business. Cambridge, MA: Massachusetts Institute of Technology.

Arkes, Hal R., Victoria A. Shaffer, and Mitchell A. Medow. 2007. Patients derogate physicians who use a computer-assisted diagnostic aid. *Medical Decision Making* 27 (2) (March 1): 189–202.

Arkes, Hal R., Robert L. Wortmann, Paul D. Saville, and Allan R. Harkness. 1981. Hindsight bias among physicians weighing the likelihood of diagnoses. *Journal of Applied Psychology* 66 (2) (April): 252–254.

Arrow, Kenneth J. 1963. Uncertainty and the welfare economics of medical care. *American Economic Review* 53 (5) (December): 941–973.

Ashraf, Nava, James Berry, and Jesse M. Shapiro. 2010. Can higher prices stimulate product use? Evidence from a field experiment in Zambia. *American Economic Review* 100 (5) (December): 2383–2413.

Ayanian, John Z., and Donald M. Berwick. 1991. Do physicians have a bias toward action? *Medical Decision Making* 11 (3) (August): 154–158.

Bagwell, Kyle, and Michael H. Riordan. 1991. High and declining prices signal product quality. *American Economic Review* 81 (1) (March): 224–239.

Bakwin, Harry. 1945. Pseudodoxia pediatrica. *New England Journal of Medicine* 232 (24) (June 14): 691–697.

Bar-Eli, Michael, Ofer H. Azar, Ilana Ritov, Yael Keidar-Levin, and Galit Schein. 2007. Action bias among elite soccer goalkeepers: The case of penalty kicks. *Journal of Economic Psychology*, 28 (5) (October): 606–621.

Baron, Jonathan. 2008. *Thinking and deciding*, 4th ed. Cambridge, UK, and New York: Cambridge University Press.

Barsky, Robert B., F. Thomas Juster, Miles S. Kimball, and Matthew D. Shapiro. 1997. Preference parameters and behavioral heterogeneity: An experimental approach in the health and retirement study. *Quarterly Journal of Economics* 112 (2) (May): 537–579.

Bateman, Ian, Daniel Kahneman, Alistair Munro, Chris Starmer, and Robert Sugden. 2005. Testing competing models of loss aversion: An adversarial collaboration. *Journal of Public Economics* 89 (8) (August): 1561–1580.

Becker, Gary S., and Julio Jorge Elías. 2007. Introducing incentives in the market for live and cadaveric organ donations. *Journal of Economic Perspectives* 21 (3) (Summer): 3–24.

Becker, Gary S., and Kevin M. Murphy. 1988. A theory of rational addiction. *Journal of Political Economy* 96 (4) (August): 675–700.

Blank, Hartmut, Steffen Nestler, Gernot von Collani, and Volkhard Fischer. 2008. How many hindsight biases are there? *Cognition* 106 (3) (March): 1408–1440.

Blumberg, Linda J., Matthew Buettgens, and Judy Feder. 2012. *The individual mandate in perspective*. Washington, DC: The Urban Institute.

Borgida, Eugene, and Richard E. Nisbett. 1977. The differential impact of abstract vs. concrete information on decisions. *Journal of Applied Social Psychology* 7 (3) (September): 258–271.

Bornstein, Brian H., A. Christine Emler, and Gretchen B. Chapman. 1999. Rationality in medical treatment decisions: Is there a sunk-cost effect? *Social Science & Medicine* 49 (2) (July): 215–222.

Botti, Simona, and Sheena S. Iyengar. 2006. The dark side of choice: When choice impairs social welfare. *Journal of Public Policy & Marketing* 25 (1) (Spring): 24–38.

A Breast Cancer Preview. 2009. *Wall Street Journal.* November 19: A20.

Breast Cancer Screening Recommendations: Hearings before the Health Subcommittee of the House Energy and Commerce Committee. 111th Congress (December 2, 2009).

Brickman, Philip, Dan Coates, and Ronnie Janoff-Bulman. 1978. Lottery winners and accident victims: Is happiness relative? *Journal of Personality and Social Psychology* 36 (8) (August): 917–927.

Britney Spears is single again. January 5, 2004. Retrieved on October 29, 2012, from www.thesmokinggun.com/documents/celebrity/britney-spears-single-again.

Brook, Robert H., John E. Ware, William H. Rogers, Emmett B. Keeler, Allyson R. Davies, Cathy A. Donald, George A. Goldberg, Kathleen N. Lohr, Patricia C. Masthay, and Joseph P. Newhouse. 1983. Does free care improve adults' health? *New England Journal of Medicine* 309 (23) (December 8): 1426–1434.

Cabana, Michael D., Cynthia S. Rand, Neil R. Powe, Albert W. Wu, Modena H. Wilson, Paul-Andre C. Abboud, and Haya R. Rubin. 1999. Why don't physicians follow clinical practice guidelines? A framework for improvement. *JAMA: The Journal of the American Medical Association* 282 (15) (October 20): 1458–1465.

Camerer, Colin F. 1989. Does the basketball market believe in the "hot hand'? *American Economic Review* 79 (5) (December): 1257–1261.

Caplan, Robert A., Karen L. Posner, and Frederick W. Cheney. 1991. Effect of outcome on physician judgments of appropriateness of care. *JAMA: The Journal of the American Medical Association* 265 (15) (April 17): 1957–1960.

Carman, Kristin L., Maureen Maurer, Jill Mathews Yegian, Pamela Dardess, Jeanne McGee, Mark Evers, and Karen O. Marlo. 2010. Evidence that consumers are skeptical about evidence-based health care. *Health Affairs* 29 (7) (July): 1400–1406.

Carmon, Ziv, and Dan Ariely. 2000. Focusing on the foregone: How value can appear so different to buyers and sellers. *Journal of Consumer Research* 27 (3) (December): 360–370.

Carrier, Emily R., James D. Reschovsky, Michelle M. Mello, Ralph C. Mayrell, and David Katz. 2010. Physicians' fears of malpractice lawsuits are not assuaged by tort reforms. *Health Affairs* 29 (9) (September): 1585–1592.

Carter, K. Codell, and Barbara R. Carter. 1994. *Childbed fever: A scientific biography of Ignaz Semmelweis.* Contributions in medical studies. Vol. 39. Westport, CT: Greenwood Press.

Cassar, Gavin, and Justin Craig. 2009. An investigation of hindsight bias in nascent venture activity. *Journal of Business Venturing* 24 (2) (March): 149–164.

Centers for Disease Control and Prevention. 2002. Guideline for hand hygiene in health-care settings: Recommendations of the healthcare infection control practices advisory committee and the HICPAC/SHEA/APIC/IDSA hand hygiene task force. *Morbidity and Mortality Weekly Report* 51 (RR-16) (October 25): 1–45.

Chaudhry, Basit, Jerome Wang, Shinyi Wu, Margaret Maglione, Walter Mojica, Elizabeth Roth, Sally C. Morton, and Paul G. Shekelle. 2006. Systematic review: Impact of health information technology on quality, efficiency, and costs of medical care. *Annals of Internal Medicine* 144 (10) (May 16): 742–752.

Chen, M. Keith, Venkat Lakshminarayanan, and Laurie R. Santos. 2006. How basic are behavioral biases? Evidence from capuchin monkey trading behavior. *Journal of Political Economy* 114 (3) (June): 517–537.

Chinander, Karen R., and Maurice E. Schweitzer. 2003. The input bias: The misuse of input information in judgments of outcomes. *Organizational Behavior and Human Decision Processes*, 91 (2) (July): 243–253.

Christensen, Caryn, Paul Heckerling, Mary Mackesy-Amiti, Lionel M. Bernstein, and Arthur S. Elstein. 1995. Pervasiveness of framing effects among physicians and medical students. *Journal of Behavioral Decision Making* 8 (3) (September): 169–180.

Claxton, Mark, Bianca DiJulio, Benjamin Finder, Janet Lundy, Megan McHugh, Awo Osei-Anto, Heidi Whitmore, Jeremy Pickreign, and Jon Gabel. 2010. *Employer health benefits: 2010 annual survey.* Menlo Park, CA, and Chicago: Kaiser Family Foundation and Health Research & Educational Trust.

Cohen, Jessica, and Pascaline Dupas. 2010. Free distribution or cost-sharing? Evidence from a randomized malaria prevention experiment. *Quarterly Journal of Economics* 125 (1) (February): 1–45.

Coval, Joshua D., and Tyler Shumway. 2005. Do behavioral biases affect prices? *Journal of Finance* 60 (1) (February): 1–34.

Creamer, Robert. 2009. Memo to Congress: On health care vote you must choose between insurance companies and average Americans. Retrieved on October 29, 2012, from www.huffingtonpost.com /robert-creamer/memo-to-congress-on-healt_b_348353.html.

Cromwell, Jerry, and Janet B. Mitchell. 1986. Physician-induced demand for surgery. *Journal of Health Economics* 5 (4) (December): 293–313.

Croskerry, Pat. 2009. A universal model of diagnostic reasoning. *Academic Medicine* 84 (8) (August): 1022–1028.

———. 2003. Cognitive forcing strategies in clinical decisionmaking. *Annals of Emergency Medicine* 41 (1) (January): 110–120.

Cummings, Janet, Thomas Rice, and Yaniv Hanoch. 2009. Who thinks that Part D is too complicated? Survey results on the Medicare prescription drug benefit. *Medical Care Research and Review* 66 (1) (February): 97–115.

Damasio, Antonio R. 1994. *Descartes' error: Emotion, reason, and the human brain.* New York: G. P. Putnam.

Dartmouth Institute for Health Policy and Clinical Practice. 2011. *Dartmouth atlas of health care.* Lebanon, NH: Dartmouth Institute for Health Policy and Clinical Practice. Retrieved on November 4, 2011, from www.dartmouthatlas.org/.

Deci, Edward L., Richard Koestner, and Richard M. Ryan. 1999. A meta-analytic review of experiments examining the effects of extrinsic rewards on intrinsic motivation. *Psychological Bulletin* 125 (6) (November): 627–668.

Deci, Edward L., and Richard M. Ryan. 1985. *Intrinsic motivation and self-determination in human behavior.* Perspectives in social psychology. New York: Plenum.

DeKay, Michael L., and David A. Asch. 1998. Is the defensive use of diagnostic tests good for patients, or bad? *Medical Decision Making* 18 (1) (January): 19–28.

DellaVigna, Stefano, and Ulrike Malmendier. 2004. Contract design and self-control: Theory and evidence. *Quarterly Journal of Economics* 119 (2) (May): 353–402.

DeNavas-Walt, Carmen, Bernadette D. Proctor, and Jessica C. Smith. 2010. *Income, poverty, and health insurance coverage in the United States: 2009.* Washington, DC: U.S. Census Bureau, Current Population Reports, P60–238.

DiMatteo, M. Robin. 2004. Variations in patients' adherence to medical recommendations: A quantitative review of 50 years of research. *Medical Care* 42 (3) (March): 200–209.

DiMatteo, M. Robin, Patrick J. Giordani, Heidi S. Lepper, and Thomas W. Croghan. 2002. Patient adherence and medical treatment outcomes: A meta-analysis. *Medical Care* 40 (9) (September): 794–811.

Dranove, David, and Paul Wehner. 1994. Physician-induced demand for childbirths. *Journal of Health Economics* 13 (1) (March): 61–73.

Druckman, James N. 2001. Using credible advice to overcome framing effects. *Journal of Law, Economics, and Organization* 17 (1) (April): 62–82.

Druckman, James, and Rose McDermott. 2008. Emotion and the framing of risky choice. *Political Behavior* 30 (3) (September): 297–321.

Eisenberg, John M. 1979. Sociologic influences on decision-making by clinicians. *Annals of Internal Medicine* 90 (6) (June): 957–964.

Elstein, Arthur S., Lee S. Shulman, and Sarah A. Sprafka. 1978. *Medical problem solving: An analysis of clinical reasoning.* Cambridge, MA: Harvard University Press.

Elster, Jon. 1989. Social norms and economic theory. *Journal of Economic Perspectives* 3 (4) (Fall): 99–117.

Epstein, Arnold M. 2010. Geographic variation in Medicare spending. *New England Journal of Medicine* 363 (1) (July 1): 85–86.

Epstein, Ronald M. 1999. Mindful practice. *JAMA: The Journal of the American Medical Association* 282 (9) (September 1): 833–839.

Esserman, Laura, Yiwey Shieh, and Ian Thompson. 2009. Rethinking screening for breast cancer and prostate cancer. *JAMA: The Journal of the American Medical Association* 302 (15) (October 21): 1685–1692.

Evans, Jonathan St. B. T. 2008. Dual-processing accounts of reasoning, judgment, and social cognition. *Annual Review of Psychology* 59: 255–278.

Evans, Robert G. 1984. *Strained mercy: The economics of Canadian health care.* Toronto: Butterworths.

Fehr, Ernst, and Urs Fischbacher. 2004. Social norms and human cooperation. *Trends in Cognitive Sciences* 8 (4) (April): 185–190.

Feinstein, Alvan R. 1985. The "chagrin factor" and qualitative decision analysis. *Archives of Internal Medicine* 145 (7) (July): 1257–1259.

Fendrick, A. M., and Michael E. Chernew. 2007. Value-based insurance design: A "clinically sensitive, fiscally responsible" approach to mitigate the adverse clinical effects of high-deductible consumer-directed health plans. *Journal of General Internal Medicine* 22 (6) (June): 890–891.

Finkelstein, Amy. 2009. E-ZTax: Tax salience and tax rates. *Quarterly Journal of Economics* 124 (3) (August): 969–1010.

Fischer, Michael A., Margaret R. Stedman, Joyce Lii, Christine Vogeli, William H. Shrank, M. A. Brookhart, and Joel S. Weissman. 2010. Primary medication non-adherence: Analysis of 195,930 electronic prescriptions. *JGIM: Journal of General Internal Medicine* 25 (4) (April): 284–290.

Fischhoff, Baruch. 1975. Hindsight is not equal to foresight: The effect of outcome knowledge on judgment under uncertainty. *Journal of Experimental Psychology: Human Perception and Performance* 1 (3) (August): 288–299.

Fischhoff, Baruch, Paul Slovic, Sarah Lichtenstein, Stephen Read, and Barbara Combs. 1978. How safe is safe enough? A psychometric study of attitudes towards technological risks and benefits. *Policy Sciences* 9 (2) (April): 127–152.

Fisher, Elliott S., David E. Wennberg, Therese A. Stukel, Daniel J. Gott-lieb, F. L. Lucas, and Etoile L. Pinder. 2003a. The implications of regional variations in Medicare spending. Part 1: The content, quality, and accessibility of care. *Annals of Internal Medicine* 138 (4) (February 18): 273–287.

———. 2003b. The implications of regional variations in Medicare spending. Part 2: Health outcomes and satisfaction with care. *Annals of Internal Medicine* 138 (4) (February 18): 288–298.

Fowler, Floyd J., Patricia M. Gallagher, Denise L. Anthony, Kirk Larsen, and Jonathan S. Skinner. 2008. Relationship between regional per capita Medicare expenditures and patient perceptions of quality of care. *JAMA: The Journal of the American Medical Association* 299 (20) (May 28): 2406–2412.

Francke, Anneke L., Marieke C. Smit, de Veer, Anke J. E., and Patriek Mistiaen. 2008. Factors influencing the implementation of clinical guidelines for health care professionals: A systematic meta-review. *BMC Medical Informatics & Decision Making* 8 (1) (January): 1–11.

Frank, Richard G. 2007. Behavioral economics and health economics. In *Behavioral economics and its applications*, eds. Peter Diamond and Hannu Vartiainen, 195–234. Princeton, NJ: Princeton University Press.

Fredrickson, Barbara L., and Daniel Kahneman. 1993. Duration neglect in retrospective evaluations of affective episodes. *Journal of Personality and Social Psychology* 65 (1) (July): 45–55.

Freeman, Joseph D., Srikanth Kadiyala, Janice F. Bell, and Diane P. Martin. 2008. The causal effect of health insurance on utilization and outcomes in adults: A systematic review of US studies. *Medical Care* 46 (10) (October): 1023–1032.

Friedman, Milton, and L. J. Savage. 1948. The utility analysis of choices involving risk. *Journal of Political Economy* 56 (4) (August): 279–304.

Frølich, Anne, Jason A. Talavera, Peter Broadhead, and R. Adams Dudley. 2007. A behavioral model of clinician responses to incentives to improve quality. *Health Policy* 80 (1) (January): 179–193.

Fuchs, Victor R. 1978. The supply of surgeons and the demand for operations. *Journal of Human Resources* 13 (Supplement): 35–56.

———. 1975. *Who shall live? Health, economics, and social choice.* New York: Basic Books.

Garg, Amit X., Neill K. J. Adhikari, Heather McDonald, M. Patricia Rosas-Arellano, P. J. Devereaux, Joseph Beyene, Justina Sam, and R. Brian Haynes. 2005. Effects of computerized clinical decision support systems on practitioner performance and patient outcomes. *JAMA: The Journal of the American Medical Association* 293 (10) (March 09): 1223–1238.

Gawande, Atul. 2010. *The checklist manifesto: How to get things right.* New York: Metropolitan Books.

———. 2009. The cost conundrum. *New Yorker* (June 1): 36–44.

Gigerenzer, Gerd, and Wolfgang Gaissmaier. 2011. Heuristic decision making. *Annual Review of Psychology* 62: 451–482.

Gigerenzer, Gerd, Peter M. Todd, and ABC Research Group. 1999. *Simple heuristics that make us smart.* Evolution and cognition. New York: Oxford University Press.

Gilbert, Daniel Todd. 2007. *Stumbling on happiness.* New York: Vintage.

Gilovich, Thomas, Dale W. Griffin, and Daniel Kahneman. 2002. *Heuristics and biases: The psychology of intuitive judgement.* Cambridge, UK, and New York: Cambridge University Press.

Gilovich, Thomas, Robert Vallone, and Amos Tversky. 1985. The hot hand in basketball: On the misperception of random sequences. *Cognitive Psychology* 17 (3) (July): 295–314.

Gneezy, Uri, and Aldo Rustichini. 2000a. A fine is a price. *The Journal of Legal Studies* 29 (1) (January): 1–17.

———. 2000b. Pay enough or don't pay at all. *Quarterly Journal of Economics* 115 (3) (August): 791–810.

Goodman-Delahunty, Jane, Pä Granhag, Maria Hartwig, and Elizabeth F. Loftus. 2010. Insightful or wishful: Lawyers' ability to predict case outcomes. *Psychology, Public Policy, and Law* 16 (2) (May): 133–157.

Graber, Mark L., Nancy Franklin, and Ruthanna Gordon. 2005. Diagnostic error in internal medicine. *Archives of Internal Medicine* 165 (13) (July): 1493–1499.

Grant, Adam M., and David A. Hofmann. 2011. It's not all about me. *Psychological Science* 22 (12) (December): 1494–1499.

Gregg, Judd. 2009. We need truly bipartisan, fiscally responsible healthcare reform. *The [Manchester, NH] Union-Leader*, Dec. 16.

Griffith, R. M. 1949. Odds adjustments by American horse-race bettors. *The American Journal of Psychology* 62 (2) (April): 290–294.

Grol, Richard, and Jeremy Grimshaw. 2003. From best evidence to best practice: Effective implementation of change in patients' care. *Lancet* 362 (9391) (October 11): 1225–1230.

Groopman, Jerome E. 2007. *How doctors think*. Boston: Houghton Mifflin.

Gruber, Jonathan, and Botond Köszegi. 2001. Is addiction "rational"? Theory and evidence. *Quarterly Journal of Economics* 116 (4) (November): 1261–1303.

Gruber, Jonathan, and Maria Owings. 1996. Physician financial incentives and cesarean section delivery. *RAND Journal of Economics* 27 (1) (Spring): 99–123.

Halpern, Scott D., Amelie Raz, Rachel Kohn, Michael Rey, David A. Asch, and Peter Reese. 2010. Regulated payments for living kidney donation: An empirical assessment of the ethical concerns. *Annals of Internal Medicine* 152 (6) (March 16): 358–365.

Hammack, Judd, Gardner Mallard Brown, and Resources for the Future. 1974. *Waterfowl and wetlands: Toward bio-economic analysis*.

Washington: Resources for the Future; distributed by the Johns Hopkins University Press, Baltimore.

Handwashing Liaison Group. 1999. Hand washing: A modest measure—with big effects. *British Medical Journal* 318 (7185) (March 13): 686.

Hanoch, Yaniv, Stacey Wood, Andrew Barnes, Pi-Ju Liu, and Thomas Rice. 2011. Choosing the right Medicare prescription drug plan: The effect of age, strategy selection, and choice set size. *Health Psychology* 30 (6) (November): 719-727.

Haynes, R. Brian, Elizabeth Ackloo, Navdeep Sahota, Heather P. McDonald, and Xiaomei Yao. 2008. *Interventions for enhancing medication adherence.* London: The Cochrane Collaboration.

Health care repeal debate. 2011. Retrieved on October 12, 2012, from www.c-spanvideo.org/videoLibrary/clip.php?appid=599428034.

Health Resources and Services Administration. 2009. *2009 annual report of the U.S. organ procurement and transplantation network and the scientific registry of transplant recipients: Transplant data 1999–2008.* Washington, DC: U.S. Department of Health and Human Services, Health Resources and Services Administration.

Heberlein, T. A., and R. C. Bishop. 1986. Assessing the validity of contingent valuation: Three field experiments. *Science of the Total Environment* 56 (November 15): 99–107.

Henrich, Joseph, Steven J. Heine, and Ara Norenzayan. 2010. The weirdest people in the world? *Behavioral and Brain Sciences* 33 (2-3) (June): 61–83.

Heyman, James, and Dan Ariely. 2004. Effort for payment: A tale of two markets. *Psychological Science* 15 (11) (November): 787–793.

Hozo, Iztok, and Benjamin Djulbegovic. 2008. When is diagnostic testing inappropriate or irrational? Acceptable regret approach. *Medical Decision Making* 28 (4) (July/August): 540–553.

Hunt, Dereck L., R. Brian Haynes, Steven E. Hanna, and Kristina Smith. 1998. Effects of computer-based clinical decision support systems on physician performance and patient outcomes. *JAMA: The*

Journal of the American Medical Association 280 (15) (October 21): 1339–1346.

Idle, Eric. 2005. *The song that goes like this.* Hal Leonard Music Publishing.

Illegal aliens can receive benefits under House health care bill. Aug. 26, 2009. Federation for American Immigration Reform. Retrieved on March 18, 2011, from www.fairus.org/site/News2?page=NewsArticle &id=21317&security=1601&news_iv_ctrl=1741

In Massachusetts, individual mandate sparks little outcry. 2012. *Boston Herald*, June 6: A1.

Ioannidis, John P. A. 2005. Why most published research findings are false. *PLOS Medicine* 2 (8) (August): 696–701.

Iyengar, Sheena. 2010. *The art of choosing.* New York: Twelve.

Iyengar, Sheena S., and Mark R. Lepper. 2000. When choice is demotivating: Can one desire too much of a good thing? *Journal of Personality and Social Psychology* 79 (6) (December): 995–1006.

Johnson, Eric J., and Daniel Goldstein. 2003. Do defaults save lives? *Science* 302 (5649) (November 21): 1338–1339.

Johnson, Eric J., John Hershey, Jacqueline Meszaros, and Howard Kunreuther. 1993. Framing, probability distortions, and insurance decisions. *Journal of Risk and Uncertainty* 7 (1) (August): 35–51.

The Joint Commission. 2009. *Measuring hand hygiene adherence: Overcoming the challenges.* Oakbrook Terrace, IL: The Joint Commission.

Jones, Jeffrey M. 2007. *Latest Gallup update shows cigarette smoking near historical lows.* Washington, DC: The Gallup Organization.

———. 2006. *Smoking habits stable; Most would like to quit.* Washington, DC: The Gallup Organization.

Kahneman, Daniel. 2011. *Thinking, fast and slow.* New York: Farrar, Straus & Giroux.

Kahneman, Daniel, and Shane Frederick. 2002. Representativeness revisited: Attribute substitution in intuitive judgment. In *Heuristics and biases: The psychology of intuitive judgement*, eds. Thomas Gilovich,

Dale Griffin, and Daniel Kahneman, 49–81. Cambridge, UK, and New York: Cambridge University Press.

Kahneman, Daniel, Jack L. Knetsch, and Richard H. Thaler. 1990. Experimental tests of the endowment effect and the Coase theorem. *Journal of Political Economy* 98 (6) (December): 1325–1348.

———. 1986. Fairness as a constraint on profit seeking: Entitlements in the market. *The American Economic Review* 76 (4) (September): 728–741.

Kahneman, Daniel, and Dale T. Miller. 1986. Norm theory: Comparing reality to its alternatives. *Psychological Review* 93 (2) (April): 136–153.

Kahneman, Daniel, Paul Slovic, and Amos Tversky. 1982. *Judgment under uncertainty: Heuristics and biases.* Cambridge, UK, and New York: Cambridge University Press.

Kahneman, Daniel, and Amos Tversky. 1979. Prospect theory: An analysis of decision under risk. *Econometrica* 47 (2) (March): 263–291.

———. 1972. Subjective probability: A judgment of representativeness. *Cognitive Psychology,* 3 (3) (July): 430-54.

Kaiser Commission on Medicaid and the Uninsured. 2010. *The uninsured: A primer.* Washington, DC: Kaiser Family Foundation, December.

Kaiser health tracking poll: March 2012. 2012. Menlo Park, CA: The Henry J. Kaiser Family Foundation.

Kaiser health tracking poll: February 2011. 2011. Menlo Park, CA: The Henry J. Kaiser Family Foundation.

Kaiser health tracking poll: August 2010. 2010. Menlo Park, CA: The Henry J. Kaiser Family Foundation.

Kassirer, Jerome P. 1989. Our stubborn quest for diagnostic certainty. *New England Journal of Medicine* 320 (22) (June 1): 1489–1491.

Kassirer, Jerome P., John B. Wong, and Richard I. Kopelman. 2010. *Learning clinical reasoning,* 2nd ed. Baltimore, MD: Lippincott Williams & Wilkins.

Kearns, Janine M. 2009. Letter to the editor. *New York Times.* November 18.

Keren, Gideon, and Yaacov Schul. 2009. Two is not always better than one: A critical evaluation of two-system theories. *Perspectives on Psychological Science* 4 (6) (November): 533–550.

Kim, E. H., Adair Morse, and Luigi Zingales. 2006. What has mattered to economics since 1970. *Journal of Economic Perspectives* 20 (4) (Fall 2006): 189–202.

Klevens, R. Monina, Jonathan R. Edwards, Chesley L. Richards Jr., Teresa C. Horan, Robert P. Gaynes, Daniel A. Pollock, and Denise M. Cardo. 2007. Estimating health care-associated infections and deaths in U.S. hospitals, 2002. *Public Health Reports* 122 (2) (March–April): 160–166.

Knetsch, Jack L. 1989. The endowment effect and evidence of nonreversible indifference curves. *American Economic Review* 79 (5) (December): 1277–1284.

Kohn, Linda T., Janet Corrigan, and Molla S. Donaldson. 2000. *To err is human: Building a safer health system.* Washington, DC: National Academy Press.

Kolstad, Jonathan T., and Amanda E. Kowalski. 2010. *The impact of health care reform on hospital and preventive care: Evidence from Massachusetts.* Working Paper 16012 ed. National Bureau of Economic Research.

Kruger, Justin, and David Dunning. 1999. Unskilled and unaware of it: How difficulties in recognizing one's own incompetence lead to inflated self-assessments. *Journal of Personality and Social Psychology* 77 (6) (December): 1121–1134.

Kuhn, Thomas S. 1965; 1962. *The structure of scientific revolutions.* International encyclopedia of unified science. Vol. 2, no. 2. Chicago: University of Chicago Press.

Kunreuther, Howard, Nathan Novemsky, and Daniel Kahneman. 2001. Making low probabilities useful. *Journal of Risk and Uncertainty* 23 (2) (September): 103–120.

Lacetera, Nicola, Mario Macis, and Robert Slonim. 2012. Will there be blood? Incentives and displacement effects in pro-social behavior.

American Economic Journal: Economic Policy 4 (1) (February): 186–223.

Lancaster, Kelvin. 1990. The economics of product variety: A survey. *Marketing Science* 9 (3) (Summer): 189–206.

Lawthers, Ann G., A. Russell Localio, Nan M. Laird, Stuart Lipsitz, Liesi Hebert, and Troyen A. Brennan. 1992. Physicians' perceptions of the risk of being sued. *Journal of Health Politics, Policy and Law* 17 (3) (Fall): 463–482.

Lehrer, Jonah. 2010. The truth wears off. *New Yorker.* (December 13): 52–57.

Lester, Helen, Julie Schmittdiel, Joe Selby, Bruce Fireman, Stephen Campbell, Janelle Lee, Alan Whippy, and Philip Madvig. 2010. The impact of removing financial incentives from clinical quality indicators: Longitudinal analysis of four Kaiser Permanente indicators. *British Medical Journal* 340 (May 11, 2010).

Lilienfeld, Scott O., Rachel Ammirati, and Kristin Landfield. 2009. Giving debiasing away: Can psychological research on correcting cognitive errors promote human welfare? *Perspectives on Psychological Science* 4 (4) (July): 390–398.

List, John A. 2003. Does market experience eliminate market anomalies? *Quarterly Journal of Economics* 118 (1) (February): 41-71.

Loewenstein, George. 2005. Hot–cold empathy gaps and medical decision making. *Health Psychology* 24 (4) (July): S49–S56.

———. 2000. Emotions in economic theory and economic behavior. *American Economic Review* 90 (2) (May): 426–432.

———. 1996. Out of control: Visceral influences on behavior. *Organizational Behavior and Human Decision Processes* 65 (3) (March): 272–292.

Loewenstein, George, Troyen Brennan, and Kevin G. Volpp. 2007. Asymmetric paternalism to improve health behaviors. *JAMA: Journal of the American Medical Association* 298 (20) (November 28): 2415-2417.

Loewenstein, George, Ted O'Donoghue, and Matthew Rabin. 2003. Projection bias in predicting future utility. *Quarterly Journal of Economics* 118 (4) (November): 1209–1248.

Loewenstein, George, Elke U. Weber, Christopher K. Hsee, and Ned Welch. 2001. Risk as feelings. *Psychological Bulletin* 127 (2) (March): 267–286.

Lorber, Janie. 2009. *G.O.P. women attack mammogram guidelines.* Retrieved on October 29, 2012, from http://thecaucus.blogs.nytimes.com/2009/11/18/gop-women-attack-breast-cancer-findings/.

Lundy, Janet, and Benjamin D. Finder. 2009. *Cost sharing for health care: France, Germany, and Switzerland.* Menlo Park, CA: Kaiser Family Foundation, Report 7852.

Madrian, Brigitte C., and Dennis F. Shea. 2001. The power of suggestion: Inertia in 401(k) participation and savings behavior. *Quarterly Journal of Economics* 116 (4) (November): 1149–1187.

Mandelblatt, Jeanne S., Kathleen A. Cronin, Stephanie Bailey, Donald A. Berry, Harry J. de Koning, Gerrit Draisma, Hui Huang, et al. 2009. Effects of mammography screening under different screening schedules: Model estimates of potential benefits and harms. *Annals of Internal Medicine* 151 (10) (November 17): 738–747,W243–W247.

Manning, Willard G., Joseph P. Newhouse, Naihua Duan, Emmett B. Keeler, Arleen Leibowitz, and M. S. Marquis. 1987. Health insurance and the demand for medical care: Evidence from a randomized experiment. *American Economic Review* 77 (3) (June): 251–277.

McGlothlin, William H. 1956. Stability of choices among uncertain alternatives. *The American Journal of Psychology* 69 (4) (December): 604–615.

McNeil, Barbara J., Stephen G. Pauker, Harold C. Sox, and Amos Tversky. 1982. On the elicitation of preferences for alternative therapies. *The New England Journal of Medicine* 306 (21) (May 27): 1259–1262.

Mellstrom, Carl, and Magnus Johannesson. 2008. Crowding out in blood donation: Was Titmuss right? *Journal of the European Economic Association* 6 (4) (June 15): 845–863.

Mick, David G. 2001. From the editor: Announcing a new section in JCR: Reinquiries. *Journal of Consumer Research* 28 (1) (June): 1–5.

Mikulski, Senator Barbara A. December 3, 2009. *Press release: Senate approves Mikulski amendment making women's preventive care affordable and accessible.* Washington, DC.

Milgrom, Paul, and John Roberts. 1986. Price and advertising signals of product quality. *Journal of Political Economy* 94 (4) (August): 796–821.

Mogilner, Cassie, Tamar Rudnick, and Sheena S. Iyengar. 2008. The mere categorization effect: How the presence of categories increases choosers' perceptions of assortment variety and outcome satisfaction. *Journal of Consumer Research* 35 (2) (August): 202–215.

Montopoli, Brian. 2011. Michele Bachmann: Health care law "crown jewel of socialism." Retrieved on October 29, 2012, from www .cbsnews.com/8301-503544_162-20028978-503544.html.

Moonesinghe, Ramal, Muin J. Khoury, A. Cecile, and J. W. Janssens. 2007. Most published research findings are false—but a little replication goes a long way. *PLOS Medicine* 4 (2) (February): 218–221.

Murray, Shailagh. 2009. Senate turns to health bill's major obstacles. *The Washington Post.* December 8.

National Breast Cancer Coalition. 2009. NBCC commends revised U.S. Preventive Services Task Force breast cancer screening recommendations. *Women's Health Weekly* (December 3): 266.

National Center for Health Statistics, 2010. *National ambulatory medical care survey: 2008 summary tables.* Atlanta, GA: Centers for Disease Control and Prevention.

Nelson, Heidi D., Kari Tyne, Arpana Naik, Christina Bougatsos, Benjamin K. Chan, Peggy Nygren, and Linda Humphrey. 2009. *Screening for breast cancer: Systematic evidence review update for the U.S. Preventive Services Task Force.* Portland: Oregon Evidence-based Practice Center, AHRQ Publication No. 10-05142-EF-1.

Nelson, Heidi D., Kari Tyne, Arpana Naik, Christina Bougatsos, Benjamin K. Chan, and Linda Humphrey. 2009. Screening for breast cancer: An update for the U.S. Preventive Services Task Force. *Annals of Internal Medicine* 151 (10) (November 17): 727–737,W237–W242.

New England Healthcare Institute. 2009. *Thinking outside the pillbox: A system-wide approach to improving patient medication adherence for chronic disease.* Cambridge, MA: New England Healthcare Institute.

Newport, Frank. 2010. *Smoking and age: The baby boomer bulge.* Washington, DC: The Gallup Organization.

Nisbett, Richard E., and Lee Ross. 1980. *Human inference: Strategies and shortcomings of social judgment.* Century psychology series. Englewood Cliffs, NJ: Prentice-Hall.

Nordgren, Loran F., Joop van der Pligt, and Frenk van Harreveld. 2006. Visceral drives in retrospect: Explanations about the inaccessible past. *Psychological Science* 17 (7) (July): 635–640.

O'Brien, Michael. 2011. Pelosi: Democrats' "first test" is defending healthcare reform. Retrieved on October 29, 2012, from http://thehill.com/blogs/blog-briefing-room/news/136141-pelosi-democrats-first-test-is-defending-health-reform.

O'Donoghue, Ted, and Matthew Rabin. 1999. Doing it now or later. *American Economic Review* 89 (1) (March): 103–124.

OHRI Emergency Medicine Research. Ottawa ankle rules. Retrieved on October 29, 2012, from www.ohri.ca/emerg/cdr/ankle_formats.html.

Oppenheimer, Judy. 2009. Letter to the editor. *The Washington Post.* November 20.

Organ Procurement and Transplantation Network. 2011. Transplants by donor type, U.S. transplants performed: January 1, 1988–April 30, 2011. Available from http://optn.transplant.hrsa.gov.

Orient, Jane M., and Joseph D. Sapira. 2000. *Sapira's art & science of bedside diagnosis,* 2nd ed. Philadelphia: Lippincott Williams & Wilkins.

Orszag, Peter. May 29, 2008. Health care and behavioral economics. Paper presented at Growing Risks for Workers and Growing Fiscal Deficits: Challenges for Social Insurance, Washington, DC.

Osterberg, Lars, and Terrence Blaschke. 2005. Adherence to medication. *New England Journal of Medicine* 353 (5) (August 4): 487–497.

Oswald, Andrew J., and Nattavudh Powdthavee. 2008. Does happiness adapt? A longitudinal study of disability with implications for economists and judges. *Journal of Public Economics* 92 (5–6) (June): 1061–1077.

Palin, Sarah. 2009. *Statement on the current health care debate.* Aug. 7. Retrieved on October 29, 2012, from www.facebook.com /note.php?note_id=113851103434.

Parker, Tom. 2008. *Rules of thumb: A life manual.* New York: Workman Publishing.

Pauker, Stephen G., and Jerome P. Kassirer. 1987. Decision analysis. *New England Journal of Medicine* 316 (5) (January 29): 250–258.

———. 1980. The threshold approach to clinical decision making. *New England Journal of Medicine* 302 (20) (May 15): 1109–1117.

Pauly, Mark V. 1968. The economics of moral hazard: Comment. *American Economic Review* 58 (3) (June): 531–537.

Peters, Ellen. 2006. The functions of affect in the construction of preferences. In *The construction of preferences*, eds. Sarah Lichtenstein and Paul Slovic, 454–463. Cambridge, UK, and New York: Cambridge University Press.

Pinker, Steven. 1997. *How the mind works.* New York: Norton.

Pittet, Didier. 2001. Improving adherence to hand hygiene practice: A multidisciplinary approach. *Emerging Infectious Diseases* 7 (2) (March–April): 234–240.

Pittet, Didier, Anne Simon, Stephane Hugonnet, Carmen Pessoa-Silva, Valerie Sauvan, and Thomas V. Perneger. 2004. Hand hygiene among physicians: Performance, beliefs, and perceptions. *Annals of Internal Medicine* 141 (1) (July 6): 1–8.

Plous, Scott. 1993. *The psychology of judgment and decision making.* Philadelphia: Temple University Press.

Pohl, Rüdiger F., and Wolfgang Hell. 1996. No reduction in hindsight bias after complete information and repeated testing. *Organizational Behavior and Human Decision Processes* 67 (1) (July): 49–58.

Prelec, Drazen, and George Loewenstein. 1998. The red and the black: Mental accounting of savings and debt. *Marketing Science* 17 (1) (Winter): 4–28.

Pronin, Emily. 2007. Perception and misperception of bias in human judgment. *Trends in Cognitive Sciences* 11 (1) (January): 37–43.

Pronin, Emily, Thomas Gilovich, and Lee Ross. 2004. Objectivity in the eye of the beholder: Divergent perceptions of bias in self versus others. *Psychological Review* 111 (3) (July): 781–799.

Pronovost, Peter, Christine Goeschel, Elizabeth Colantuoni, Sam Watson, Lisa H. Lubomski, Sean Berenholtz, David A. Thompson, et al. 2010. Sustaining reductions in catheter related bloodstream infections in Michigan: Observational study. *British Medical Journal* 340: c309.

Pronovost, Peter, Dale Needham, Sean Berenholtz, David Sinopoli, Haitao Chu, Sara Cosgrove, Bryan Sexton, et al. 2006. An intervention to decrease catheter-related bloodstream infections in the ICU. *New England Journal of Medicine* 355 (26) (December 28): 2725–2732.

Pronovost, Peter J., and Eric Vohr. 2010. *Safe patients, smart hospitals: How one doctor's checklist can help us change health care from the inside out.* New York: Hudson Street Press.

Putler, Daniel S. 1992. Incorporating reference price effects into a theory of consumer choice. *Marketing Science* 11 (3) (Summer): 287–309.

Rabin, Roni Caryn. 2009a. New guidelines on breast cancer draw opposition. *New York Times*, November 17.

———. 2009b, November 18. *Our bodies, our breast exams.* Well. Tara Parker-Pope on Health (blog). Retrieved on October 29, 2012, from http://well.blogs.nytimes.com/author/tara-parker-pope/.

Reason, J. T. 1990. *Human error.* Cambridge, UK, and New York: Cambridge University Press.

Redelmeier, Donald A., and Eldar Shafir. 1995. Medical decision making in situations that offer multiple alternatives. *JAMA: The Journal of the American Medical Association* 273 (4) (January 25): 302–305.

Reinhardt, Uwe. 1972. A production function for physician services. *The Review of Economics and Statistics* 54 (1) (February): 55–66.

Rice, Thomas, Yaniv Hanoch, and Janet Cummings. 2010. What factors influence seniors' desire for choice among health insurance options? Survey results on the Medicare prescription drug benefit. *Health Economics, Policy and Law* 5(4) (October): 437–457.

Rifkin, William. 2009. Letter to the editor. *New York Times*. November 18.

Riis, Jason, George Loewenstein, Jonathan Baron, Christopher Jepson, Angela Fagerlin, and Peter A. Ubel. 2005. Ignorance of hedonic adaptation to hemodialysis: A study using ecological momentary assessment. *Journal of Experimental Psychology: General* 134 (1) (February): 3–9.

Robert Wood Johnson Foundation. 2011. *Call for proposals: Applying behavioral economics to perplexing health and health care challenges.* Princeton, NJ: Robert Wood Johnson Foundation.

Robinson, James C., and Paul B. Ginsburg. 2009. Consumer-driven health care: Promise and performance. *Health Affairs* 28 (2) (March/April): W272–W281.

Roebuck, M. Christopher, Joshua N. Liberman, Marin Gemmill-Toyama, and Troyen A. Brennan. 2011. Medication adherence leads to lower health care use and costs despite increased drug spending. *Health Affairs* 30 (1) (January): 91–99.

Roth, Alvin E. 2007. Repugnance as a constraint on markets. *Journal of Economic Perspectives* 21 (3) (Summer): 37–58.

Rottenstreich, Yuval, and Christopher K. Hsee. 2001. Money, kisses, and electric shocks: On the affective psychology of risk. *Psychological Science* 12 (3) (May): 185–190.

Rozenblit, Leonid, and Frank Keil. 2002. The misunderstood limits of folk science: An illusion of explanatory depth. *Cognitive Science* 26 (5) (September-October): 521–562.

Rucker, Philip. 2009. S.C. senator is a voice of reform opposition. *The Washington Post.* July 28.

Ryan, Josiah. 2011, January 19. Weiner: Play health care reform drinking game responsibly. Retrieved on October 29, 2012, from http://thehill

.com/blogs/floor-action/house/138861-weiner-play-health-care
-reform-drinking-game-responsibly.

Sabate, Eduardo. 2003. *Adherence to long-term therapies: Evidence for action*. Geneva: World Health Organization.

Sack, Kevin. 2009. Culture clash in medicine. *New York Times*, November 20.

Sackett, David L., and John C. Snow. 1979. The magnitude of compliance and noncompliance. In *Compliance in health care*, eds. R. Brian Haynes, D. W. Taylor, and David L. Sackette, 11–22. Baltimore, MD: Johns Hopkins University Press.

Sayette, Michael A., George Loewenstein, Kasey M. Griffin, and Jessica J. Black. 2008. Exploring the cold-to-hot empathy gap in smokers. *Psychological Science* 19 (9) (September): 926–932.

Scheibehenne, Benjamin, Rainer Greifeneder, and Peter M. Todd. 2010. Can there ever be too many options? A meta-analytic review of choice overload. *The Journal of Consumer Research* 37 (3) (October): 409–425.

Schelling, Thomas C. 1978. *Micromotives and macrobehavior*. Fels lectures on public policy analysis. New York: Norton.

Schkade, David A., and Daniel Kahneman. 1998. Does living in California make people happy? *Psychological Science* 9 (5) (September): 340-346.

Schram, Arthur, and Joep Sonnemans. 2011. How individuals choose health insurance: An experimental analysis. *European Economic Review* 55 (6) (August): 799–819.

Schwartz, Barry. 2004. *The paradox of choice*. New York: HarperCollins.

———. 2000. Self-determination: The tyranny of freedom. *American Psychologist* 55 (1) (January): 79–88.

Schwartz, Janet A., and Gretchen B. Chapman. 1999. Are more options always better? The attraction effect in physicians' decisions about medications. *Medical Decision Making* 19 (3) (August 1): 315–323.

Schwartz, Lisa M., Steven Woloshin, Floyd J. Fowler, and H. Gilbert Welch. 2004. Enthusiasm for cancer screening in the United States.

JAMA: The Journal of the American Medical Association 291 (1) (January 7): 71–78.

Schwartz, Lisa M., Steven Woloshin, Harold C. Sox, Baruch Fischhoff, and H. Gilbert Welch. 2000. US women's attitudes to false-positive mammography results and detection of ductal carcinoma in situ: Cross sectional survey. *British Medical Journal* 320 (7250) (June 17): 1635–1640.

Scott, Anthony, Peter Sivey, Driss Ait Ouakrim, Lisa Willenberg, Lucio Naccarella, John Furler, and Doris Young. 2011. The effect of financial incentives on the quality of health care provided by primary care physicians. *Cochrane Database of Systematic Reviews*, 9.

Sears, David O. 1986. College sophomores in the laboratory: Influences of a narrow data base on social psychology's view of human nature. *Journal of Personality & Social Psychology* 51 (3) (September): 515–530.

Shah, Anuj K., and Daniel M. Oppenheimer. 2008. Heuristics made easy: An effort-reduction framework. *Psychological Bulletin* 134 (2) (March): 207–222.

Shampanier, Kristina, Nina Mazar, and Dan Ariely. 2007. Zero as a special price: The true value of free products. *Marketing Science* 26 (6) (November-December): 742–757.

Shaneyfelt, Terrence M. 2001. Building bridges to quality. *JAMA: The Journal of the American Medical Association* 286 (20) (November 28): 2600–2601.

Shaw, Gienna. 2011. Does decision support make docs look dumb? *HealthLeaders*. April: 42.

Shefrin, Hersh, and Meir Statman. 1985. The disposition to sell winners too early and ride losers too long: Theory and evidence. *Journal of Finance* 40 (3) (July): 777–790.

Sherbino, Jonathan, Kelly L. Dore, Eric Siu, and Geoffrey R. Norman. 2011. The effectiveness of cognitive forcing strategies to decrease diagnostic error: An exploratory study. *Teaching and Learning in Medicine* 23 (1) (January): 78–84.

Silen, William, and Zachary Cope. 2010. *Cope's early diagnosis of the acute abdomen.* 22nd ed. Revised by William Silen, ed. New York: Oxford University Press.

Simon, Herbert A. 1957. *Models of man: Social and rational; mathematical essays on rational human behavior in a social setting.* New York: Wiley.

———. 1956. Rational choice and the structure of environments. *Psychological Review* 63 (2) (March): 129–138.

———. 1955. A behavioral model of rational choice. *Quarterly Journal of Economics* 69 (1) (February): 99–118.

Sirovich, Brenda, Patricia M. Gallagher, David E. Wennberg, and Elliott S. Fisher. 2008. Discretionary decision making by primary care physicians and the cost of U.S. health care. *Health Affairs* 27 (3) (May): 813–823.

Sirovich, Brenda E., Daniel J. Gottlieb, H. G. Welch, and Elliott S. Fisher. 2006. Regional variations in health care intensity and physician perceptions of quality of care. *Annals of Internal Medicine* 144 (9) (May 2): 641–649, W143–W146.

Sirovich, Brenda E., Steven Woloshin, and Lisa M. Schwartz. 2011. Too little? Too much? Primary care physicians' views on U.S. health care: A brief report. *Archives of Internal Medicine* 171 (17) (September 26): 1582–1585.

Slovic, Paul, Melissa L. Finucane, Ellen Peters, and Donald G. MacGregor. 2007. The affect heuristic. *European Journal of Operational Research* 177 (3) (March 16): 1333–1352.

———. 2004. Risk as analysis and risk as feelings: Some thoughts about affect, reason, risk, and rationality. *Risk Analysis: An International Journal* 24 (2) (April): 311–322.

Smith, Adam. 1790/2009. *The theory of moral sentiments.* 6th ed. New York: Penguin Books.

Snowberg, Erik, and Justin Wolfers. 2010. Explaining the favorite–long shot bias: Is it risk-love or misperceptions? *The Journal of Political Economy* 118 (4) (August): 723–746.

Sox, Harold C. 1988. *Medical decision making.* Boston: Butterworths.

Stein, Rob, and Dan Eggen. 2009. White House backs off cancer test guidelines. *The Washington Post,* November 19: A1.

Steinhauer, Jennifer. 2009. New mammogram advice finds a skeptical audience. *New York Times,* November 18: sec A.

Stigler, George J., and Gary S. Becker. 1977. De gustibus non est disputandum. *American Economic Review* 67 (2) (March): 76–90.

Stubbs, Joseph W. 2009, November 24. Statement on the politicization of evidence-based clinical research. In American College of Physicians [database online]. Retrieved on October 29, 2012, from www.acponline.org/pressroom/pol_ebcr.htm.

Studdert, David M., Michelle M. Mello, and Troyen A. Brennan. 2004. Medical malpractice. *New England Journal of Medicine* 350 (3) (January 15): 283–292.

Sunstein, Cass R., and Richard H. Thaler. 2003. Libertarian paternalism is not an oxymoron. *The University of Chicago Law Review* 70 (4) (Fall): 1159–1202.

Svenson, Ola. 1981. Are we all less risky and more skillful than our fellow drivers? *Acta Psychologica* 47 (2) (February): 143–148.

Tasic, Slavisa. 2009. The illusion of regulatory competence. *Critical Review* 21 (4): 423–436.

Taubes, Gary. 1997. The breast-screening brawl. *Science* 275 (5303) (February 21): 1056-1059.

Taylor, Shelley E., and Suzanne C. Thompson. 1982. Stalking the elusive "vividness" effect. *Psychological Review* 89 (2) (March): 155–181.

Tetlock, Philip E. 2005. *Expert political opinion.* Princeton, NJ: Princeton University Press.

Thaler, Richard H. 1999. Mental accounting matters. *Journal of Behavioral Decision Making* 12 (3) (September): 183–206.

Thaler, Richard H., and Cass R. Sunstein. 2008. *Nudge: Improving decisions about health, wealth, and happiness.* New Haven, CT: Yale University Press.

Titmuss, Richard Morris. 1970. *The gift relationship, from human blood to social policy.* London: Allen & Unwin.

Tufte, Edward R. 2007. *The visual display of quantitative information*. 2nd ed. Cheshire, CT: Graphics Press.

Tversky, Amos, and Daniel Kahneman. 1986. Rational choice and the framing of decisions. *Journal of Business* 59 (4) (October): S251–S278.

———. 1981. The framing of decisions and the psychology of choice. *Science* 211 (4481) (January 30): 453–458.

———. 1974. Judgment under uncertainty: Heuristics and biases. *Science* 185 (4157) (September 27): 1124–1131.

———. 1973. Availability: A heuristic for judging frequency and probability. *Cognitive Psychology* 5 (2) (September): 207–232.

———. 1971. Belief in the law of small numbers. *Psychological Bulletin* 76 (2) (August): 105–110.

Ubel, Peter A., Andrea M. Angott, and Brian J. Zikmund-Fisher. 2011. Physicians recommend different treatments for patients than they would choose for themselves. *Archives of Internal Medicine* 171 (7) (April): 630–634.

U.S. Preventive Services Task Force. 2011, April 8. Description of the task force. Retrieved on October 29, 2012, from www.uspreventive servicestaskforce.org/.

———. 2009. Screening for breast cancer: U.S. Preventive Services Task Force recommendation statement. *Annals of Internal Medicine* 151 (10) (November 17): 716–726.

———. 2008. *Procedure manual*. Rockville, MD: Agency for Health-care Research and Quality.

Van Boven, Leaf, David Dunning, and George Loewenstein. 2000. Egocentric empathy gaps between owners and buyers: Misperceptions of the endowment effect. *Journal of Personality and Social Psychology* 79 (1) (July): 66–76.

Van Boven, Leaf, and George Loewenstein. 2003. Social projection of transient drive states. *Personality and Social Psychology Bulletin* 29 (9) (September): 1159–1168.

Van Den Bos, Jill, Karan Rustagi, Travis Gray, Michael Halford, Eva Ziemkiewicz, and Jonathan Shreve. 2011. The $17.1 billion problem:

The annual cost of measurable medical errors. *Health Affairs* 30 (4) (April): 596–603.

Volpp, Kevin G., David A. Asch, Robert Galvin, and George Loewenstein. 2011. Redesigning employee health incentives—Lessons from behavioral economics. *New England Journal of Medicine* 365 (5) (August 4): 388–390.

Volpp, Kevin G., Leslie K. John, Andrea B. Troxel, Laurie Norton, Jennifer Fassbender, and George Loewenstein. 2008. Financial incentive-based approaches for weight loss: A randomized trial. *JAMA: The Journal of the American Medical Association* 300 (22) (December 10): 2631–2637.

Volpp, Kevin G., Mark V. Pauly, George Loewenstein, and David Bangsberg. 2009a. P4P4P: An agenda for research on pay-for-performance for patients. *Health Affairs* 28 (1) (January): 206–214.

Volpp, Kevin G., Andrea B. Troxel, Mark V. Pauly, Henry A. Glick, Andrea Puig, David A. Asch, Robert Galvin, et al. 2009b. A randomized, controlled trial of financial incentives for smoking cessation. *The New England Journal of Medicine* 360 (7) (February 12): 699–709.

Waber, Rebecca L., Baba Shiv, Ziv Carmon, and Dan Ariely. 2008. Commercial features of placebo and therapeutic efficacy. *JAMA: The Journal of the American Medical Association* 299 (9) (March 5): 1016–1017.

Weinstein, Michael M. 2009, December 13. Paul A. Samuelson, Nobel Economist, Dies at 94. *New York Times*, A1.

Weinstein, Neil D. 1989. Effects of personal experience on self-protective behavior. *Psychological Bulletin* 105 (1) (January): 31–50.

Welch, H. G. 2009. Overdiagnosis and mammography screening. *BMJ: British Medical Journal* 339 (7714) (September 25): 182–183.

Wennberg, John, and Alan Gittelsohn. 1973. Small area variations in health care delivery. *Science* 182 (4117) (December 14): 1102–1108.

Winslow, Ron, and Shirley S. Wang. 2009. In cancer testing, less is now better. *Wall Street Journal*. November 21: A3.

World Health Organization. 2009. *WHO guidelines on hand hygiene in health care*. Geneva: World Health Organization.

Young, Neal S., John P. A. Ioannidis, and Omar Al-Ubaydli. 2008. Why current publication practices may distort science. *PLOS Medicine* 5 (10) (October): 1418–1422.